T0331913

Praise for The Smart Financial Advisor

"As an advisor you know the prime directive in financial advisory: care about your client's goals and values, and advise accordingly. What you may not have noticed, because the tide has been turning slowly, is that technology, analytics and data transparency have been colluding to reveal to your clients just how well or poorly you are fulfilling your prime directive. Bill Martin's *The Smart Financial Advisor* is your guidebook to building your craft to safely and successfully navigate this turning tide. It is a foundational text for the 21st century advisor disguised as common sense. Fortunately for you, Martin managed to get this book to print before the tide has consumed your practice. I urge you to take advantage of the timing and read this book."

— Mark J. Nitzberg, Ph.D., Berkeley AI Research Lab, University of California, Co-Founder, and former CTO, Smartleaf, Inc.

"Bill Martin's *The Smart Financial Advisor* is a thoughtful guide on how financial advisors should future-proof their practice in the new millennium – embrace goals-based planning and the Fintech tools that enable it. Advisors thinking about connecting robo advice and digital financial planning into their practice should read this book, or face technological extinction."

— Lex Sokolin, Global Director Fintech Strategy & Partner at Autonomous Research

"*The Smart Financial Advisor* offers a thoroughly practical guide for financial advisors to achieve better outcomes both for their clients and for themselves. Over the last decade we have gained new insights about client behaviors that are demanding a fundamental shift in client interactions and investment decisioning. This book's uniqueness lies in its articulation of how advisors can not only achieve a more collaborative client relationship and better investment outcomes through highly personalized goals-based investing, but also how those benefits can be scaled and extended using advanced financial technology tools and solutions. This clarity of vision provides a tangible roadmap for all advisors seeking to better service their clients while also growing their practices. I thoroughly recommend this book."

— Simon Algar, Founder and Principal, wealth-reports

"*The Smart Financial Advisor* hits on many of the issues that derail investor and advisor success. Advisors would do well to heed Bill Martin's recommendations and understand the current and future environment; adapting to an ever-quickening pace of change. In the end, we are all human: it's those human emotions that may be the difference between success and failure. Bill provides the tools to navigate your fears or exuberance towards clients' ultimate goals."

— Steve Lockshin, Founder, AdvicePeriod

"*The Smart Financial Advisor* is a valuable resource that challenges advisors to work differently. By embracing the ideas in this book, advisors will learn how to blend the power of technology with human judgement. As a result, they will become an indispensable partner in helping clients gain clarity and control over their entire financial lives."

— Joe Duran, Founder and CEO, United Capital Financial Partners

"Goals-based investing is one of the simplest, most powerful, and most consistently overlooked tools at the disposal of financial advisors. In this well-researched and engaging book, Bill Martin speaks to both the why and how of goals-based investing in a way that will improve both investor and advisor outcomes."

— Dr Daniel Crosby, author of *The Laws of Wealth: Psychology and the Secret to Investing Success*

"With a $3 trillion wealth transfer underway, the future is very bright for wealth management. However, advisors must adapt and innovate to participate in this unprecedented opportunity. *The Smart Financial Advisor* provides powerful and practical insights for advisors to thrive in the future by embracing technology and adopting a holistic approach to managing wealth."

— April Rudin, Global Wealth Management Strategist, Founder and CEO, The Rudin Group

"The financial industry revolution is in fast-forward, and it has never been more exciting. But misapplication without a thoughtful advisory thesis will lead to misdirected energy and lackluster results. Bill Martin's *The Smart Financial Advisor* eloquently distills complex aspects today's advisors must navigate to channel a meaningful impact in their clients' future. This book is how financial advisors need to be thinking about the role of professional advice."

— Aaron Schumm, Founder and CEO, Vestwell

"As wealth management continues to change and evolve, leading advisors are embracing a fiduciary approach, leveraging technology to present the client's entire financial situation on any device, anytime. Bill Martin completely captures this new paradigm in *The Smart Financial Advisor*, making the book an essential resource for financial advisors everywhere."

— David Benskin, CEO, Wealth Access

"Bill Martin's *The Smart Financial Advisor* is a practical and easy-to-read guide for advisors who wish to embrace the future of wealth management. In simple and engaging language, Mr Martin explains where current practices fall short and how advisors can do better by centering their practices on helping clients achieve their goals. Part how-to manual, part manifesto, this book describes what being an advisor can and should mean."

— Gerard Michael, President & Co-Founder, Smartleaf, Inc.

"I've known Bill Martin professionally for many years. He is smart, thoughtful, and forward looking. And so is his book. The wealth management industry is today being disrupted by multiple simultaneous forces – technology, demographics, shifting investor preferences, product development, and legal and regulatory evolutions. In this book, Bill focuses on the two disruptive trends the advisor has the most control over – fintech and goals-based planning. By doing so he lays out a framework for how wealth management will be delivered over the next decade or more, and how advisors can adopt and adapt to these disruptive forces in order to deliver a differentiated client experience. I recommend this book to anyone seeking to deliver exceptional wealth management services to end investors."

— Scott Welch, CIMA®, Chief Investment Officer,
Dynasty Financial Partners

The *Smart*
Financial
Advisor

Every owner of a physical copy of this edition of

The *Smart* Financial Advisor

can download the eBook for free direct from us at Harriman House, in a DRM-free format that can be read on any eReader, tablet or smartphone.

Simply head to:

ebooks.harriman-house.com/smartfinacialadvisor

to get your copy now.

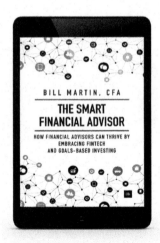

The *Smart* Financial Advisor

How *Financial Advisors* can *Thrive* by *Embracing Fintech* and *Goals-Based Investing*

Bill Martin, CFA

Hh | Harriman House

HARRIMAN HOUSE LTD
18 College Street
Petersfield
Hampshire
GU31 4AD
GREAT BRITAIN
Tel: +44 (0)1730 233870
Email: enquiries@harriman-house.com
Website: www.harriman-house.com

First published in Great Britain in 2017
Copyright © Bill Martin

Hardback ISBN: 978-0-85719-583-8
eBook ISBN: 978-0-85719-584-5

British Library Cataloguing in Publication Data
A CIP catalogue record for this book can be obtained from the British Library.

Contents

Part 1. Hazards that Derail Investor Goals

Part 2. Improving Investor Outcomes with Goals-Based Investing

Part 3. A Collaborative Framework for Success

About the author

Bill Martin, CFA

Chief Investment Officer

INTRUST Bank

www.linkedin.com/in/billmartincfa

Bill leads investment strategy for INTRUST Bank, emphasizing goals-based client solutions, portfolio construction using multifactor risk analysis, and tax-aware portfolio optimization. Prior to joining INTRUST, Bill served as director of managed account services at SunGard Advisor Technologies and Folio Dynamix. In this role, he consulted with and delivered investment solutions to wealth and retirement firms across the US. He has authored numerous industry articles and whitepapers and is a frequent speaker on investment strategies and industry innovation. Bill serves as a wealth management advisory board member for the American Bankers Association and participates on several client advisory councils of fintech and asset management companies. Moreover, as an active board member of Exploration Place, he advocates for science and technology learning across generations. Bill holds an MBA from the University of Kansas, is a CFA Charterholder, and has more than 20 years of investment-related experience.

Disclosure statements

The information contained herein is not meant as a source of specific investment recommendations, and the author and Harriman House make no implied or express recommendations concerning the manner in which any investor's accounts should or would be handled, as appropriate investment decisions depend upon the investor's investment objectives. The information is general in nature and is not intended to be, and should not be construed as, legal or tax advice. The author and Harriman House make no warranties with regard to the information or results obtained by its use and disclaim any liability arising out of your use of, or reliance on, the information. The views expressed are those of the author, are subject to change, and are not those of INTRUST Financial Corporation or its affiliates. Past performance is no guarantee of future results.

Acknowledgements

Without the ongoing encouragement from my wife, family, and colleagues, this work would not have been possible. I am indebted to their sacrifices and grateful for their constant support. Also, I am thankful to work for an organization that is deeply committed to serving clients, providing a platform to put the principles of this book into practice. Furthermore, I sincerely appreciate Harriman House for giving me the opportunity to share my passion for goals-based investing with an international audience. Lastly, I thank you, my fellow practitioner, for investing in this book and committing to make our profession even better in the future.

Preface

Financial advisors face an overwhelming amount of industry change. Regulatory requirements are expanding, advisory fees are compressing, and emerging technologies are disrupting long-standing business models. As a result, traditional investment firms are increasingly encountering competitive pressures.

Investors face many challenges, too. Their success is lackluster, at best. Numerous studies confirm that average investor returns barely keep pace with inflation. Behavioral biases and other hazards contribute to these dismal results. Furthermore, a proliferation of investment products and advisory services create a confusing maze of options for investors to navigate.

This book was written to help financial advisors not just survive amid a precarious environment, but to thrive. Also, the aim is to help advisors significantly improve investor outcomes. The keys to realizing these benefits are revealed and explained herein.

Part 1 of *The Smart Financial Advisor* examines seven hazards of traditional investing that derail investors from achieving their goals. Even astute advisors and investors find themselves ensnared by these dangers that superficially appear to be smart strategies for building wealth. By unpacking these seven hazards, this book challenges financial advisors and investors to rethink traditional investing and begs the question, "Is there a smarter way to manage wealth?"

Part 2 answers this question by introducing goals-based investing and shows how this approach circumvents the hazards that often impede investor progress. Through engaging stories, examples, and practical applications, Part 2 illustrates how goals-based investing identifies and evaluates investor needs, wants, and wishes. The importance of assessing investors' risk willingness as well as investors' capacity and necessity for risk is explained in easy-to-understand language. Methods to construct strategies that align with investor risk constraints and goals are outlined. Additionally, enhanced strategies to increase the probability of goal attainment are examined, such as asset location and tax-smart withdrawal sequencing. The section closes by reviewing the importance of using technology to deliver transparent reporting and to engage investors within a goals-based framework.

Unlike traditional investment approaches, goals-based investing requires focused collaboration between investors and their advisors. Part 3 explores the changing roles of the investor-advisor relationship and how fintech solutions can further enhance this partnership and position advisory practices for sustainable growth. The book concludes by highlighting two examples of transformation resulting from the adoption of goals-based investing, leaving readers inspired and ready to embrace this approach.

The Smart Financial Advisor will appeal to new advisors as well as seasoned financial veterans. Wealth managers can adopt the book's principles to transform their practices, gaining insights into the latest fintech innovations and best practices for goals-based investing. It will also help advisors prosper amid escalating industry disruption and regulation by discovering ways to increase efficiencies and improve client engagement. Ultimately, the ideas here will make financial advisors smarter, and in turn, improve client outcomes.

Introduction

A smarter way to manage wealth

> "Begin with the end in mind."
>
> – Stephen Covey

I RECALL THE CONVERSATION was civil. Nonetheless, my client's words punched hard. *"I'm moving my money elsewhere…"*

Losing any investor from an advisory practice hurts. But loss of a longstanding, eight-figure client is exceptionally painful. I wondered, how did this happen?

Answers to this agonizing question eluded me. Our team's service was superior. The portfolio's long-term performance had outpaced its benchmark. The firm's track record in client retention was stellar.

So what went wrong?

After much soul searching, I finally stumbled upon understanding. I had been evaluating the loss from my perspective and knowledge of the wealth management industry. But it was not until I looked at the experience from my ex-client's perspective did explanations surface.

Here is what I discovered.

The advisory team – which included me and several of my colleagues – had spent hundreds of hours working through complex issues for the client. Most of these items were not directly related to the client's portfolio. We evaluated wealth transfer and gifting strategies. The team worked diligently to reduce the portfolio's tax liabilities. And we proactively coordinated our activities with the client's CPA and attorney.

However, each time we met with the client, the meeting centered on the markets and account performance. Supporting materials highlighted the economy, equity and fixed income markets, and portfolio performance compared to broad market indices. Typically, all of the behind-the-scenes work the team had done for the client was only mentioned in passing.

Inadvertently, these investment-centric meetings trained the client to assess the firm's value primarily on investment performance. Although we were aware of our broader value proposition, we failed to adequately communicate and demonstrate this reality to the client.

The year in which this client fired the team, our equity performance lagged the S&P 500 Index. Since the client's perceived value of the relationship had been reduced to investment returns and our 12-month performance trailed the market, the client chose to walk away.

In retrospect, I realized I was largely to blame. My single-minded focus on investments with the client was a primary reason we lost this relationship.

Misplaced focus of traditional investing

Similar to my misfortunate story, many financial advisors continue to manage client wealth using the traditional investment approach – focusing on market dynamics, investment products, and account performance. However, trying to predict the market is a fool's game. Chasing products with strong past returns often disappoints. And overemphasizing investment returns can lead to dissatisfied client relationships, as I found out the hard way.

Traditional investing measures advisory success by comparing investment returns to market indices. Even though the primary aim of this approach is to outperform the market, actual investor results are tragically poor. This fact is illustrated in Figure A, which shows the 20-year annualized returns of major asset classes compared to the average investor return of only 2.1% per year for the period ending December 31, 2015.

Financial markets cannot be blamed for these dismal investor results. Nor can investment products assume most of the liability. Rather, the actions and misplaced focus of financial advisors and investors are the primary drivers of underperformance. Too often practitioners and investors react to external factors outside their control.

For example, markets rally, and investors get overly exuberant. Meanwhile, advisors may fuel enthusiasm by peddling hot products to capitalize on the buying frenzy. When markets correct and begin to freefall, investors dump their holdings in hoards. And by advising clients to go to cash, financial advisors contribute to retreating prices. The result is that investments are bought at high valuations and sold at low prices, forfeiting opportunities for investors and leaving financial aspirations beyond reach.

Figure A. 20-year annualized returns by asset class (1996–2015)

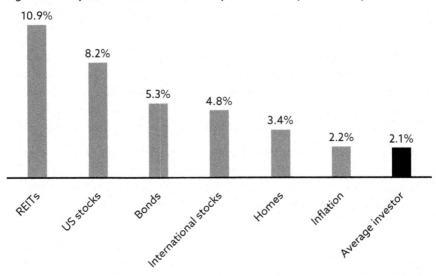

Sources: Bloomberg – indices used include NAREIT Equity REIT Index (for REITs), S&P 500 Index for (US Stocks), Barclays US Aggregate (for Bonds), MSCI EAFE (for International Stocks), Median sale price of existing single-family homes (for Homes) and CPI (for inflation). Average Investor return from: www.qidllc.com.

Most advisors who rely on traditional investment approaches claim that their advice aligns with the best interests of clients. Yet, advisory actions often suggest otherwise. Traditional investing focuses on the means for achieving client goals (investment products and performance) rather than actual desired client outcomes.

This now seems backwards to me.

As I am drafting this Introduction, I am traveling on a plane. When booking the flight, I was not informed much about the plane I would be traveling on. Rather, the booking process centered on my departure location and final destination. This methodology gave me a reasonable degree of confidence that I will end up in New Orleans later today – the location for my conference speaking engagement.

Financial advisors typically take the opposite approach when interacting with clients. They focus on the mode of transportation, reviewing in detail information about stocks, bonds, mutual funds, ETFs, and their related performance. Discussion around the clients' final destinations are generally afterthoughts or ignored altogether. Practitioners need to remember investment vehicles are merely the means to a much greater end – achieving the client's long-term financial goals. What clients care most about is being able to sustain their basic needs for life and having a reasonable chance of funding further non-essential luxuries or aspirational wishes.

Consider this example. A client account appreciates 5% in 2016, underperforming the S&P 500 Index. Is this good or bad? If the client goal is to outperform this benchmark, then the answer is obvious. But what if the purpose of the portfolio is to fund the client's future retirement income? A one-year return such as 5% tells us very little about the success or failure of progressing toward this goal.

A better assessment is measuring the probability of fully funding the client's retirement income goal. A 5% return in 2016 is relatively immaterial if the client's likelihood of goal attainment is in a high-confidence range. What ultimately matters is whether the client is on track to realize the goal and can take comfort in a well-designed wealth strategy.

Unfortunately, too many wealth advisors miss this bigger picture. They continue holding on to traditional investing practices, even though this approach is frequently hazardous to investor wealth.

Smart financial advisors understand the misplaced focus of traditional investing and its common pitfalls. Accordingly, they learn to identify the hazards associated with this type of investing, as described in Part 1. By knowing and recognizing these dangers, practitioners find ways to circumvent such traps. They proactively seek better ways to manage client wealth. One such method, known as goals-based investing, is increasingly being embraced by leading practitioners.

A better approach – goals-based investing

A goals-based approach changes the priorities of traditional investing; it begins with the end in mind. Early in the advisor-client relationship, time is spent understanding the investor's long-term goals and assessing the probability of achieving these outcomes. Unlike investment-centric approaches that focus solely on client assets, goals-based investing is holistic and takes into consideration a client's entire balance sheet. Present and future assets are managed against current and prospective liabilities to avoid the underfunding of client goals. Examples of financial goals include maintaining a quality lifestyle throughout retirement, funding college education for children and grandchildren, leaving assets to the next generation, and granting of charitable gifts.

In many ways, this approach is similar to the process of managing a well-run pension plan, whereby pension assets (e.g. investments and contributions) are appropriately matched to pension liabilities (e.g. current and future retirement benefits). Success or failure is not measured in terms of investment returns. Rather, success or failure is defined by the overall funding status of the pension. Underfunded pensions will likely have a difficult time fully meeting their future obligations unless additional corporate contributions are made. Likewise, if a client has an underfunded retirement income goal, the client will need to save more or adopt a more aggressive retirement savings strategy in order to meet this future liability.

Five benefits of goals-based investing

Goals-based investing has many benefits – both for advisors and clients. Five of these benefits are noted below, and many more are revealed throughout this book.

1. Enables advisors to manage more of their clients' wealth

For a goals-based approach to be truly effective, advisors need to understand their clients' complete financial picture. A Russell Investments study found that nearly 40% of taxable client assets are held away from their primary advisors.[1] Therefore, it is critical that clients provide their advisor with 401(k) statements, assets with other wealth managers, self-managed investments, and other assets – in addition to the assets managed by the advisor. The benefit for the client is coordinated and holistic advice. The benefit for the advisor is an increased potential of managing the client's held-away assets at some point in the future.

2. Better matches assets and liabilities

Knowing client goals makes it easier to help families understand how much they need to save and how much they can afford to reasonably spend. By earmarking a client's current assets to future liabilities, advisors can help ensure clients do not fail to meet their goals or incur debt.

3. Determines optimal asset allocation

Goals-based investing helps evaluate a client's capacity and necessity to take on risk given the client's resources, goals, and time horizon. Traditional risk tolerance questionnaires used by many advisors assess a client's willingness to take on risk, but they do not necessarily measure financial capacity and the amount of risk required to fund client goals. By understanding client risk preferences in a more comprehensive manner, advisors can provide better guidance on determining a client's optimal asset allocation.

---

[1]   'More Conversation Needed on Best Practices for Tax-Aware Portfolios', www. lifehealth.com (August 5, 2015).

4. Minimizes taxes

Goals-based practices intentionally minimize the tax liabilities of their clients by utilizing tax-smart strategies. Some of these methods include estate planning, tax-aware investing, intelligent asset location, and optimal income sourcing. With a goals-based approach, a client's taxable and tax-advantaged accounts are coordinated to reduce taxes in the current period and to minimize taxes in the future. Generating tax alpha – the after-tax benefit from implementing tax-smart strategies – typically has a higher degree of certainty than generating excess investment returns. Smart advisors leverage this reality for the benefit of their clients.

5. Increases an advisor's value

If clients perceive value limited to investment performance, fees may come under pressure and client relationships will likely be less sticky. By providing holistic advice, wealth advisors can demonstrate a deeper value proposition. Also, tools such as goals-based planning software and goal progress reports help advisors connect emotionally with clients, resulting in loyalty, retention, and client referrals.

Fintech within a goals-based investing framework

Within the goals-based framework, progress is tracked against investor goals that are prioritized as basic needs, lifestyle wants, or legacy aspirations. Financial technology, commonly referred to as fintech, enables advisors to effectively and efficiently manage, monitor, and report goal progress. Also, fintech solutions help foster collaboration between advisors and clients, facilitating understanding of client total wealth, goals, financial priorities, risk preferences, life changes, and advisor recommendations. In the end, goals-based investing helps investors know if they have enough money to accomplish their long-term financial objectives. It also helps investors understand if they can do even more with their money.

Advisory practices that proactively embrace fintech solutions will be better positioned for survival in the digital era than firms that do not make technology initiatives a priority. Smart advisors will not let their practices be found among the wreckage of the slow-dying wealth management shops. They will learn from other tech-savvy advisors, leveraging technology throughout their practices. Smart advisors will use fintech to engage their clients. And they will develop and train their teams to fully utilize technology, fostering practice growth and driving better client outcomes.

Turning loss into opportunity

My loss of a sizeable client relationship fundamentally changed my beliefs about wealth management and the client experience. I learned that investment-centric wealth practices marginalize advisor value. Fortunately, I also discovered a better approach – goals-based investing.

As a witness to the transformational benefits of a goals-based framework, I have seen how this approach truly enhances the overall client experience and creates opportunities for stronger practice growth. Moreover, I have experienced firsthand how goals-based investing – supported with collaborative fintech solutions – provides clients with more confidence in their ability to reach their financial goals and aspirations. As a result, this holistic approach positions the practitioner to function like the family's CFO; a true trusted advisor.

I am a passionate advocate for goals-based investing. The last decade of my career has been dedicated to transforming an investment-centric industry to a client-focused one. The wealth management industry has a long way to go. However, I am encouraged as more firms and advisors explore and embark on transforming their practices. Through this change, wealth management is rightfully becoming a noble profession.

As you read, you will discover that goals-based investing is ultimately a win-win proposition. By adopting the principles here, you will help clients sidestep the hazards of traditional investing and improve client outcomes by focusing on the achievement of their long-term goals. Also, by embracing goals-based investing and supporting this framework with innovative fintech solutions, your practice will likely grow – enabling you to thrive amid a constantly changing environment.

PART 1

Hazards
— *that Derail* —
Investor Goals

The purpose of Part 1 is to identify and explain the common perils of traditional investment approaches. Each chapter begins with an engaging story drawn from various disciplines that highlights a given hazard. Following the illustrations are research findings and professional examples that demonstrate how the hazards erode investor wealth. The chapters conclude by foreshadowing how goals-based investing sidesteps the identified dangers of traditional investing.

I

Reacting to External Factors

The hazard of reactionary behavior

> "It is always darkest just before the day dawneth."
>
> — Thomas Fuller

SCIENTIFICALLY THE MOMENT just before dawn is not the darkest, but from an emotional perspective Thomas Fuller's quote rings true. This reality is especially evidenced when observing investor behavior.

Consider investor actions during bear markets. In times of distress, asset prices wane, then continue falling, and eventually capitulate. Darkness permeates the markets when valuations are most severely depressed. Buyers are few and far between. Sellers saturate the markets.

At times like this, fear rules. Emotions become elevated and prompt investors to flee tumultuous environments. This reactionary response is an inherent safety mechanism. Humans are wired to run away from danger.

Even though our emotional responses are meant to protect us, the opposite occurs for investors. Fleeing oversold markets leads to counterproductive results. Just as masses of investors are throwing in the towel and dumping their holdings, markets tend to recover. Consequently, investors lock in losses at market troughs and miss out on the upswing.

Figure 1.1 compares investor flows into and out of equity mutual funds to the 12-month returns of the S&P 500 Index.

Figure 1.1. US equity net fund flows compared to 12-month S&P 500 Index returns

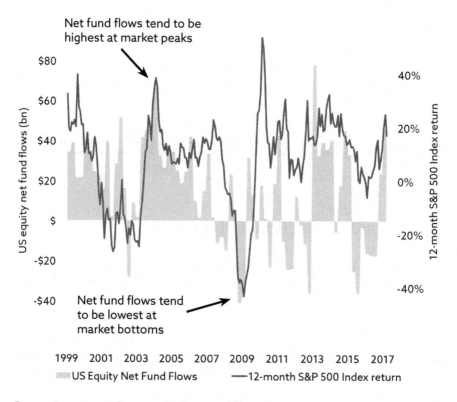

Source: Investment Company Institute and Bloomberg.

Note that when stock prices are low and previous 12-month returns are bad, money usually flows out of equity mutual funds. Net withdrawals of funds are at their highest levels when the market is at its lowest points. For example, in the third quarter of 2008, investors sold equity mutual funds at record levels amid the worst financial crisis in recent history. Subsequently, the stock market made a sharp comeback in 2009. But many investors were out of the market and missed the opportunity to recover their losses.

Moreover, financial advisors are not immune to the behavioral traps that ensnare investors. Advisors tend to let emotions control their responses during periods of market stress, too.

The temptation to counsel clients to react amid freefalling markets is ever present. Clients expect their advisors to do something when prices are plummeting. And advisors do not want to be perceived as nonresponsive and risk losing relationships. So they recommend that clients realign portfolios to be much more conservatively positioned. Others suggest selling assets and increasing cash allocations. In moments of crisis, protectionism trumps all other factors – investors overvalue safety and advisors are highly motivated to defend the sustainability of their practices. This harmful combination too often results in financial advisors acquiescing to behavioral pressures and advising clients to convert distressed assets to cash or ultra conservative investments.

Unfortunately, advisors and investors alike are inclined to overreact to external factors like market swings. Despite knowing that buying low and selling high is foundational to investment success, financial professionals and investors tend to do exactly the opposite. Emotions prevail over rational thought. As a result, opportunities are forfeited, and investor goals may be beyond reach.

I cannot stand the pain any longer!

An advisor friend of mine told me he may never forget the sound of his client's panic-stricken voice. He said it trembled with fear, as if news of a tragic death was just received.

The call came in January of 2009. Moments before, the client had gone to the mailbox and opened his year-end investment statement. The report revealed his portfolio lost 20% in 2008. The advisor recalls the client desperately pleading, "I cannot stand the pain any longer!"

A few years prior to this call, the client and his business partner sold their manufacturing firm for a hefty sum. My friend got the privilege to manage both partners' assets. The clients were near retirement age and had more than enough wealth to support their income needs and other financial goals for life. They both agreed with their advisor to portfolios with a 50/50 mix of stocks and bonds.

In early 2009, the two clients' paths diverged. My friend was unable to persuade the frantic partner from overreacting. When he demanded that his portfolio be liquidated and remain in cash until further instruction, reluctantly, the advisor followed the client's orders. The other, more level-headed partner heeded my friend's advice and remained fully invested.

A few months after the panicky client went to cash and the other partner decided to stay the course, the market swiftly began to recover. 2009 ended up being a great year for the markets, with the S&P 500 Index advancing more than 26%.

Eventually, the anxious client instructed his advisor to invest in an ultra-conservative bond portfolio. He never recovered all of his losses after selling at the market's bottom. In contrast, the partner that followed my friend's advice fully recovered his unrealized losses within a few years and subsequently has seen his portfolio gain more than 50% in cumulative value.

As this story illustrates, overreacting to external, uncontrollable factors can be very costly for investors. The penalty of lost returns from reactionary behavior is sometimes referred to as the *behavior gap*, as explained in more detail below.

Behavior gap

Research suggests a wide chasm exists between the higher returns investors *could* earn, and the lower returns they *actually* realize. What investors really earn is not the official performance from their investments reported as time-weighted returns in fund prospectuses. Instead, actual investor returns are a function of the timing of their contributions and withdrawals into an investment, also known as an investor's money-weighted returns.

Destructive behavior, such as panicking during market downturns and chasing performance when markets rally, is often cited as the cause of the difference between potential and actual returns. Studies estimate the size of this behavior gap to range from slightly more than 1% per year to more than 3%, as shown in Figure 1.2. The results vary due to calculation methodology or the period analyzed, but most research agrees that investor behavior reduces return potential.

DALBAR, a financial services market research firm, has been measuring the behavior gap since 1994. Their research consistently validates that average investors earn much less than reported mutual fund performance because of bad investor timing decisions. As illustrated in Figure 1.2, DALBAR's research for the 20-year period ending December 31, 2015 estimates the annual gap between the average equity investor's returns and S&P 500 Index performance to be 3.5%. DALBAR uses monthly mutual fund sales, redemption, and exchange data from the Investment Company Institute to calculate the "average investor return". Other 20-year periods have behavior gaps in excess of six percentage points annually, according to DALBAR's past research.[2]

Financial advisors may believe they are immune from the behavioral gap. But that is not the case. At a 2015 CFA Institute conference, Carl Richards, author of *The Behavior Gap*, pointed out, "Most of the money in a mutual fund is advised; it gets there because an advisor put it there." Richard's observation indicts financial advisors rather than exonerating them. The reality is that too

---

2   'DALBAR's 22nd Annual Quantitative Analysis of Investor Behavior', www.qidllc. com (2016).

many financial advisors are accommodating destructive investor behavior, and thus further contributing to the behavior gap.[3]

Figure 1.2. Estimates of the behavior gap

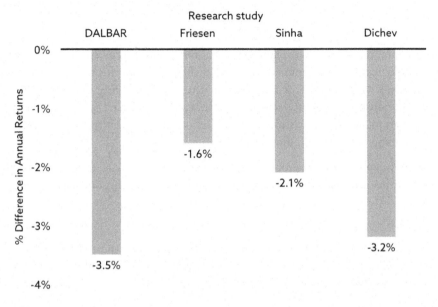

Sources: DALBAR's 22nd Annual Quantitative Analysis of Investor Behavior', www. qidllc.com (2016); Geoffrey C. Friesen and Travis R. A. Sapp, 'Mutual fund flows and investor returns: An empirical examination of fund investor timing ability', CBA Faculty Publications (September 2007); Rajeeva Sinha and Vijay Jog, 'Fund Flows And Performance: A Study of Canadian Equity Funds', www.people.hbs.edu; and Ilia D. Dichev and Gwen Yu, 'Higher risk, lower returns: What hedge fund investors really earn', *Journal of Financial Economics* (January 2011).

To avoid the hazard of overreacting, advisors first must recognize and understand the causes that yield dismal investor outcomes.

3   David Allison, 'How Financial Advisers Can Help Close the Behavior Gap', blogs. cfainstitute.org/investor (July 27, 2015) and Carl Richards, 'The Behavior Gap', www. cfapubs.org (September 2013).

Five behavioral causes of poor investment decisions

Like all humans, advisors and investors may behave irrationally when faced with certain triggers. Psychological misperceptions also may produce unreasonable responses. Emotion-based behavior, when void of logic, leads advisors and investors to make bad timing judgments and poor investment decisions. Underperformance subsequently results.

Behavioral finance helps explain these irrational responses by studying various psychological biases of humans. Although these predispositions serve natural purposes such as providing a protective instinct when facing loss, they often lead to foolish investment decisions. Understanding human biases provides an explanation for why investment anomalies occur, like seemingly unfounded sell-offs and rallies amid efficient markets.

Below, I explore five common behavioral traps that ensnare investors. These include: loss aversion, confirmation bias, herding, anchoring, and recency bias.

1. Loss aversion

Humans are hardwired to fear losses more than they enjoy gains. This tendency is referred to as loss aversion by behavioral psychologists. A number of research studies have estimated people weigh losses more than twice as much as potential gains.

The first study to introduce the principle of loss aversion was conducted by Professors Daniel Kahneman and Amos Tversky in 1979. In this ground-breaking research, Kahneman and Tversky presented a concept called prospect theory which contends people value gains and losses differently, making decisions based on perceived gains rather than perceived losses. For example, if an investor were presented with two equivalent investment options – one expressed in terms of potential gains and the other in potential losses – the investor typically would choose the option framed in terms of gains, even when both investments are expected to generate the same returns.[4]

Loss aversion helps explain a number of irrational financial behaviors. For instance, the pain associated with losses causes some people to avoid investments with long-term growth potential because of the possibility of negative returns in the near term. As a result, these risk averse investors tend to gravitate toward ultra conservative investments that may limit their ability to achieve their financial goals.

---

[4]   Daniel Kahneman and Amos Tversky, 'Prospect Theory: An Analysis of Decision under Risk' (1979).

In other situations, investors may shun selling concentrated holdings with capital gains to avoid the loss incurred by paying taxes. Although diversifying a concentrated investment helps reduce the risk of overexposure to a single asset, some investors prefer not to incur taxes instead of diversifying their portfolios. The theory of loss aversion provides insight as to why some investors make this potentially imprudent choice.

2. Confirmation bias

Confirmation bias refers to behavior that selectively seeks evidence to support an opinion while dismissing contradictory evidence. Individuals are blinded from carefully evaluating facts and data with an open mind as a result of their confirmation bias. Instead of remaining impartial when forming opinions, people generally only look for points of view that reinforce their currently held perspectives.

Confirmation bias is exhibited by advisors and investors when they latch on to information that supports their investment thesis but ignore data that contradicts it. Consequently, this skewed perspective may result in faulty conclusions and bad investment decisions.

For example, consider an advisor who hears about a top-performing mutual fund and becomes convinced his clients should own this fund. Before offering this investment, the advisor conducts *research* on the fund and learns the entire management team that generated the fund's past performance recently left the firm. Despite this glaring red flag, the advisor ignores the information and chooses to focus on the fund's top-ranking track record, its impressive historical statistics, and the fund family's sterling reputation. With supporting evidence in hand, the advisor concludes the mutual fund is a good choice and begins offering it to his clients. Such a situation would be confirmation bias at work.

3. Herding

Humans are tribal creatures. We habitually run in herds. This natural tendency leads people to blindly follow popular trends with little forethought. Behavioral finance experts often blame herding as the cause of irrational exuberance at stock market peaks and why so few buyers can be found when markets tank.

Herding occurs for several reasons. First, peer pressure is a powerful force. People naturally desire to be accepted by a group and avoid being perceived as outcasts. Second, individuals find safety in numbers. We rationalize that opinions of a large group must be right. These two influences result in people mimicking the actions of large crowds, even if the behaviors are foolish.

I experienced firsthand the absurdness of herding while living in Phoenix in the mid-to-late 2000s. We had sold our home, and the title company's front-desk assistant was assigned to oversee the signing of our paperwork at closing. (All of the title officers were unavailable due to the sheer volume of transactions taking place near the market's peak.) During our closing, the assistant shared a story with my wife and me, about recently purchasing her fifth investment property. She had learned about the home from a local taxi driver whose neighbor's house was about to be put up for sale.

The assistant told us how she quickly jumped on the tip, secured financing (from a fly-by-night lender), and was well on her way to becoming a real estate mogul. I could not fathom how an hourly worker could own five investment properties without having to put down any equity. The only explanation was the market had gone completely mad as a result of herding. No one wanted to miss out. Lenders did not. Appraisers did not. Even front-desk assistants had to get in the game. Shortly thereafter, Phoenix experienced one of the worst housing boom-to-bust cycles in US history.

Herd mentality does not only inflict novice investors. It can also significantly influence financial professionals. For example, whenever a new investment fad surfaces, many clients begin asking their advisors about investing in this hot, new strategy. Not wanting to lose clients to more trendy financial professionals, advisors may succumb to herding pressure and begin offering the latest investment gimmick to their clients. An advisor can rationalize this decision, because clients will remain loyal if the strategy pans out. And if it does not, clients likely will not leave, as nearly everyone else will have experienced similar losses.

Unquestionably, herd behavior erodes investor wealth. By the time the newest trend is commonly known, future appreciation is likely limited. Herd followers typically enter the fad too late and experience losses instead of gains. This was certainly the case of the front-desk assistant helping with my house closing, as well as countless other makeshift real estate investors in the mid-to-late 2000s. When family and friends begin touting lucrative investment strategies, herd warning signs should be flashing brightly. Smart advisors and investors recognize these signs and have the courage to swim upstream.

4. Anchoring

People tend to overweight the importance of psychological benchmarks, rules-of-thumb, or baseline numbers when making decisions. These reference points serve as mental anchors – even if they are irrelevant to the present set of circumstances.

Anchoring can negatively affect investment decisions. For example, the purchase price of an investment can serve as an anchor by which future buy and sell considerations are referenced. If the current price of a stock is below its acquisition cost, the price may seem cheap. This cognitive bias prompts the investor to buy more of the stock even though the company's deteriorating fundamentals warrant the lower valuation.

Another example of anchoring is making investment decisions based on arbitrary index numbers. For instance, a Dow Jones Industrial Average reading of 20,000 may serve as a trigger to buy or sell investments, regardless of the benchmark's underlying valuation considerations.

5. Recency bias

People are hard-wired to make decisions that are heavily influenced by recent events or experiences. Recency bias suggests new opinions are often formed by extrapolating the latest circumstances into the future.

Behavioral psychologists have found people tend to overestimate the likelihood of being in a car crash if they recently witnessed a wreck. Vivid memories of the experience make the prospect of such an occurrence feel tangible and real, and thus seem more probable than actual crash statistics support. Similarly, investors are more likely to fear the onset of a bear market after recently experiencing a market correction. Fresh and painful memories of the financial setback influence investor behavior on a go-forward basis.

Institutional investors and advisors are not immune from recency bias. For example, Bloomberg surveys market strategists each week, asking for their recommended asset allocation weightings. During the last two decades, the market strategists' highest average weighting to equities came just after the dot-com peak in early 2001. And their lowest average weighting to stocks followed just after the financial crisis low point in early 2009. As this example shows, even financial professionals' opinions can be biased and skewed by recent events.[5]

A perfect storm

Independently, each of these five behavioral biases may induce irrational financial actions by advisors and investors. However, when multiple behavioral traps interact, a perfect storm for wealth destruction emerges. At such times, it is imperative that these cognitive biases are recognized.

---

[5]   Alistair Byrne and Stephen Utkus, 'Understanding how the mind can help or hinder investment success', www.vanguard.co.uk (2013).

Consider the wealth erosion experienced by an investor who is negatively impacted by the convergence of multiple behavioral biases. Due to loss aversion, this investor holds on to a large mutual fund investment below its cost basis. As time goes on, the market swoons, and the fund continues to lose value. Recency bias takes hold, and the investor believes the losses will continue. Moreover, the investor succumbs to confirmation bias by focusing on the financial media's obsession with the sell-off, but gives no credence to an analyst's new, positive report about the investor's mutual fund.

Meanwhile, the market sell-off continues, fueled by herding behavior. And after the Dow falls another 500 points to a 12-month low, anchoring kicks in. The investor finally sells the mutual fund based on this irrelevant benchmark threshold. Huge losses are realized. Shortly thereafter, the market sharply rebounds, and the investor entirely misses the fund's largest gain in three years.

This illustration may seem farfetched. Yet, the average investor's dismal return, as explained by the behavioral gap, suggests otherwise.

Besides loss aversion, confirmation bias, herding, anchoring, and recency bias, a number of other cognitive theories have emerged to explain irrational investor behavior. An exhaustive study of these behavioral biases is beyond the scope of this book. Advisors wanting to learn more about this subject may find *The Laws of Wealth* by Daniel Crosby to be a helpful resource.

Smart financial advisors deter clients from overreacting

My home state of Kansas is notorious for tornados. Remaining outside when a tornadic storm approaches may result in severe injury or death. Thus, a person's innate behavior to flee and take refuge amid a tornado is a helpful, life-saving response.

However, this same reaction to bolt from danger can produce the opposite effect for advisors and their clients in situations when markets appear perilous. Succumbing to reactionary behavior often is hazardous to investor wealth as demonstrated in this chapter.

Smart advisors deter their clients from making harmful, reactionary decisions. Instead of enabling clients to fall prey to their behavioral biases, they coach their clients through tumultuous market environments. For example, smart advisors help clients remain calm by refocusing conversations on long-term client goals instead of external circumstances. These discussions, when reinforced by analysis from goals-based technology, provide investors with a basis for staying in the market when others are fleeing.

Prior to periods of market stress, advisors using a goals-based investing approach proactively evaluate client risk, investment strategies, and goals under multiple scenarios. This analysis helps advisors construct investor-specific solutions to weather difficult conditions. It also gives clients confidence to heed advisor guidance that feels counterintuitive when markets are spiraling downward. Chapter 8 explains these concepts in more detail.

Emotions are powerful. They strongly influence human behavior. But when investors overreact to them, results may be disastrous. By helping clients manage their behavioral biases through a goals-based investing framework, smart advisors are better able to position clients for long-term success.

2

Failing to Plan

The hazard of directionless investing

> "By failing to prepare, you are preparing to fail."
>
> — Benjamin Franklin

ON A WARM Friday afternoon in September of 2010, Ed Rosenthal, 68, set out for a celebratory hike up 4,900-foot Warren View, a peak in Joshua Tree National Park in south-eastern California. Hiking this five-mile up-and-back trek was Ed's longstanding ritual after closing big real estate deals. He took a small, half-quart hydration pack and a daypack with a few essentials, but left his jacket, phone, and map in the car. In his zest to conquer the mountain, Ed forgot to tell his wife – or anyone else – that he was going on the hike.

Within an hour and a half, Ed had reached the summit. He soaked in the expansive desert vista for a few minutes and silently congratulated himself for being at the top of his game. He then decided to head back. But something was wrong. Ed could not find the little-used rock trail. So he picked a spot to descend, hoping he would cross the trail on his way down. He never did. Instead, he found himself lost in the middle of the Mojave Desert.

Six hours after starting the hike, Ed hunkered down for the night. After a fitful rest, dawn awakened him. He was already dehydrated, as he had finished his water the afternoon before. He resumed his search to find the trail, but his wandering only resulted in further exhaustion under the scorching desert sun. Thirsty, tired, and depleted, Ed stumbled to a lone evergreen and crawled under its branches for relief and shade. Day turned to night, and the situation became exceedingly dire.

The next day, Ed mustered enough strength to continue looking for a way out of the desert, but soon collapsed in a shaded area near a small canyon. He thought about his wife and daughter and how he missed them. Ed scribbled a message to each of them and prepared that he might soon die. When night arrived, he could see the lights of civilization ten miles in the distance, promising deliverance. But he was too thirsty and exhausted to move, and he began to drift in and out of consciousness.

If the intermittent rain showers had not sprung up, Ed's chance of survival would have been slim to none. Finally, six days after embarking on the hike, a search and rescue crew found Ed clinging to life. Fortunately, he lived and subsequently made a full recovery.[6]

Too often, advisors and investors make the same mistake that Ed made when he set out for his celebratory hike in the California desert. They fail to adequately plan. Ed's lack of preparation – not taking a map, phone, and layers of clothes, and telling no one of his whereabouts – nearly cost him his life. Failing to plan can be very costly for investors, too. When plans are not developed or left discarded, financial goals may go unrealized.

Most people start investing with a general idea of where they are heading. A common example is building wealth for retirement. But without specific plans, investors are merely guessing at how much money is needed to accomplish their objectives, and these guesses may be way off. Accordingly, they may find themselves lost along the way and miss their desired destinations.

Preparing adequately is essential for investor success. A well-designed plan – created with the help of an experienced financial advisor – provides a blueprint for accomplishing broad objectives and dynamically reflects life and financial changes over time. Furthermore, it identifies investor goals such as saving for retirement or major purchases, and estimates the amount of money likely needed to meet these goals. Financial plans then can serve as benchmarks to evaluate the distance between where an investor is currently positioned and where he or she would like to be in the future. In other words, goal-based plans help answer the question – are you on track or not?

In this chapter, the prevalence of investors and advisors failing to plan is considered, and the consequences of directionless investing are examined, including the pending retirement crisis. The chapter concludes by highlighting how smart advisors position their practices to avoid this hazard.

6   Joshua Prestin, 'Out Alive: Lost in the Desert', www.backpacker.com (October 3, 2014).

Failing to plan is a common mistake made by investors

Most investors recognize the importance of planning, yet fail to take action. A 2015 Wells Fargo/Gallup survey found that 89% of US investors acknowledge they desire to be financially secure for the long term versus having cash in hand today. Despite valuing long-term results associated with a deliberate planning process, only 38% of US investors had a written financial plan to help them achieve their investment and retirement goals. The study found that retired investors tend to prepare better than those still working, with results of 43% and 36% with financial plans, respectively.

When those with no written financial strategy were asked why they lacked one, two top reasons emerged. The number one reason investors gave was that they had not taken the time (29%). The second top reason given was they had not thought about it (27%). These reasons sound more like excuses given by a teenager when asked why his room was not clean than a rationale for why adults are failing to plan for a secure financial future.[7]

In another study, the Society of Actuaries commissioned Mathew Greenwald & Associates in 2015 to research US investors' awareness of potential financial risks in retirement and how this awareness affects the management of their assets. The study found that many investors never consult a financial professional to help craft a written financial plan. Only 15% of pre-retirees reported having consulted with a financial advisor at least once a year for help with decisions about retirement and financial planning. Another quarter do so as needed, while about one-in-ten consult a financial professional less than once a year. However, based on this study, more than half of investors acknowledged they have never consulted with a financial advisor.[8]

These two studies, along with many others, suggest that failing to plan is a common mistake made by investors. But what about advisors? Do they make the same error when managing their own assets? Surprisingly, the answer is yes.

Failing to plan is prevalent among advisors, too

One presumes that professionals heed their own advice in matters relevant to their expertise. But this expectation does not consistently hold true. Take physicians as an example. Doctors routinely counsel patients about eating well and maintaining a healthy weight. Yet, there are many doctors who have poor

---

7   Jeffrey M. Jones, 'More Nonretired U.S. Investors Have a Written Financial Plan' www.gallup.com (July 31, 2015).

8   '2015 Risks and Process of Retirement Survey' www.soa.org (2015).

dietary habits and are overweight. Financial professionals, likewise, do not always practice what they preach. This reality is especially true when it comes to advisors adequately preparing for their own financial futures.

In a 2016 survey conducted by Bob Veres, a financial services author and consultant, more than 1000 US advisors were asked if they buy for themselves financial advisory and planning services they provide for their clients. The survey revealed only 50% of advisors have a financial plan for themselves. Furthermore, a relatively small number of respondents (19%) receive planning services from another advisor at their firm. And a mere 4% work with a planner at another firm. Accordingly, very few advisors are buying the same services that they provide to clients.

The study also asked advisors how often they review their own financial situation. Figure 2.1 shows the results of this question.

Figure 2.1. How often financial advisors review their portfolios

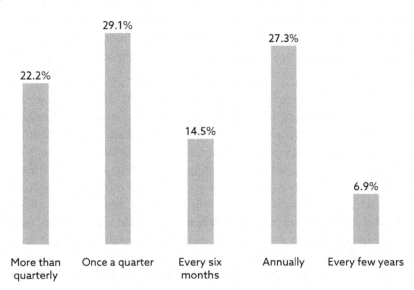

Figure 2.1 suggests advisors may not be giving their own financial circumstances as much attention as they give to those of their clients. In fact, more than one-third of the surveyed advisors review their own portfolios only once a year or every few years – frequencies that would likely get them fired if they managed client assets the same way.[9]

9   Bob Veres, 'Our Survey Results: How Good are Advisors at Their Own Financial

Consequences of failing to plan

Both investors and advisors too often fail to plan for their financial futures. This hazard can be very costly. Consequences for directionless investing include having to reduce living standards, assuming more risk, not being able to achieve financial goals, and possibly even outliving one's resources.

Having to reduce living standards

Failure to plan may result in having to live on less in later years. Without appropriate planning, income generated during working years too often is spent on funding current living standards without setting aside adequate savings for retirement. When this occurs, accumulated cash and investment assets may be insufficient to maintain pre-retirement living standards throughout retirement.

Research commissioned by the Society of Actuaries found retirees do little planning and often do not have long-term financial goals. The majority of surveyed retirees did not have a financial plan upon retirement; nor did they generally have one later in their retirement years. Given this widespread failure to plan, the study revealed retirees had to adapt spending in retirement, with unexpected expenses often contributing to them having to become more frugal than they were during their working years.

The research found retirees generally encountered similar, unanticipated expenditures, including housing repairs and maintenance, giving/lending children money, health care, marital changes, investment losses, inflation, and taxes. These types of expenses certainly can occur at any time in life. Yet without planning for such expenditures, funding them can be especially difficult in retirement. Cash reserves, investment accounts, and other assets set aside for maintaining living standards throughout retirement may have to be depleted to fund these unforeseen expenses. When asked about their financial picture, most retirees indicated they hoped to sustain their wealth at current levels in the future. But past spending experiences of retirees indicate this outcome may be unlikely for many elderly people as they age – especially in the absence of planning.[10]

Assuming more risk

Another consequence of failing to plan is having to assume more financial risk. People who fail to plan in earlier working years face hard decisions as they get

Planning?', www.advisorperspectives.com (March 1, 2016).
[10]   'Post-Retirement Experiences of Individuals Retired for 15 Years or More', www.soa. org (2016).

closer to retirement – choosing between working longer, living on less money, or taking on more investment risk in an attempt to reach financial goals.

Unfortunately, working longer is not always an option because of factors such as difficult work environments, family needs, and health problems. People generally plan to retire at a considerably older age than current retirees actually retired. For example, recent empirical research has found that workers typically retire at age 60 (median actual retirement age), but pre-retirees normally expect to retire at age 65 (median expected retirement age). Furthermore, this research revealed nearly 20% of pre-retirees intend to work until age 68 or longer, and 14% indicated they do not plan to ever retire.[11]

This disconnect between expected and actual retirement dates combined with inadequate planning leaves people having to assume more investment risk in later years. In such instances, increasing portfolio allocations to potentially higher-returning, more volatile investments like equities and high-yield bonds may be the only way to conceivably reach long-term financial goals.

However, taking on more investment risk can be perilous. Consider near-retirees who over-allocated to riskier assets leading up to the Great Recession in the late 2000s. Those who bet their financial futures on the hope of higher returns saw their retirement savings plummet in 2008, with many experiencing their portfolio values fall 30%–50% or more.

Not attaining financial goals

A third consequence of failing to plan is having to abandon certain financial goals. Some investors may be able to sustain their lifestyles throughout retirement, but because of inadequate planning (not lack of resources), they are unable to attain aspirational and legacy goals. These wishes may include leaving money to heirs and/or making philanthropic gifts.

Legacy ambitions often are thwarted by poor planning and the absence of having sound strategies in place for the future. My professional experience has shown this reality to hold true for investors with moderate savings as well as people with sizeable estates.

Outliving resources

A fourth consequence of directionless investing is outliving one's resources.

Northwestern Mutual's 2015 Planning and Progress study revealed that longevity risk, the possibility of outliving a person's savings, is a common financial fear

---

[11] '2015 Risks and Process of Retirement Survey', www.soa.org (2015).

among Americans. The findings also exposed that this risk has largely gone unaddressed. According to this research, 31% of US adults believe they will likely outlive their assets, while another 24% of Americans are unsure if their savings will last. Despite these beliefs, more than half (52%) have not taken any action to address longevity risk.[12]

Each of the aforementioned consequences of failing to plan point toward an impending retirement crisis. This stark reality is examined below.

Retirement savings crisis

Individual saving for retirement has always been important. However, the changing landscape of the US retirement system has put more importance on personal responsibility in recent years. For example, consider the findings of a 2015 research report published by the National Institute on Retirement Security titled *The Continuing Retirement Savings Crisis*. The report quantified the share of retirees receiving defined benefit (DB) pension income from their or their spouse's former employer fell from 52% in the late 1990s to 43% in 2010, and has since further declined.[13]

In addition to fewer retirees receiving DB pension income, Americans are increasingly concerned about the future viability of Social Security. A 2016 study conducted by the Harris Poll found that only a quarter of US adults 18 years and older believe that Social Security is extremely likely to be there when they retire. Additionally, the study showed that 49% of current retirees expect Social Security to be their sole or primary source of retirement income, compared to just 35% of pre-retirees who have this expectation.[14]

Given these beliefs about the future availability of Social Security and the reality that fewer retirees are receiving DB benefits, Americans are faced with having to save and invest more of their wages in order to adequately fund retirement. Unfortunately, the average pre-retiree household – even those close to retirement – has virtually no retirement savings. Figure 2.2 illustrates this alarming fact.

As shown in Figure 2.2, the median retirement account balance for all working-age households in the US is a mere $2,500. Just as alarming is the fact that households near retirement (ages 55–64) have saved on average only $14,500. These miniscule amounts leave no doubt that Americans have severely undersaved for retirement.

---

[12] 'Planning and Progress Study 2015', www.northwesternmutual.com (2015).
[13] Nari Rhee and Ilana Boivie, 'The Continuing Retirement Savings Crisis', www.nirsonline.org (March 2015).
[14] 'Planning and Progress Study 2016', www.northwesternmutual.com (2016).

Figure 2.2. Median US retirement household account balances by age

Source: Nari Rhee and Ilana Boivie, 'The Continuing Retirement Savings Crisis', www.nirsonline.org (March 2015).

Making matters worse is that pre-retirees often do not know how much to be saving for retirement. The Employment Benefit Research Institute's 2016 Retirement Confidence Survey found that less than half (48%) of working households have done a retirement needs calculation. Furthermore, those who have calculated their retirement savings number likely used a method lacking sound rationale. For example, 39% arrive at their number by simply guessing. Others merely read or heard how much they should be saving. Only 26% calculated their required savings by consulting a financial advisor.[15]

Given these findings, it is not surprising that a 2016 JP Morgan study of 401(k) participants discovered that less than four-in-ten US workers are confident about how much to save to stay on track for a comfortable retirement. Figure 2.3 highlights that very few 401(k) participants have a clear understanding of how to set a retirement savings goal.

[15]   Ruth Helman, Craig Copeland and Jack VanDerhei, 'The 2016 Retirement Confidence Survey – Worker Confidence Stable, Retiree Confidence Continues to Increase', EBRI Issue Brief, no. 422 (Employee Benefit Research Institute, March 2016).

Figure 2.3. Retirement planning confidence among 401(k) participants

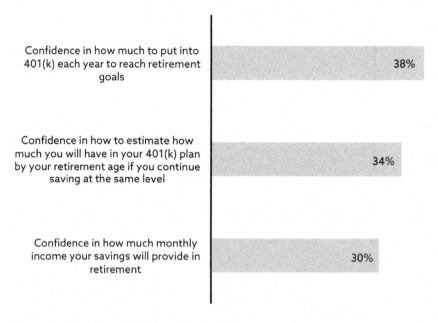

Source: 'Guiding participants from intent to action 2016. Defined Contribution Plan Participant Survey Findings' am.jpmorgan.com (July 2016).

The looming retirement savings crisis in America cannot be easily solved. The trend toward fewer employer-sponsored DB plans will likely continue. Also, the long-term viability of Social Security remaining in its current form is somewhat questionable. These challenges place the retirement savings burden squarely on the shoulders of individuals. Yet, pre-retirees are not saving nearly enough – largely due to failing to adequately plan.

With the help of financial advisors, these trends can be reversed. When advisors are engaged, investor confidence and financial outcomes tend to improve. According to the 2015 Wells Fargo/Gallup poll about retirement optimism, pre-retirees with a written plan tend to be confident in their ability to reach their retirement goals. The study found that 42% are highly confident of this, with another 48% somewhat confident. And the vast majority of workers with a written plan (74%) developed their plan with the help of a financial advisor.[16]

[16] Jeffrey M. Jones, 'More Nonretired U.S. Investors Have a Written Financial Plan', www.gallup.com (July 31, 2015).

Smart financial advisors help clients plan by establishing and prioritizing goals

Failing to plan contributes to outcomes not being realized. Personal experience has taught me this truth. A few years ago I made a New Year's resolution to lose weight. However, I did not create a specific strategy to accomplish this worthwhile objective. Instead, I hit the gym for the first few weeks of the year and attempted to eat less. Quickly, bad habits returned, though. By the end of the year, I was heavier than I had ever been.

More recently, a friend introduced me to a health and fitness app called MyFitnessPal. He shared how this tool helped him set weight-loss goals and track progress. For me, the proof was visual. My friend looked as thin as he had in college. So I decided to give the app a try.

First, I entered my weight goal. From there, the app calculated my necessary daily calorie intake. With a specific target weight determined and a daily calorie plan in place, I started my journey toward better health. This required me to daily input my food intake and any calories burned from exercise. The app made this easy by a simple interface with preset calorie information on thousands of foods. It is also integrated with exercise apps that link calories expended on activities like running or biking.

Weekly I entered my current weight into the app. At first, progress was slow, but I stuck with the plan. The app further helped me by tracking my progress and sending mobile reminders to input daily calories if I had forgotten to do so. As the weeks passed, I noticed my clothes were beginning to fit better. After about four months, I was shopping for new clothes, because much of my wardrobe was too large. Eventually, I hit my target weight, and I have been able to maintain this goal ever since.

I believe this story contains clues about how smart financial advisors can help clients attain long-term goals. Similar to me, most people have general ideas about long-term objectives – whether it is to get healthier or to be able to afford retiring someday. But like my weight-loss example, these basic objectives absent specific plans and goals are not sufficient to make effective, sustainable progress. Accordingly, a key factor to long-term outcome achievement is to create a plan that includes specific goals.

This commonsense, straightforward approach laid the foundation for my return to a healthier weight. Likewise, I believe this method of proactive planning better positions advisors to deliver successful investor outcomes. To help clients avoid the hazard of failing to plan, advisors need to collaborate with clients, identifying long-term financial goals and quantifying reasonable accumulation and spending targets. Additionally, advisors should work with clients to

33

prioritize from a range of goals that may otherwise compete with one another. By doing so, the foundations of a well-structured, goals-based plan are put in place.

3

Quarantining Portfolios

The hazard of isolation

> "Isolation is a self-defeating dream."
>
> — Carlos Salinas de Gortari

QUARANTINE IS NORMALLY a medical term. In this context, to quarantine means keeping a person away from others to prevent spreading a disease.

In October of 2014, the governor of New Jersey mandated quarantines for people exposed to Ebola. The intent of this rule was to protect citizens from individuals who came into contact with the deadly virus. However, this controversial policy created conflict between personal liberties and public protection.

On the day this mandate was enacted, nurse Kaci Hickox was quarantined in New Jersey. She had just returned from treating Ebola patients in West Africa. Despite showing no symptoms of Ebola and testing negative for the disease, she was held in isolation for three days in New Jersey before being allowed to return to her home in Maine. Ms. Hickox subsequently sued the governor of New Jersey. According to a statement released by her attorneys, she claimed, "My liberty, my interests, and consequently my civil rights were ignored."[17]

Ms. Hickox's quarantine proved to be unnecessary. Similarly, financial advisors who needlessly manage portfolios in isolation restrict client success.

---

[17]　B. Chappell, 'Christie Defends Quarantine And Jabs At CDC Over Ebola', www.npr. org (October 26, 2014); and L. Wagner, 'New Jersey Governor Facing Lawsuit From Nurse Quarantined During Ebola Scare', www.npr.org (October 22, 2015).

High net worth clients generally have multiple investment accounts such as taxable accounts, tax-deferred accounts, and tax-free accounts. Sometimes these accounts are managed by one advisor. At other times, an investor engages multiple advisors. When advisors quarantine portfolios, they manage each client account separately without regard for a client's other accounts.

This practice is prevalent when multiple advisors are managing an investor's wealth. Coordination is more difficult with multiple advisors than a single advisor. Yet, quarantining portfolios is surprisingly common, even when an investor engages just one advisor to manage all assets. In both circumstances, each client account is managed on a standalone basis rather than in a coordinated, holistic approach.

The dangers of quarantining portfolios are evidenced when a client's individually-managed accounts are viewed on a combined basis. One account may be conservatively invested. Another may be aggressively allocated. Quarantined portfolios often work against each other, lacking a unified strategy that is aligned with a client's overall goals.

For example, consider two financial advisors who are both servicing the same 58-year-old male investor who is hoping to retire in five years. The client has three accounts – a taxable account, a tax-deferred individual retirement account (IRA), and an employer-sponsored 401(k). Each account's value is approximately equal. The taxable account is managed by one advisor; the IRA is managed by the other advisor. The 401(k) is self-directed by the client. Each account is invested on a standalone basis without full consideration of how the other accounts are invested.

To determine the portfolio mix of the managed accounts, risk tolerance questionnaires are used by the advisors. The advisor managing the taxable account scores the client as a balanced investor and allocates the portfolio with 50% to equities and 50% to bonds. The second advisor scores the client to a moderate growth portfolio comprised of 60% equities and 40% bonds. Ignoring how the managed accounts are invested, the client allocates his 401(k) assets evenly among the three top-performing fund choices in the plan, which all happen to be equity funds.

When all three accounts are combined, the client has approximately 70% of his assets invested in equities. Given the 58-year old hopes to retire in five years, this allocation is likely too aggressive and may jeopardize his retirement goal. His early retirement dreams could be erased with just one, untimely down market. Because the client's portfolios are being managed in isolation, this considerable risk goes unnoticed by his advisors.

As shown in this example, when advisors quarantine portfolios, the management of an investor's multiple accounts is not coordinated. Consequently, the ability of advisors to manage a client's wealth in harmony with the client's holistic goals is limited. Moreover, tax-smart coordination among an investor's accounts becomes difficult for advisors to effectively execute when managing portfolios separately.

Quarantining portfolios is hazardous; it obscures a client's complete wealth picture. It is like attempting to construct a client's comprehensive wealth strategy without a full blueprint of the client's resources and desired outcomes.

A partial blueprint

The first home my wife and I owned was a newly constructed house. Six months prior to moving into our new home, we selected a lot and hired the builder. Before construction began, we reviewed a number of house plans and selected a design that we both liked. The architect made a few tweaks to the floor plan to accommodate our specific lot and personal preferences.

With the final blueprints in hand, the builder and subcontractors began moving dirt. Before long, the foundation was poured and framing was underway. The blueprints served as the primary source of instructions for how we intended the house to be built. Whenever construction or design questions arose, the blueprints became the definitive guide for the builder.

The construction process presented challenges at times. Bad weather caused delays. Subcontractors occasionally did not show up when scheduled. Also, my wife and I had to make interior finishing decisions while living three hours away. Despite these setbacks, in the end, our finished home was exactly as we had hoped it to be.

This successful outcome would have been very different if our builder had a partial blueprint. What if our house plans contained drawings for only one room, such as the kitchen? We would have likely enjoyed our eating space, but the rest of the house may have been unliveable based on our needs.

Building a home with incomplete blueprints is a ridiculous scenario. No one would ever take this approach. Yet, financial advisors commonly manage client wealth with only a partial picture. The hazards of this myopic practice are often overlooked by advisors and investors.

Four underlying dangers of quarantining portfolios

In order to effectively sidestep the pitfall of managing portfolios in isolation, financial advisors need a better understanding of the underlying dangers. Four of these risks are examined below.

1. Blocked view

One underlying danger is that financial advisors cannot see the entirety of their clients' wealth with a single view.

I work downtown and when my schedule permits, I will run on nearby paths along the Arkansas river. A satellite image from Google Maps shows the river is a few blocks from my office in the direction my window faces. However, I cannot see the river because adjacent buildings block my view. If my only knowledge of downtown was derived from my window's view, I would never know the river existed.

Likewise, quarantining portfolios results in blocked views. This approach restricts financial advisors from operating with a complete perspective of their client's goals, assets, and liabilities. Consequently, opportunities to holistically manage client wealth are missed.

2. Pay more; get less

Another danger of quarantining portfolios is that it often results in investors paying more, but getting less.

No one likes to overpay for a purchase. The frustration of overpaying is exacerbated when a pricey item delivers less satisfaction than a cheaper option. Paying more and getting less is a bad combination.

When portfolios are quarantined, clients generally end up incurring higher fees and owing more taxes. Investments spread across multiple advisors likely cost investors more in fees than if assets were consolidated with a primary advisor. The opportunity for a client to get asset-based discounts from advisors is decreased, because each of the client's advisors end up with a smaller portion of the client's overall wallet share. And higher fees over time erode investor wealth.

Furthermore, when portfolios are managed in isolation, a coordinated, tax-smart approach becomes much more difficult to execute. Offsetting gains with losses from one portfolio to the next is challenging for multiple advisors to effectively coordinate. Also, wash sale violations become more common. These violations occur under the Internal Revenue Service rules when an investment is sold at a loss and within 30 days after the sale the same or similar security is repurchased. Accordingly, investors cannot deduct wash sale losses. Research by Parametric

Portfolio Associates shows that ineffective tax management of portfolios can annually reduce investor returns by 0.7–2.5 percentage points, depending on market conditions.[18]

3. Mismatched strategies

A third danger of quarantining portfolios is the pitfall of mismatched strategies. Uncoordinated investments work against each other and often produce suboptimal results.

The example of the 58-year-old client at the beginning of the chapter illustrates this point. He had three separate investment accounts. Two portfolios were managed by different advisors with dissimilar allocations. The third account was self-managed and entirely misaligned with his other two accounts. Nevertheless, the three accounts shared a common purpose – to fund the investor's retirement. Because each account was constructed in isolation versus a coordinated approach, the resulting mix of the client's total assets was incompatible with his near-term retirement goal.

Mismatched investments are common when financial advisors manage portfolios in isolation. On a standalone basis, each account's strategy may seem well designed. However, when combined at the household level, the collective strategies will likely be out of place, and will fail to complement one another. In aggregate, household assets may be completely misaligned with the client's overall goals and objectives. Incongruent investments will eventually detract from an investor's long-term success.

4. Regulatory risk

The fourth danger of operating in isolation is that this approach may jeopardize an advisor's ability to meet the fiduciary standard. This standard requires financial advisors to do what is best for their clients and is the basis of the Department of Labor's rule that regulates how advisors provide retirement advice.

To comply with the best interest standard, advisors should have a complete understanding of a client's financial situation. When investors work with multiple advisors, meeting this regulatory obligation becomes much more challenging for each advisory firm. Also, when advisors manage a client's multiple accounts separately, they inadvertently may not be investing the entirety of the client's assets in the overall best interest of the client.

---

[18] P. Bouchey, R. Santodomingo and J. Sireklove, 'Tax Efficient Investing: Tactics and Strategies', www.parametricportfolio.com (January/February 2015).

Failure to meet the fiduciary standard has steep penalties. Advisors may face regulatory censure or fines, and expose themselves to litigation.[19]

Why financial advisors quarantine portfolios

If managing portfolios in isolation is hazardous to investor wealth, why is this practice widely adopted by financial advisors?

Two reasons exist. First, investors at times do not share their broader financial circumstances with their advisors. Second, financial advisors may be limited by industry practices, technology, or expertise in holistically managing client wealth.

1. When investors are to blame

High net worth individuals tend to spread their assets across multiple firms and financial advisors. According to a Cisco survey of 1000 wealthy US investors, nearly one-third of investors with a financial advisor have more than one advisor. Reasons for engaging multiple advisors include getting varied investment perspectives and reducing risk. In addition, some wealthy clients seek multiple advisors for procuring different areas of expertise.[20]

When investors have assets managed by multiple firms and advisors, quarantining portfolios can easily occur. Portfolio transparency from one advisor to the next is often limited. Clients may intentionally withhold this information. In other situations, financial advisors simply do not ask clients to share their outside holdings. Without knowledge of the other advisors' actions, a financial advisor is forced to act independently.

2. When financial advisors are to blame

Closemouthed investors using more than one advisor are not the only cause of portfolios being quarantined. At times, financial advisors are the source of this hazard.

Based on the same Cisco study, more than two-thirds of clients who engage advisors consolidate their assets with a single advisor. This should imply that the problem of quarantining does not apply for the majority of investors. But,

---

[19]   M. Rieker 'When a Client Has More Than One Adviser', *Wall Street Journal*, www.wsj.com (March 20, 2015).
[20]   J. Loucks, R. Waitman and J. Ericsson, 'Winning the Battle for the Wealthy Investor: New Cisco IBSG Study Uncovers Significant Opportunity To Address Needs of Wealthy Under-50 Investors', Cisco Internet Business Solutions Group, www.cisco.com (January 2011).

even with full knowledge of an investor's balance sheet, financial advisors are apt to manage portfolios in isolation.

One reason is found in the history of the financial advisory industry. Other causes contributing to assets being quarantined include system limitations and existing advisory practices.

Historical challenges

The origins of many retail investing strategies can be traced back to ideas first used by institutional investors such as banks, pension funds, and university endowments. For instance, institutional investors traditionally have measured success based on portfolio performance compared to specified benchmarks. Financial advisors subsequently began adopting this type of performance reporting for their individual clients. Even though institutions and individuals have different investment goals and constraints, evaluating success became centered on the same factor – relative account performance.

Through the widespread usage of account-specific performance reporting, the financial advisory industry taught clients to value their services based primarily on individual portfolio performance. Account-level performance reporting developed as the standard method for conveying relative worth to clients. Accordingly, advisory success became measured at the account level instead of holistically. Advisors, in turn, concentrated efforts on maximizing the results of accounts on a standalone basis. Unfortunately, the industry's historical focus on account-specific performance reinforced the practice of quarantining portfolios among financial advisors.

System limitations

Financial advisors are also confronted with technology deficiencies that inhibit them from holistically managing an investor's wealth. Most established portfolio accounting and rebalancing systems are based on a single account structure. For example, many widely-adopted portfolio management systems can efficiently rebalance thousands of single accounts. However, these same systems typically cannot synchronize the rebalancing of a client's multiple accounts in a scalable, coordinated manner.

Financial advisors operating on legacy technology depend on inefficient manual processes in order to manage an investor's multiple accounts in an integrated fashion. For instance, client data can be exported from many account-based portfolio management systems and imported into Excel. Client accounts then can be grouped at the household level and evaluated on a more holistic basis. Subsequently, coordinated trade recommendations generated in Excel may be able to be imported back into the portfolio management system for execution.

Relying on this type of approach introduces more chance of human error and presents inefficiencies that may impair advisory growth and profitability. Faced with the competing trade-offs of holistic management and system limitations, financial advisors frequently resort to quarantining portfolios.

Existing advisory practices

Besides the industry's historical challenges and system limitations, existing advisory practices may reinforce the hazardous approach of managing wealth in isolation. Examples include the use of risk tolerance questionnaires and investment policy statements. These tools are important components in managing investor wealth. Yet, they can unintentionally support a segregated approach to portfolio management.

Determining a client's investment strategy commonly begins with the use of a risk tolerance questionnaire. These tools for assessing a client's risk appetite typically generate a score that maps to a corresponding portfolio. However, the investment models are generally account-level solutions, not holistic, household-based strategies.

For example, an advisor managing multiple accounts of an investor is required by her firm to use a risk tolerance questionnaire for each account. The client's risk score corresponds to an appropriate risk-based model portfolio maintained by the advisor's firm. Because the firm's risk tolerance questionnaire drives the recommended portfolio, each account of the client gets mapped to the same model, regardless of the account type. This compliance-driven practice leaves no leeway for the advisor to implement different allocations among a client's accounts to take advantage of their tax status using asset location. As highlighted by this illustration, using account-based risk tolerance scoring systems reinforces the implementation of quarantined portfolios.

However, if the advisor was able to manage the accounts holistically in this example, she would locate the less tax-efficient assets in the tax-deferred and tax-free client accounts and the more tax-efficient assets in the taxable accounts. The investor's overall household allocation still would correspond with an appropriate mix of assets for his or her risk appetite. But by treating the accounts holistically rather than on a standalone basis, the advisor is able to generate higher after-tax results for the client simply by using a smart asset location strategy across the client's accounts. In chapter 13, this type of goals-based tax strategy is explained in more detail.

The advisory practice of using investment policy statements also may lead to similar, constrained outcomes, as evidenced in use of account-based risk tolerance questionnaires. An investment policy statement (IPS) is a document drafted between a financial advisor and a client that provides guidelines for how a portfolio will be managed, including the determined asset mix, risk tolerance, and liquidity requirements. Using an IPS with clients is a good practice. It establishes an agreed-upon foundation for the advisor-client relationship.

Nevertheless, investment policy statements have their limitations. More often than not, IPS generation is based on a single account – not the household level. Similar to the previous example that illustrated limitations of account-based risk tolerance questionnaires, IPS documents based on a single account structure lead to suboptimal results when viewed at the household level. This is true because advisors are constrained by this process of treating each of a client's accounts distinctly, and holistic-based strategies such as asset location are not possible with this approach. Consequently, the practice of using an IPS with clients may inadvertently lead to managing portfolios separately from each other, unless financial advisors and their firms adopt a holistic IPS approach.

Smart financial advisors avoid quarantining portfolios

As evidenced in this chapter, quarantining portfolios is hazardous to investor outcomes.

When assets are managed in isolation, it is possible for financial advisors to soundly construct individual portfolios. However, a client's total wealth may be entirely misaligned with the desired household goals. Long-term investor priorities tend to get off track. And when portfolios are quarantined, broad objectives may not be fully realized. As a result, investment success is marginalized, and client net worth is constrained.

Smart financial advisors avoid the hazards of quarantining portfolios. Instead of managing client portfolios in isolation, they manage investor assets holistically. They develop client balance sheets, implementing investment strategies that match client assets to their liabilities, as explained in more detail in chapter 10. By managing client relationships as a whole instead of compartmentalizing accounts, financial advisors are able to achieve more successful outcomes for their clients.

4

Mismanaging Risks

The hazard of badly managing risks

> "Risk is like fire: If controlled it will help
> you; if uncontrolled it will rise up and
> destroy you."

> — Theodore Roosevelt

EXTREME SPORTS COMMONLY lure adrenaline junkies – daredevils who thrive from the sensation of exhilaration associated with risky behaviors. Amongst the most hazardous of athletic endeavors is wingsuit BASE jumping. This sport involves leaping from a building, antenna, span, or earth (hence the acronym BASE) using a bodysuit made from parachute-like material connecting the legs and running between the arms and legs. Wingsuit jumpers land by deploying a small parachute. Not surprisingly, BASE jumping is much riskier than skydiving from a plane, because these jumps occur at considerably lower heights.

Dean Potter, an iconic extreme athlete and genuine adrenaline junkie, was drawn to wingsuit BASE jumping and other dangerous sports like free climbing and slacklining. Dean rose to fame by making solo, ropeless ascents up some of the most hazardous cliffs in the US. His endeavors pushed the boundaries of extreme sports, setting records for successfully accomplishing numerous, life-threatening feats. For example, Dean was the first athlete to BASE jump from a slackline suspended hundreds of feet in the air. He also claimed *National Geographic's* adventurer of the year award after completing a record wingsuit BASE jump flight lasting 2 minutes and 50 seconds from Eiger North Face in the Swiss Alps.

In the spring of 2014, Dean was interviewed by *Outside Magazine* about his dangerous exploits and his approach to fear, risk, and safety. After commenting about the high death rates of wingsuit jumping, Dean remarked, "I stay well within my abilities and never go to those places that are too harsh to handle."

One year following this interview, Dean and Graham Hunt, a fellow extreme athlete, died while attempting an illegal wingsuit BASE jump from Taft Point, a promontory rising 3,500 feet above Yosemite Valley in California. Dean was 43. Graham was 29. Both athletes had made this dangerous flight before. However, the jump required precisely navigating through a narrow, V-shaped notch between rock walls. Graham hit a side wall. Dean cleared the notch and then crashed. They died on impact. Neither of their parachutes had deployed.

Unfortunately, Dean's words from a year earlier rung hollow on the day of this tragic accident. Risk had been mismanaged. And the costly penalty was two untimely deaths.[21]

Similar to this sad story, investor risk – when mismanaged – can be enormously costly. For example, financial goals may go unfulfilled when too much portfolio risk backfires and aggressive investments tumble under excess downside volatility. Another example is delayed retirement caused by investing all of one's savings in ultra conservative strategies with insufficient risk for wealth to adequately grow in time for a desired retirement date.

In extreme circumstances, lives may even be lost by mismanaging financial risks. This was the case for Adolf Merckle, head of a German pharmaceutical and engineering conglomerate. In 2008, he was among the world's 100 richest people with a net worth in excess of $9 billion. But his miscalculated risk regarding his Volkswagen shares and the subsequent credit collapse of his businesses resulted in financial ruin for Mr. Merckle. Rather than face the loss of his vast wealth, he chose to take his own life at the age of 74.[22]

Undoubtedly, mismanaging investor risks can have steep penalties for advisors and the clients they serve. To better understand this hazard, two common risk misperceptions are explained and three types of investor risks are explored in this chapter. Also, two ways that advisors mismanage client risks are identified. The chapter concludes by suggesting how smart financial advisors manage investor risks to achieve better outcomes for their clients.

---

[21]   'Dean Potter Lived Life on the Edge', www.outsideonline.com (May 18, 2015).
[22]   Liz Robbins, 'The High Cost of Losing Money', thelede.blogs.nytimes.com (January 6, 2009).

Risk misperceptions

Risk is broadly defined as a chance of loss or failure. In the realm of finance, risk is the chance that an investment's actual return will differ from its expected return, including the possibility of losing a portion or all of the invested capital.

A foundational concept in finance is the relationship between risk and return. Modern Portfolio Theory (MPT) proposes that investors are risk averse. For example, if two portfolios have the same expected return, the one with less risk is preferred. In order to take on more risk, rational investors require commensurate compensation in the form of higher expected returns.

In reality, however, people tend to perceive the same risks differently. Personal judgements are made regarding the severity and probability of a given risk. These subjective differences result in two common risk misperceptions – underestimating and overestimating risk. To illustrate these blunders, the risk misperceptions of two investors evaluating the same S&P 500 Index fund are considered below.

Underestimating risk

The first investor makes the mistake of underestimating the risks associated with this investment. Since the index mutual fund is comprised of hundreds of large US company stocks, this investor inaccurately perceives the risk of the fund to be less than it really is. As a result, the investor overweights the asset in his portfolio relative to the level of risk he is comfortable taking. Later, when US equities take a hit, the investor's portfolio tumbles due to the overexposure in stocks – a costly consequence of misperceiving the index fund's actual volatility.

Overestimating risk

The second investor makes the opposite mistake. She overestimates the magnitude of the index fund's risk and opts to exclude this investment (as well as any equity exposure) from her portfolio. Yet, this investor has a long time horizon before the funds are required. She also has the willingness and financial margin to assume a moderate level of risk. Nevertheless, her risk misperception results in a very conservatively constructed portfolio that likely will fail to achieve adequate growth for her long-term goals.

These opposing risk misperceptions about the same mutual fund led to the creation of suboptimal portfolios for both investors. Although MPT suggests this should not happen, reality indicates this is a common occurrence. As these two examples illustrate, misjudgments – leading to underestimating or overestimating investment risk – can jeopardize the health of a portfolio and lessen an investor's ability to attain desired financial outcomes. Accordingly, it is essential for advisors to understand these risk misperceptions when managing client wealth.

Types of investor risks

It is also important for advisors to help clients clearly understand that all investments have embedded risks. The exposure and magnitude of these risks varies depending on the underlying investment, but, generally, as investment risk increases, the expectation of higher returns likewise rises.

Since investment risk cannot be entirely eliminated, a key to smart investing is to take calculated risks, not reckless risks. Thus, advisors should take the time to educate clients about the risks of an investment opportunity, communicating the importance of taking calculated risks and making sensible investment decisions.

With that in mind, let's look at what types of risks advisors face when managing client portfolios. Three broad categories encompass most investor risks. These include investment-specific risks, behavioral risks, and goal risks.

1. Investment-specific risks

Seven major investment-specific risks are summarized below. The first four represent market risks; the remaining three are diversifiable risks.

Market risks, also known as systematic risks, are comprised of universal factors that affect overall performance of financial markets. Systematic risks cannot be completely diversified away, but they can be hedged or managed. They include:

(i) Interest rate risk

Interest rate risk is the risk associated with changes in interest rates. Investments that are sensitive to this risk will experience valuation fluctuations as interest rates move, spreads between two rates change and the shape of the yield curve shifts. These changes generally affect investments inversely. For example, when interest rates rise, fixed income prices normally fall. And when interest rates fall, fixed income prices usually rise. Advisors can reduce interest rate risk by diversifying among fixed income instruments with different maturities and durations, or by hedging using interest rate swaps.

(ii) Inflation risk

Inflation risk is the reduction in purchasing power caused by increases in the prices of goods and services over time. For instance, consider a bond with a 3% coupon rate. If inflation is 2%, the real return of this investment is a mere 1%.

Ironically, relatively conservative investments such as certificates of deposit (CDs) and high-quality bonds have more exposure to inflation risk than higher volatility investments such as equities. This is because fixed-rate investments may not generate sufficient returns to keep pace with price increases, thereby reducing an investor's purchasing power. On the other hand, equities tend to preserve the inflation-adjusted value of capital over the long run as companies normally can pass price increases to their customers. Advisors should pay close attention to inflation risk when managing retirement assets, because these portfolios often have significant weightings to conservative, fixed-rate investments that inherently expose retiree wealth to the risk of inflation over time.

(iii) Currency risk

Currency risk (or exchange-rate risk) results from changes in the relative value of a currency. This risk affects investors making international investments. For example, if US dollars are converted to a foreign currency to buy an international investment, then exchange rate fluctuations will impact the investment's gain or loss when it is sold and converted back into US dollars. Smart practitioners can reduce currency risk by currency hedging and by diversifying international investments across various countries and regions.

(iv) Macro risk

Macro risk, also known as geopolitical risk, is the risk associated with political changes or instability and unrest in a country or region. Concerns arising from volatile and unpredictable situations across the globe can negatively affect investment returns. Examples of macro risk include political elections, changes in government, war, natural disasters, epidemics, widespread unemployment, and terrorist attacks. Longer-term investments generally have more exposure to macro risk than short-term investments, since geopolitical events become increasingly difficult to forecast as time horizons lengthen.

Unlike the four market risks noted above, advisors can essentially eliminate the remaining three investment risks from client portfolios through broad diversification. These diversifiable risks, sometimes referred to as unsystematic risks, originate from company-specific circumstances or unique factors associated with a specific asset class. They include:

(v) Credit risk

Credit risk is the risk associated with a borrower unable to make required payments on its debt. Credit risk tends to surface when a company incurs excessive debt. If such a company encounters financial difficulties in the operation of its business, it may be unable to repay its debt. As a result, bondholders, preferred stockholders, and lenders may not receive, in part or in full, the interest or principal owed them. Since credit risk is a company-specific risk, advisors can significantly reduce the impact of this unsystematic risk in client portfolios by diversifying across many debt issuers.

(vi) Liquidity risk

Liquidity risk refers to the possibility that an investor is unable to convert an asset quickly into cash with little or no loss in value. This risk may occur because there is no active market for the asset, or because trading it will result in a considerable loss. Investments with limited liquidity typically have unusually wide bid-ask spreads.

Liquidity risk tends to be inversely related to the numbers of shares or units outstanding of a security. For instance, a stock with limited float – the amount of shares of company that are publicly tradeable – generally will have higher liquidity risk than a blue chip stock with millions of publicly tradeable shares and a high daily trading volume.

Advisors can decrease investor exposure to liquidity risk by keeping a portion of client portfolios in cash, cash equivalents, or highly liquid assets. Also, practitioners should keep in mind that liquidity risk is greater for investors with financial goals with short time horizons, as assets normally must be sold to fund near-term expenditures associated with such goals.

(vii) Company-specific risk

Company-specific risk, also referred to as idiosyncratic risk, is the risk associated with a particular corporate enterprise. This risk arises from microeconomic factors that affect a specific asset, such as a stock and its underlying company. If a company's business degenerates and its prospects look bleak, the market value of its securities may fall sharply.

Examples of company-specific risk include changes in a firm's profitability or operating environment; other examples include an unfavorable outcome of litigation, assessment of a regulatory penalty, or an employee strike for a given company. Unlike market risks, advisors can substantially mitigate or eliminate company-specific risk from a portfolio by sufficiently diversifying investment holdings.

2. Behavioral risks

The study of behavioral finance attempts to explain why people make investment decisions that are suboptimal and how human emotions influence the investment decision-making process. Although traditional finance theories assume investors behave rationally when confronted with investment risks, behavioral finance theories suggest otherwise. Investors can be their own worst enemies, and their behavior patterns often lead to poor investment decisions. Behavioral risk refers to the tendency of investors to omit the use of sound logic when investing, letting emotions take over in this process instead.

Chapter 1 explains in more detail how behavioral influences such as loss aversion and herding induce counterproductive investment actions that result in a behavioral gap – the difference between potential and actual returns realized by investors. Despite this well-documented gap in performance, behavioral risk is still often overlooked by both advisors and investors.

In a study about behavioral risk, Prudential Financial engaged behavioral finance experts Dr. V Kumar and Denish Shah from the University of Connecticut School of Business to explore the impact of investor emotions on retirement investment decisions. More than 1000 US investors within five years of retirement were surveyed. The study found nearly all investors let emotions guide retirement investment decisions to some extent, indicating that most people have some exposure to behavioral risk. The research also revealed that a significant percentage of both men and women were moderately or highly influenced by emotions when making investment decisions (72% and 80%, respectively). Yet, only 35% of the participants in the study believed emotions impact their investment decisions.[23]

Investors certainly need to know about financial markets and investment risks. But they also need to understand themselves and how their behaviors may represent substantial risk to their successful goal attainment. Because people are typically unaware of the impact of behavior risk, it is important for financial advisors to discover the emotional and cognitive biases of investors adversely impacting investor success.

For example, advisors should recognize that investors influenced by aversion to losses may be less inclined to take necessary risk to realize their long-term financial goals. At the opposite extreme, financial professionals should be mindful of how people biased to be overly aggressive may assume unhealthy levels of investment risk, disregarding the adoption of prudent risk management strategies in their portfolios.[24]

In reference to these behavioral risks, Ben Graham, the father of value investing, observed, "Individuals who cannot master their emotions are ill-suited to profit

[23] 'Prudential Financial's Four Pillars of Retirement Series: Behavioral Risk in The Retirement Red Zone®', www.retirementmadesimpler.org (2007).
[24] H. Kent Baker and Victor Ricciardi, 'Understanding Behavioral Aspects of Financial Planning and Investing', www.onefpa.org (March 2015).

from the investment process." With a clearer understanding of these risks, advisors can make better investment recommendations for their clients and be cognizant of emotional factors that may lead investors astray.[25]

3. Goal risks

Investment risks and behavioral risk can wreak havoc on investor portfolios if poorly understood and mismanaged. Additionally, a third type of risk – goal risk – can equally be damaging to investor outcomes.

Goal risk is the risk associated with failing to reach a specific financial goal. In other words, this risk is less about portfolio volatility or an investor's feelings toward risk; rather, it is defined by the risk of the goal itself. One way to evaluate goal risk is to identify the required rate of return needed to achieve the goal. A high tolerance for goal risk essentially means an investor requires a low investment return to adequately fund future expected expenditures. Conversely, a low tolerance for goal risk equates to an investor needing a high rate of return to have a chance of reaching a goal.

Consider the following two examples. If a goal requires a higher expected return given an investor's available resources and future savings, the investor will need to assume more risk in order to potentially achieve the necessary return to attain the desired outcome. On the other hand, if a client has accumulated sufficient wealth to fund her goals, this client's goal risk to maintain this fully funded status over time is low. In this second case, the value of additional gains potentially generated by taking on higher degrees of risk is much less important than avoiding goal implosion resulting from large losses.[26]

Within a goals-based investing framework, advisors can assess a client's goal risk by measuring the client's probability of success using Monte Carlo analysis (see chapters 10 and 11). Another consideration when evaluating a client's goal risk is to factor in the priority of a stated goal. If a goal represents a client need or necessity for basic living, failure to meet this goal can be devastating. Accordingly, a higher probability of success should be required (e.g. 90% probability). For lower priority goals, such as desired wants and aspirational wishes, a lower level of confidence in goal attainment may be appropriate (e.g. 70% probability of success).[27]

---

[25]   Michael Pompian, 'Risk Profiling Through A Behavioral Finance Lens', www.cfapubs. org (February 2016).

[26]   Michael Kitces, 'Don't Just Focus On Risk Tolerance For The Portfolio, Because Goal Risk Tolerance Matters Too!', www.kitces.com (September 2, 2015).

[27]   'Goals-based planning: A personalized service for strengthening client relationships', www.ey.com (2016).

When goal risk is ignored, investors may be exposed to undesirable outcomes. For instance, if a client invests aggressively due to a high willingness to assume investment risk, but his necessity for goal risk is low given ample savings, market drawdowns can be detrimental and needlessly impair goal progress. Unfortunately, in the mid-to-late 2000s, this situation was an unnecessary reality for many aggressive savers nearing retirement with overexposure to equities. When the Great Recession of 2008 hit, funded retirements became severely underfunded, resulting in delayed retirements or a substantial reduction in living standards.

Two ways advisors mismanage client risks

As illustrated by the aforementioned lesson of the late 2000s, it is vital for advisors to gauge an investor's tolerance to withstand investment and emotional risks, and to appropriately determine an investor's required risk needed to attain their goals.

However, traditional investment approaches often ignore or gloss over goal risk as a factor when constructing investor portfolios. This results in two common advisor mistakes when managing client risks: assessing only a client's willingness to assume investment risk, and improperly balancing between a client's investment, behavioral, and goal risks.

Mistake 1. Assessing only a client's willingness to assume investment risk

The previous chapter pointed out that a common advisory practice is the use of risk tolerance questionnaires. This traditional approach assesses how much risk a client can reasonably withstand, resulting in a recommended investment strategy consistent with the determined risk tolerance level. The problem with this approach is that recommended portfolios may not be properly aligned with client goals.

For example, a portfolio suggested by a risk tolerance questionnaire may be more aggressive than necessary to attain a client's goal. In other situations, a conservatively-scored risk tolerance may result in a recommended portfolio with insufficient risk to have a reasonable probability of reaching a client's desired outcomes.

To avoid recommending portfolios that are mismatched with client goals, advisors should not solely rely on risk tolerance questionnaires. They should also determine whether a goal is appropriate in light of a client's resources, anticipated savings and willingness to assume investment risk.[28]

Mistake 2. Improperly balancing between the three types of investor risks

A second mistake advisors make is to identify a client's investment, behavioral, and goal risks, but then overemphasize one risk relative to the others. This improper balancing of risks results in a partial view of the dangers impacting client outcomes.

For example, an advisor may focus predominately on the required risk to reach a client goal, while minimizing the importance of investment and behavioral risks. If the required goal risk for a client is high, but willingness to withstand market volatility is low and financial capacity is low, an overly aggressive portfolio may be recommended. A more prudent response in this situation may be for the advisor to help the client identify a realistic goal that better matches the client's risk tolerance and financial capacity.

A smarter way for advisors to manage client risks

Investor risks – if managed properly by advisors – can play an important role in helping to achieve client needs, wants, and wishes. However, when investor risks are mismanaged, misperceived, partially assessed or improperly balanced, financial goals are placed in jeopardy.

Smart financial advisors recognize the importance of managing client risks well. One way this is accomplished is for advisors to adequately understand a client's investment, behavioral, and goal risks. Advisors can use well-designed risk tolerance questionnaires to assess a client's willingness to assume investment risks. Furthermore, they can determine a client's financial risk capacity and required risk needed to achieve client goals. Throughout this process, advisors should clearly document and clarify with the client his or her risk considerations. By doing so, the investor will have a better understanding of how his or her risks can be managed to achieve the highest probability of long-term goal success.

Best practices for evaluating and managing client risks are explored in more detail in chapter 11.

---

[28] Michael Kitces, 'Don't Just Focus On Risk Tolerance For The Portfolio, Because Goal Risk Tolerance Matters Too!', www.kitces.com (September 2, 2015).

5

Relying on Alluring Stories

The hazard of investing based on opportunistic tales

> "The more inspired a story makes me feel,
> very often the more nervous I get."
>
> — Tyler Cowen, an American Economist

ON NOVEMBER 9, 2016 – the day after the US presidential election – Eric Tucker, a 35-year-old marketing entrepreneur, snapped a picture of parked buses near downtown Austin, Texas. He posted the picture and tweeted that paid demonstrators had been bused in to protest the election results.

Although Eric had only about 40 Twitter followers, his tweet went viral. It was shared over 16,000 times on Twitter and more than 350,000 times on Facebook. The story, summarized in 136 characters, fueled a nationwide conspiracy theory. However, the tweet was not accurate. The buses had not transported paid protestors. Rather, they were brought in to transport attendees of a large software conference being held in downtown Austin.

The fact that the news was fake was seemingly irrelevant. The tweet promoted a narrative that energized a group of voters, quickly spreading like wildfire. A few days following this frenzy, Eric deleted his tweet. Hardly anyone noticed.[29]

In a matter of moments, alluring stories – ones that blur, bend, or omit facts like Eric Tucker's misinformed tweet – can go viral on social media. This

---

[29] Sapna Maheshwari, 'How Fake News Goes Viral: A Case Study', www.nytimes.com (November 20, 2016).

phenomenon exists because people love juicy gossip, even if such chatter contains little to no truth.

But our desire for tantalizing stories does not go without consequences. Friendships can be damaged. Reputations can become tarnished. Even fortunes can be lost.

America's most innovative company

Lost fortunes befell many unsuspecting investors in 2001 who had become enthralled by an enticing story spun by the company Enron. In the months and years leading up to this financial disaster, a constant stream of fake news had been circulated by this rapidly-growing energy conglomerate via creative accounting. Top Enron executives, including Chairman and CEO Kenneth Lay, recognized the power of a compelling story and made their pitch by cooking the company's books.

Hordes of folks bought Enron's story hook, line, and sinker – including the financial press. In fact, *Fortune* magazine named Enron "America's Most Innovative Company" for six consecutive years. The year before the fraud was uncovered, the magazine wrote:

> "No company illustrates the transformative power of innovation more dramatically than Enron. Over the past decade Enron's commitment to the invention – and later domination – of new business categories has taken it from a $200 million old-economy pipeline operator to a $40 billion new-economy trading powerhouse."[30]

Notwithstanding the numerous accolades received from the likes of *Fortune* and Wall Street analysts, Enron's false narrative eventually became exposed. The scandal brought down Enron and its inept auditing firm. Over 22,000 employees lost their jobs. And billions of dollars of investor wealth evaporated nearly instantaneously. All of this misfortune happened because fraudsters – posing as corporate executives – preyed on people's cravings for an alluring story.

How stories ensnare investors

Generally, sourcing investment ideas from stories is a dangerous practice. Opportunistic tales – whether heard at the country club, cocktail party, or in the office – can prompt poor investment decisions. Alluring stories of quick profits, best-kept secrets, and exclusive, limited-time opportunities should be

---

[30] Nicholas Stein, 'The World's Most Admired Companies – How do you make the Most Admired list?', www.archive.fortune.com (October 2, 2000).

met with a healthy dose of skepticism. Yet, time and time again, people fall for stories – even though happy endings rarely occur as the narratives suggest.

Stories ensnare investors in a variety of ways. Common traps include misdirecting focus on products rather than financial goals, enticing a reliance on intuition instead of logic and evidence, and distorting the true merits of an opportunity. Each of these concepts is explored in more depth below.

Misdirecting focus on product, not client goals

An inherent flaw of investment stories is that their plots exclude the most important element – a focus on the investor and his or her goals. In its place, storylines center on investment products. Investors are less likely to notice false narratives, inconsistencies, and embellishments when stories are about something other than themselves, especially with content where their knowledge and expertise is limited.

A challenge for investors when sifting through investment options is to recognize that not all financial advice is offered under the same legal standards. In the US, some circumstances require practitioners to merely ensure products are suitable for investors. In other situations, advisors are required to act in the overall best interests of their clients, operating under a higher fiduciary standard. This difference results from whether a financial professional is functioning as a broker or an investment advisor, and whether or not the recommendations involve retirement accounts such as 401(k)s, pension plans, and IRAs. Moreover, the differing levels of legal responsibility between the suitability and fiduciary standards have a direct bearing on the types of stories being told to investors and the quality of investment advice that investors receive.

The suitability requirement

In recent years, many financial professionals licensed as brokers in the US have begun referring to themselves as wealth managers, investment advisors, or financial advisors. Regardless of the confusing array of titles, the main function of brokers historically has been to sell products and make money from those transactions. When brokers operate under the suitability requirement, they can legally put their interests above client interests when making investment recommendations. Investors, accordingly, should not be surprised that *suitable* investments recommended by brokers commonly pay some of the highest fees and commissions in the industry.[31]

---

[31]   Stephen Ahern, 'Registered Investment Advisors vs. Brokers: What's the difference?', www.brightscope.com.

If the recommendations involve retirement accounts, a higher fiduciary standard is required pursuant to the Department of Labor's fiduciary rule that became effective as of June 2017. Not surprisingly, a number of major brokerage houses lobbied Congress against this new rule when it was being proposed.

The fiduciary standard

In contrast to the legal requirements of brokers when operating under the suitability requirement, investment advisors licensed in the US as Registered Investment Advisors under the Securities Act of 1940 must legally act as fiduciaries under all circumstances. Law.com describes a fiduciary as "a person who has the power and obligation to act for another under circumstances which require total trust, good faith, and honesty." *Black's Law Dictionary* defines a fiduciary relationship as "one founded on trust or confidence reposed by one person in the integrity and fidelity of another." Thus, investment advisors acting as fiduciaries have both the ethical responsibility and legal requirement to act in their clients' best interests. Moreover, if an investment advisor has a conflict of interest, the advisor must eliminate the conflict or fully disclose it upfront to clients. In short, investment advisors' main role is to offer unbiased advice, making this business model more aligned with the achievement of investor goals than exists under a brokerage relationship.

Investor confusion between broker and advisor differences

Although the legal standards of brokers and investment advisors are dissimilar when dealing with non-retirement accounts, many investors unfortunately do not understand the differences and how these variances impact the investment advice given to them. A 2010 national survey of investors commissioned by the CFA Institute shows that most US investors are confused about these differences. The CFA survey found that two out of three investors (66%) wrongly believe that brokers are always held to a fiduciary standard, while most survey participants (76%) correctly understood that this high standard of care is in place for financial planners and investment advisors under all circumstances.

Investor misbeliefs that brokers and advisors are governed, at all times, by the same fiduciary principles create the opportunity for misplaced trust by investors in product stories being sold by their brokers under the suitability requirement. And when clients wrongly believe these product pitches are being offered in the context of their best interests and void of conflicts of interests, poorly informed investment decisions may occur, and investor goal attainment may become derailed.[32]

---

[32] 'U.S. Investors & The Fiduciary Standard: A National Opinion Survey', www.hastingsgroup.com (September 15, 2010).

Financial advisors operating as fiduciaries should educate investors on the differences between these standards of advice. In doing so, advisors can help investors proceed with caution when being pitched product stories in the absence of the fiduciary standard. They also can differentiate their practices from other firms that historically only were bound to the suitability standard. Furthermore, smart advisors should also encourage investors to understand the fee structures of the products being sold by brokers and to make sure they are aware of any conflicts of interest before investing.

Enticing a reliance on intuition, not logic and evidence

Besides misdirecting focus on products rather than investor goals, another way stories ensnare investors is by enticing a reliance on intuition instead of logic and evidence. Making investment decisions based on one's gut feelings is typically a really bad approach to managing wealth. As explained in chapter 1, this type of emotion-driven investing is prone to a long list of behavioral pitfalls, often leading to bad market timing decisions and tragic investment outcomes.

This unfortunate reality is highlighted in the cocktail party theory developed by Peter Lynch, former manager of one of the world's top performing mutual funds, in his bestselling book *One Up on Wall Street*. Basically, this theory illustrates the absurdity of investment stories being told in social settings.

In his book, Lynch describes four types of investment stories told at cocktail parties depending on the current state of the market. The first type of investment story is virtually non-existent. When the stock market is depressed, hardly anyone wants to talk about equities when socializing. In fact, according to Lynch, talking to the dentist about plaque is preferred over interacting with investment professionals at this stage of the market. The second type of narrative emerges when the market first begins to rebound. The party buzz is still not about stocks, but people may occasionally mention how risky the market is when bumping into financial advisors. Conversations with the dentist are still preferred at this stage.

The third type of investment story at parties surfaces when the stock market is rallying. People are gathered around investment professionals asking what stocks should be bought. At this point, party goers are enthusiastically talking about the market. The final type of investment story erupts at the height of a bull market. No longer is advice being sought from financial advisors. Instead, everyone else, including the dentist, is now offering stock tips to the investment pros. Lynch remarks, "When the neighbors tell me what to buy, and then I wish I had taken their advice, it's a sure sign that the market has reached a top and is due for a tumble."[33]

As Lynch's cocktail party theory highlights, the presence of alluring investment stories (or the lack thereof) can prompt individuals to overly rely on intuition when making investment decisions. Stories that are short on facts and unduly influenced by market-induced emotions should be avoided at all costs by investors and advisors alike.

Distorting an investment's true merits

A third way stories trap investors is by distorting an investment's true merits. Prospective opportunities associated with an investment thesis tend to get inflated when investment stories are told. Meanwhile, downside risks associated with the idea get minimized or omitted. The problem with many stories shared with investors is not that they are entirely fictional, but rather that a full, balanced perspective is missing from the narratives.

Consider what happens when certain investment stories get unfairly characterized as worthless opportunities in light of past, bad experiences. For example, after the dot-com bust in the early 2000s, pummeled tech stocks were despised by many investors at the time. However, those who shunned the likes of Apple, Microsoft, and Amazon missed out on some of the greatest opportunities of American innovation. In 2015, Amazon surpassed Walmart as the most valuable retailer in the United States by market capitalization, and in 2016 was the fourth most valuable public company.[34]

Stories can also distort downside investment risks. For instance, stock-specific stories may have valid, promising potential of the underlying companies being pitched. Yet, on a stand-alone-basis, individual stocks will likely have excessive company-specific risk – that if not adequately managed through portfolio diversification, can expose investors to substantial drawdowns. In the excitement of telling a stock's story, often the broader portfolio implications and risk exposures get overlooked.

As these examples have shown, investors should recognize that stories may distort an investment's true merits. Opportunities and risks may get overstated or inaccurately diminished in such narratives. Accordingly, it is important for advisors to encourage investors to be discerning of the messages they hear,

33   Peter Lynch, *One Up On Wall Street: How To Use What You Already Know To Make Money In The Markets* (Simon & Schuster, 2000).
34   Evelyn Cheng, 'Amazon climbs into list of top five largest US stocks by market cap', www.cnbc.com (September 23, 2016).

digging deeper into the merits of an opportunity in order to get a complete picture before investing.

Storytelling limits advisor effectiveness

Not only do stories ensnare investors, they can also harm financial advisors by limiting their effectiveness with clients. Practitioners that overly rely on telling alluring stories to generate business pigeonhole the value of their profession to that of a glorified salesperson. In such cases, clients look to their advisor for one-off investment ideas, hot stock tips, and the latest investment trends. They do not source holistic financial advice from these types of advisors in a manner consistent with their other professionals like attorneys or CPAs. When wealthy investors view their advisor's primary role as investment storytellers and advisors act accordingly, the opportunity to function as the family's vital, trusted financial counselor is sacrificed.

Consider these two contrasting examples. The first advisor is a broker operating under the suitability requirement who sells compelling new investment ideas to his clients. His compensation is derived primarily through transactions and corresponding commissions. One of the broker's clients is in the process of selling his business and developing a comprehensive estate plan. This client does not even think to consult with his broker to advise on these two significant activities. Rather, his legal and financial advice is provided by a reputable law firm and accounting practice. Once his business has sold and the estate plan developed, the client may then – and only then – look to his broker for some good investment opportunities to invest his excess funds.

In comparison, the second advisor operates as an investment advisor, adhering to the fiduciary standard. His compensation is derived from advisory services associated with assets being managed and retainer fees for developing financial plans. Any and all conflicts of interests are fully disclosed to his clients. The broker's client in the prior example has a partner in the business being sold. This partner happens to be the client of the second financial advisor. Unlike the earlier broker example, this partner solicits the advice of her investment advisor – even before calling her attorney and accountant – for preliminary counsel regarding the sale of the business. The co-owner discusses with her advisor the conduciveness of the current economic environment for a business sale, how this may impact her estate plans and what potential tax ramifications are anticipated when factoring in her other investments. As the sale draws closer, the financial advisor is at the table with the client's legal counsel and CPA to help best structure the business sale to accomplish the client's financial goals.

As these two examples illustrate, the perceived and actual value of the two advisors is starkly different. Merely being a good investment storyteller is not enough. Exciting narratives may help generate sales, but they will not get you to the table when clients are contemplating important life decisions. Only authentic, trusted advice will give you a seat when these opportunities arise.

A smarter way than relying on stories

Both investors and advisors should question the purpose of any given investment story. Is the story's central theme a product pitch rather than about investor goals? Does the story stir emotions, yet is short on facts, logic, and reason? Are the true merits of an opportunity not fully portrayed? If the answer to any of these questions is "yes", be leery of relying on such stories.

Financial advisors should use stories cautiously with clients. Embellishments, material omissions, and manipulated facts should have no place in client conversations. When it comes to investment narratives, the more accurate the picture the better.

Although practitioners should not rely on storytelling as their primary means of investor communications, sharing certain stories may be beneficial. Advisors can use stories to effectively explain hard-to-understand concepts and to help prompt discussions about client goals. For instance, I recently heard an advisor encourage a young worker to save more for retirement. To help motivate early savings for a very distant need, the advisor framed the concept in terms of how much a cheeseburger and coke may cost 40 years into the future. The number was so outrageously high, the advisor's message conveyed the importance of saving now to enjoy the basic comforts of life down the road. The story resonated with the millennial, and prompted him to start saving more.

As this chapter illustrates, alluring, enticing, and captivating stories may entertain clients, but will not necessarily help clients reach their goals. Smart financial advisors do not rely on excessive storytelling to attract and retain invsestors. Instead, they depend on a disciplined goals-based investment process – a merit-based framework that uses intelligent asset allocation and portfolio construction to help attain desired outcomes for clients. Chapter 12 explains these concepts in more detail.

6

Ignoring Taxes

The hazard of disregarding the impact of taxes on investor goals

> "Death, taxes, and childbirth! There's never
> any convenient time for any of them."
>
> – Margaret Mitchell, *Gone with the Wind*

MOST FIRST GRADERS in the US learn addition and subtraction facts for sums up to 20. Between these two concepts, subtraction tends to be more challenging to master. Addition is intuitive. The concept is linked to counting upwards – a skill most preschoolers learn. Subtraction is trickier. It requires comprehending a more abstract concept of taking something away.

"There should be a lot of time spent on experiencing and understanding what the operations mean," says Cathy Seeley, President of the National Council of Teachers of Mathematics. "If you introduce the rules when a subject is only partially set in a child's mind, he'll become confused."[35]

First graders are not the only ones confused by subtraction – so are the majority of financial advisors.

Many practitioners do not fully understand the detractive nature of taxes on portfolio returns. Others choose to merely overlook tax subtraction when managing client portfolios, fixating on gross returns instead. Frequently, sales materials, return forecasts, and client performance reports are stated on a pre-tax basis. Net returns – the amount investors actually get to keep after subtracting

---

[35] 'Adding and Subtracting', www.scholastic.com.

taxes and fees – often go unreported to clients and ignored when constructing and managing portfolios.

A survey of CFA Institute members in the US who manage private client assets was conducted to gauge the level of tax awareness among investment professionals. The research found that fewer than 8% of respondents report client performance on a tax-adjusted basis. In other words, more than 92% of advisors elect not to subtract the impact of taxes when reporting client returns. Furthermore, the survey found that among the small percentage of respondents who do report after-tax performance, a majority of them make no adjustments for potential tax liabilities on unrealized gains upon liquidation. This research suggests only a small fraction of advisors account for the full impact of taxes when reporting investment performance to clients.[36]

Not only do the majority of advisors ignore taxes when reporting client returns, they also tend to overlook taxes when managing client wealth. A 2015 survey of US financial advisors conducted by global asset manager Russell Investments found that fewer than one-in-five advisors (19%) implement tax-loss harvesting – the practice of selling securities at a loss to offset taxes on capital gains – for their high net worth clients. This tax-efficient strategy is one of the easiest and most effective ways to reduce client taxes now and in the future, yet according to the Russell Investments' survey more than 80% of advisors do not attempt to harvest client losses.

"Given clients' increasing tax burdens, one would expect tax strategies to be a major focus for advisors," remarked Frank Pape, director of consulting in Russell Investments' US advisor-sold business. "Right now, many advisors and clients don't fully appreciate the drag on returns caused by taxes, which adds up quickly, especially in a low return environment. Reducing this drag and providing clients with a more complete plan for implementing a tax-managed approach is a significant way for advisors to add value, not only to their own clients, but also their businesses."[37]

Why do so many advisors appear to be confused by basic investment subtraction, overlooking and ignoring the impact of taxes on portfolio returns? Perhaps, it is because advisors are not the ones paying their clients' tax bills. Or maybe it is because they lack the knowledge and tools to effectively implement tax-efficient strategies. Regardless of the reason, ignoring taxes is a hazardous mistake that can significantly detract from investor wealth over time.

---

36 Stephen M. Horan and David Adler, 'Tax-Aware Investment Management Practice', *Journal of Wealth Management* 12:2 (Fall 2009), pp. 71–88.
37 'More Conversation Needed on Best Practices for Tax-Aware Portfolios', www. lifehealth.com (August 5, 2015).

Reducing drag

As a recreational cyclist and triathlete, I am amazed at the power, efficiency and endurance of professional cyclists. This remarkable athleticism is on full display each summer during the Tour de France, the world's most prestigious and most difficult multi-stage bicycle race. The rider who finishes the race covering around 3,500 kilometers (2,200 miles) with the fastest cumulative time wins the Tour's famed *maillot jaune* (yellow jersey).

More often than not, the winner of the Tour is not the fastest cyclist. Sheer cycling power is not enough to win the three-week long race. A key factor to finishing first is reducing aerodynamic drag consistently over long portions of the race by riding in the main group, also known as the peloton. Cyclists in a group reduce drag by riding closely behind other riders. This strategy allows the top riders (with the help of their teams) to conserve enough energy for critical moments in the race such as the steep mountain ascents and individual time-trials.

Researchers from Monash University and the Australian Institute of Sport studied how cyclists' drag was impacted by the relative position of riders in a peloton. A solo rider is subject to a number of resistive forces, but by far the largest factor is aerodynamic drag. At race speeds, more than 90% of a cyclist's power is expended overcoming drag. The researchers found that drafting behind other riders can significantly lower this resistance, reducing the average energy expenditure necessary to maintain fast speeds. In certain locations of the peloton, they discovered cyclists riding in the pack's slipstream could experience up to a 49% drop in drag.

"Small reductions in drag leading to gains in speed across the duration of an event can mean the difference between crossing the finishing line first or second," said Nathan Barry, a PhD engineering student and key contributor to the study.[38]

This research is helping fine-tune team and individual Tour racing tactics. Such has been the case for Team Sky and their lead rider, Kenyan-born Brit Chris Froome. Although Froome was not the speediest cyclist in recent Tour events, he won his fourth Tour de France in July 2017 by combining science, skill and the support of a high-performing team.

---

[38]   Monash University, 'Cyclists: Minimizing drag to maximize results', www.sciencedaily.com (July 23, 2014).

Quantifying the impact of tax drag

Tax headwinds – when ignored or mismanaged – have the potential to decrease the likelihood of investors successfully attaining their long-term financial goals. Just as elite cyclists and their teams can benefit from understanding and reducing the subtractive nature of aerodynamic drag, so can smart advisors gain advantages by understanding the impact of tax drag on portfolios and learning how to minimize its effect. Remember, it is not what investors earn, but what they keep that matters.

Three sources of tax drag on portfolios

For US investors, there are normally three sources of tax drag on portfolios, as noted below.

1. Ordinary income tax versus capital gains tax

Investment income from interest on bonds or non-qualified stock dividends is taxed as ordinary income at the investor's highest marginal income tax rate. Typically, income tax rates are the same as, or higher than, the investor's capital gains tax rate. Accordingly, the same pre-tax return is likely to be higher on an after-tax basis if the return was generated from capital gains rather than investment income.

2. Short-term capital gains versus long-term capital gains

When investors realize capital gains on investments held less than a year, these short-term gains are taxed at a higher rate than realized gains sold after holding for more than one year. The additional tax on short-term gains can be as much as 20 percentage points higher than the tax on long-term gains. Because of this different tax treatment in capital gains, strategies with frequent trading and high-turnover rates often have a significant reduction between their pre-tax and after-tax returns.

3. Current taxes versus future taxes

The longer taxes are deferred, generally the longer investors' wealth can grow. Although long-term capital gains are taxed less than short-term gains, a tax drag still occurs when long-term gains are realized. Avoiding any type of capital gain has the potential to provide tax-deferred growth. Therefore, all else being equal, deferring taxes to some later date is better than realizing capital gains in the present. Furthermore, if an investor defers gains until he or she is in a lower marginal tax rate (such as in retirement), future capital gains may be taxed at a lower level, leaving more assets available to realize investor goals.[39]

Estimating value lost to tax drag

Tax drag is often the largest headwind on fund performance – sometimes twice or three times greater than the drag caused by mutual fund fees. Because of the significant subtractive effect of taxes on fund returns, Congress passed the Mutual Fund Tax Awareness Act of 2000. This legislation mandates that every mutual fund disclose its after-tax performance for one-, five-, and ten-year periods, and show its pre-liquidation and post-liquidation after-tax returns in the fund's prospectus.[40]

Based on this publicly available information, Russell Investments analyzed the average annual tax drag on US equity and taxable fixed income funds for the ten-year period ending June 30, 2015. Tax drag was calculated by subtracting each fund's reported after-tax return from its pre-tax return. The average fund in the equity universe lost 1.1% of its return to taxes each year. Furthermore, when factoring in the compounding effect, tax drag caused a cumulative 12% average reduction in equity returns over the ten years. The tax drag for US fixed income was even worse! The analysis found that the average taxable fixed income fund gave up 1.7% of its return to taxes per year during this ten-year period.[41]

Other research similarly validates the hazard of ignoring taxes when managing portfolios. Parametric Portfolio Associates, a US-based asset manager specializing in tax-aware investing, explored the impact of taxes on portfolio returns in various market conditions. After-tax results were simulated by randomly generating security returns for a portfolio of stocks over a period of ten years. Parametric then applied tax management to the stock portfolio by systematically harvesting losses and deferring gains. After-tax returns were compared on a year-by-year basis. The simulated results indicated tax management yielded an additional 0.7% to 2.5% annual improvement in after-tax returns, depending on market conditions. Excess after-tax returns from tax management tended to be higher during periods with lower market returns and higher security volatility levels. In comparison, excess returns were generally lower when market performance was stronger and volatility was less.[42]

---

[39]   Dan Egan, 'The Right Way to Gauge Investment Returns', www.betterment.com (January 6, 2014).
[40]   Ed Moisson, 'Finding Hidden Gems in Those Pesky Fund Documents', www.lipperalpha.financial.thomsonreuters.com (April 28, 2013).
[41]   Brad Jung, 'The value of a tax aware advisor: Where robotics get terminated', www.blog.helpingadvisors.com (August 20, 2015).
[42]   Rey Santodomingo and Jennifer Sireklove, 'Estimating Tax Alpha In Different Market

Three examples comparing the impact of taxes on portfolio returns

Figure 6.1. Tax impact on returns of three portfolios

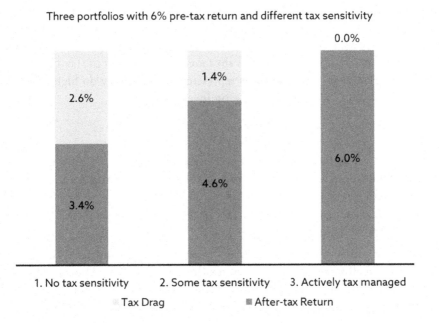

Three portfolios with 6% pre-tax return and different tax sensitivity

When investors and advisors ignore taxes, they lose sight of the long-term impact that tax drag has on portfolio returns. Moreover, when left unchecked, this limiting force can significantly impair goal attainment. Consider the following examples that compare the impact of taxes on portfolios in a given year and over a 20-year time horizon. Figure 6.1 highlights three $1,000,000 portfolios each earning a pre-tax return of 6% per year, but managed with different sensitivity to taxes:

1. The first portfolio has no tax sensitivity. In this example, 100% of the returns are from short-term capital gains and interest. The 6% pre-tax return is reduced to 3.4% on an after-tax basis.

2. The second portfolio has some tax sensitivity. In this example, 100% of the returns are from long-term capital gains. These gains are taxed at 23.8% vs. 43.4% in the first example. The result is a 4.6% after-tax return.

Environments', www.customcore.parametricportfolio.com (September 2014).

3. The third portfolio is actively tax managed. In this final example, all gains are deferred or offset by realized losses and there are no dividends. The portfolio is 100% tax efficient, and the pre-tax and after-tax returns are identical at 6%.

Over a 20-year period, the difference in after-tax growth of these examples is significant. The first portfolio with no tax sensitivity grows from $1,000,000 to approximately $2,000,000 over 20 years, whereas the 100% tax-efficient portfolio grows to around $3,200,000. In this scenario, the tax-efficient portfolio generates more than double the long-term growth of the tax-inefficient portfolio! Although these examples represent extremes, they do highlight the toll and constant drag taxes can have on investment returns.

Tax impact beyond portfolio returns

Taxes not only reduce returns at the portfolio level, they also can impact an investor's entire estate. Following are brief explanations of two other areas where taxes can further erode investor wealth.

Placement of assets

Haphazardly placing assets within an investor's taxable and tax-advantaged accounts usually creates unnecessary tax drag for investors. Also, the typical approach of keeping an investor's mix of assets roughly the same in all accounts regardless of tax status tends to reduce an investor's overall after-tax returns.

Asset location is the practice of maintaining an optimal mix of assets at the household level and placing investments in the most tax-efficient account type to minimize taxes. In contrast to randomly placing assets in an accounts or replicating the same allocation across all accounts, strategically locating assets within an investor's taxable and tax-advantaged accounts has the potential to increase investor returns on an after-tax basis by as much as 0.75% per year according to research by Vanguard. This strategy enhances after-tax returns by placing more tax-efficient investments such as passively-managed equities and municipal bonds in taxable accounts and less tax-efficient investments like taxable bonds and alternative strategies in tax-deferred accounts and tax-free accounts (e.g. in the US traditional IRAs and Roth IRAs respectively). The majority of the benefits occur when the taxable and tax-advantaged accounts are close in size, the household allocation is split fairly evenly between tax-efficient and less tax-efficient assets, and the investor is in a high tax bracket.[43]

---

43   Francis M. Kinniry Jr., Colleen M. Jaconetti, Michael A. DiJoseph, Yan Zilbering and Donald G. Bennyhoff, 'Putting a value on your value: Quantifying Vanguard Advisor's Alpha®', www.advisors.vanguard.com (September 2016).

Even though there is significant value to be garnered by strategically placing assets within various account types, many advisors and investors do not take advantage of this approach when managing wealth.

Withdrawal sequence for retirement income

Another area where taxes can further erode investor wealth is in the sourcing of retirement income. Retired investors typically do not know how to fully maximize the tax benefit when withdrawing money from their investment portfolios.

For most retirees, optimal sourcing of retirement income requires making intelligent choices about the sequence of withdrawals from taxable, tax deferred, and tax free accounts. Determining an appropriate drawdown strategy requires making assumptions, such as estimating an investor's future tax rates, future income levels, and longevity. One strategy for withdrawal sequencing is to spend from taxable accounts first, allowing the tax-advantaged accounts to grow as much as possible, and to consider converting tax-deferred retirement accounts to tax-free status during years when a retiree's tax liability is relatively low. However, investors often unintentionally pursue a less tax-optimized withdrawal sequence – they source income from their tax-advantaged accounts first, based on the understandable logic that these accounts were intentionally set up for retirement.[44]

According to Vanguard research, a well-designed drawdown strategy can add up to 1.1% in excess value per year, depending on the investor's split of assets between taxable and tax-advantaged accounts and marginal tax bracket. Similar to asset location, the greatest benefits from smart withdrawal sequencing occur when the investor's taxable and tax-advantaged accounts are similar in size and the investor is in a high tax bracket. Moreover, Ernst & Young research found that tax-aware asset location and income sourcing can increase income in retirement by as much as 33% and the remaining assets to pass on as a bequest by up to 45%.[45]

When investors spread assets across multiple advisors, maximizing the tax benefit from smart withdrawal sequencing becomes very difficult to effectively execute. Furthermore, when advisors ignore the tax benefits available from

---

44   Michael Kitces, 'Tax-Efficient Spending Strategies From Retirement Portfolios', www.kitces.com (June 22, 2016).
45   Francis M. Kinniry Jr., Colleen M. Jaconetti, Michael A. DiJoseph, Yan Zilbering and Donald G. Bennyhoff, 'Putting a value on your value: Quantifying Vanguard Advisor's Alpha®', www.advisors.vanguard.com (September 2016); and LifeYield and EY, 'Improving After-Tax Returns, Retirement Income, and Bequests Through Tax-Smart Household Management' (October 2010).

strategically ordering the drawdown of client assets in retirement, they may be jeopardizing the longevity of client assets. A poorly designed drawdown strategy often results in higher cumulative taxes throughout retirement. This unnecessary tax drag decreases the likelihood that an investor's wealth will be sufficient to last through retirement and beyond.

A smarter way for advisors to help clients reduce the impact of taxes

In the game of poker, when a player holds a winning hand but folds because of someone's bluff, this misfortunate mistake is called "leaving money on the table." If the player had played his cards right, all of the money in the pot would have been his.

Over time, this expression has taken on additional uses and meanings. In the world of finance, "leaving money on the table" commonly refers to not taking the utmost advantage of something that results in less financial benefit than is possible.

The hazard of ignoring taxes is a form of leaving money on the table that all-too-frequently plagues both investors and advisors. As illustrated in this chapter, investor returns often incur an unnecessary haircut of 1%–2% or even more per year when taxable portfolios are not managed in a tax-efficient manner. This reduction becomes especially painful in a lower return environment. Furthermore, investors regularly leave money on the table when locating assets inefficiently within taxable, tax-deferred, and tax-free accounts, and sub-optimally sourcing retirement income.

Similarly, advisors leave money on the table when they fail to manage client wealth using tax-aware strategies. According to research conducted by Russell Investments, more than four out of five investors are concerned with after-tax returns. Also, this study found that more than a third of taxable client assets (37%) are held away from their primary advisors. These statistics suggest opportunities abound for advisors to consolidate client wealth and win extra business by embracing tax-efficient practices. However, as noted earlier in this chapter, the vast majority of advisors choose to ignore taxes when managing client assets. Most do not even attempt to harvest losses in their client portfolios – one of the easiest and most basic forms of tax-aware portfolio management.[46]

Smart financial advisors recognize the importance of tax management. Not only do these advisors know that tax-aware approaches likely increase their

46 'More Conversation Needed on Best Practices for Tax-Aware Portfolios', www.lifehealth.com (August 5, 2015).

clients' overall wealth, but they also understand that tax-smart strategies also create sizeable growth opportunities for their practices. By embracing techniques such as tax loss harvesting, gain deferral, intelligent asset location, and smart withdrawal strategies, advisors are positioned to deliver more value to their clients and avoid leaving money on the table. Each of these tax-smart strategies is explained in more detail in chapter 13.

In summary, taxes are extremely hazardous when ignored. It is imperative for advisors and investors to pay close attention to the subtractive nature of taxes on portfolios and overall wealth. By reducing tax drag, investors improve their probability of reaching long-term financial goals, and advisors win by differentiating and enhancing their practices among a sea of advisors who continue to focus on pre-tax returns.

7

Focusing on Past Performance

The hazard of chasing returns

> "We drive into the future using only our rearview mirror."
>
> – Marshall McLuhan

HISTORY WAS MADE on the evening of February 22, 2017. On that night, my beloved Kansas Jayhawks men's basketball team clinched a share of its 13th consecutive Big 12 regular season title. Thirteen. Straight! Kansas' streak tied UCLA's record of 13 consecutive conference titles from 1967 to 1979 – the most in men's Division I college basketball history. UCLA's mark was reached under three coaches. Kansas accomplished this incredible feat all under one coach, Bill Self.

ESPN's Seth Greenberg attributes this historical record to Self's recruiting and coaching abilities. "To be that consistent, to be that good, to be the team – the red-letter game, the biggest game on everyone's schedule – and have that consistency, it's mind-boggling. It's phenomenal," Greenberg said. "It's even hard to fathom."

I agree with the ESPN commentator, but recognize my inherent bias as an alumnus of Kansas University. Even so, it is hard to deny that this record-setting accomplishment is one for the ages. The odds of winning 13 straight titles are next to nil from a mathematical construct. The Big 12 conference has ten teams. If any one team has the same likelihood of winning the conference title in a given year, the odds are one-in-ten. But to do so 13 straight times, the odds plummet to one-in-ten trillion! Now, let us assume KU has a 50% chance

72

of winning or sharing the Big 12 title each year instead of only a one-in-ten chance, factoring in exceptional recruiting and coaching prowess. The odds of doing so 13 times in a row are still remarkably low – a mere 1-in-8,192 chance.[47]

One explanation for this extraordinary accomplishment is random luck. But I would argue the mathematical odds suggest otherwise. Persistent skill of KU coaching and player talent significantly improved the team's chance of racking up title wins. If this belief is in fact true, as long as Bill Self is coaching the Jayhawks, his past performance is a reasonable predictor of the program's future success.

This logic of relying on past performance is used not only to predict winning sports teams, but it is applied in many facets of our everyday lives. Consider these examples. Before making a major purchase, do you research your options online and consider product reviews? Perhaps, you also get input from friends and family who already own the item you are thinking of buying. What about selecting a hotel when traveling? Do you consider past experiences with the brand? If you are like the vast majority of consumers and travelers, you answered "yes" to each of these questions. Moreover, this same logic tends to be applied when selecting people to hire. A popular interviewing technique is to assess candidates' past behaviors as a means of determining their likely job performances in the future.

As these examples suggest, people routinely rely on past performance, experiences, and behaviors when making decisions. In fact, in many circumstances, the past is one of the best predictors of the future.

If this is true, then why does the US Securities and Exchange Commission (SEC) require investment advertisements to contain a disclaimer warning that past performance does not necessarily predict future results? Is this requirement evidence of regulatory overreach?

I do not believe so. If anything, the warning may not be strong enough.

Ineffective warnings?

In a research paper titled 'Worthless Warnings?', the authors documented results of an experiment that tested the effectiveness of the SEC's past performance disclosure on investor behavior. Participants of the experiment were each shown a performance ad of an equity fund that had outperformed its peers in the past. Some were shown the ad with the SEC's warning; others were shown

---

47   Andrew Joseph, 'The 13 craziest facts from Kansas' NCAA-record 13 straight Big 12 titles', www.usatoday.com (February 22, 2017) and Jesse Newell, 'KU basketball's Big 12 streak continues to defy the odds', www.kansas.com (February 26, 2017).

the same ad, except the disclaimer was removed. After viewing the ads, the participants were asked about their likelihood to invest in the fund and about their expectations regarding its future returns. The researchers found that the SEC's warning was entirely ineffective – the disclaimer neither decreased the participants' likelihood to invest in the fund nor lessened their expectations about its future returns.

To assess if a stronger warning than the SEC's required disclaimer might influence investor behavior differently, the researchers showed other participants the same investment ad with a more blatant warning. This revised warning read, "Do not expect the fund's quoted past performance to continue in the future. Studies show that mutual funds that have outperformed their peers in the past generally do not outperform them in the future. Strong past performance is often a matter of chance."

Unlike the SEC's disclaimer, this stronger warning did affect participants' behavior. Those who saw the ad with this stronger warning demonstrated a much lower propensity to invest in the fund and expressed diminished expectations regarding its future prospects. In fact, the behaviors of these participants – actions indicative of completely dismissing the advertised past returns – were quite similar to a fourth group of participants who viewed an ad without any performance data.[48]

Based on the findings of this research, perhaps a stronger warning about advertised past investment returns is warranted.

The reality is that when it comes to investing, relying on past performance can be counterproductive. As humans, we are wired to look for patterns in data, and we want to believe that top investment results are linked to skill and hard work. However, this correlation often does not exist. And when advisors and investors blindly put faith in former winners, they generally end up being disappointed with this seemingly intuitive strategy.

Testing the persistence of past performance

Numerous research findings validate that chasing past returns can be hazardous to investor wealth. Among the studies supporting this conclusion are S&P's Persistence Scorecard, SEI's Morningstar rankings' analysis, and Callan's periodic table of investment returns. These three studies are summarized below.

---

[48]   Molly Mercer, Alan R. Palmiter and Ahmed E. Taha, 'Worthless Warnings? Testing the Effectiveness of Disclaimers in Mutual Fund Advertisements', *Journal of Empirical Legal Studies* (September 2010).

S&P Persistence Scorecard

Index provider Standard & Poor's publishes biannually the S&P Persistence Scorecard, which examines the persistence of mutual fund performance over three- and five-year consecutive 12-month periods and two non-overlapping three- and five-year periods. Relative performance, instead of absolute performance, is used by segmenting funds into quartiles. This ongoing study consistently shows very few funds remain top performers for extended periods. Following are key findings from the scorecard released in August 2016, pointing toward a lack of persistence in fund returns, mean reversion characteristics, and lower survival rates for weak performers.

Lack of persistence

Top performing funds normally lack staying power. For example, out of 641 domestic equity funds that were in the top quartile as of March 2014, only 7.3% remained in the top quartile at the end of March 2016. Furthermore, funds remaining as top performers tend to be fewer than the number expected to stay there just from random luck. For instance, only 3.7% of large-cap funds, 5.8% of mid-cap funds, and 7.8% of small-cap funds sustained top-half performance over five consecutive one-year periods. Random expectations would suggest a repeat rate of 6.3%.

An inverse relationship generally exists between the evaluation period and the ability for top-performing funds to stay on top. For example, in this study, only 0.8% of large-cap funds and no mid-cap or small-cap funds remained in the top quartile at the end of the five-year measurement period. This statistic clearly indicates excess fund returns lack long-term persistence.

Reversion to the mean

Top performers tend to fall in rankings going forward, while bottom performers generally do better in the future. These trends suggest fund returns display mean reversion characteristics, whereby returns – whether high or low – will likely move back over time toward the average return of similar funds. In fact, previously top-performing funds often do even worse going forward than the previously bottom-performing funds.

Weak performers go away

Poorly performing funds are more likely to be closed or merged into another fund – particularly funds that land in the fourth quartile. Moreover, S&P's research found bottom-quartile funds had a much higher death rate regardless of a fund's market capitalization or the period studied. For instance, approximately one-third of fourth-quartile funds disappeared over a five-year period, with

32.7% of large-cap funds, 35% of mid-cap funds, and 32% of small-cap funds in the bottom quartile being liquidated or merged. This phenomenon contributes to survivorship bias, which results in an overestimation of the actual number of funds that appear to beat their peers and the market than really do.[49]

SEI analysis of Morningstar rankings

Another study that validates the danger of focusing on past performance is SEI's analysis of Morningstar rankings. Similar to S&P's Persistence Scorecard, SEI found that investors can actually decrease their chances of realizing strong relative returns by chasing prior top-performing strategies. Yesterday's winners tend to be tomorrow's laggards.

For two consecutive five-year periods – 2006 through 2010 and then 2011 through 2015 – SEI tracked the performance of the entire large-cap blend universe of more than 4,000 funds in the Morningstar US Large Cap Blend category. As Figure 7.1 illustrates, they found that more than half of the top quartile funds in the first period fell to the bottom two quartiles (or completely out of existence) during the subsequent five-year period, while less than one-quarter of the funds remained in the first quartile for both periods.

Furthermore, SEI discovered that more than 40% of the top quartile managers from 2011–2015 were not among the funds in the first five-year period, as this group of top performers did not have a full five-year track record during the first period. Accordingly, SEI concluded that ranking investment managers by their five-year returns may not be a very reliable method in predicting future performance.[50]

49   Aye Soe, 'Does Past Performance Matter? The Persistence Scorecard', www.us.spindices. com (August 2016).
50   'Destination: Smart Investing. Wealth management services designed with your needs in mind', www.seic.com.

Figure 7.1. Past performance does not guarantee future results

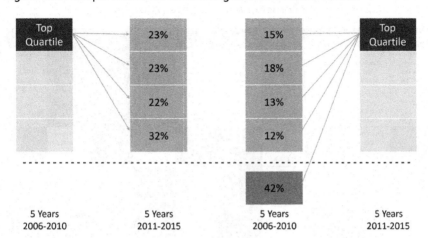

| 5 Years | 5 Years | 5 Years | 5 Years |
| 2006-2010 | 2011-2015 | 2006-2010 | 2011-2015 |

Source: SEI, Morningstar Direct, US Large Blend Universe over the entire 10-year period from 12/31/05 through 12/31/15. Based on the Morningstar universe of 4,125 US Equity Large Cap Blend managers.

Callan's periodic table of investment returns

Callan – one of the largest US consulting firms advising on more than $2 trillion in assets – annually produces a periodic table of investment returns. First published in 1999, the Callan periodic table of investment returns is patterned after Mendeleev's periodic table of the elements and shows year-by-year returns for ten asset classes, ranking them from best to worst. Figure 7.2 is an adaptation of this table of returns, highlighting annual returns for key indices ranked in order of performance for the ten-year period from 2007–16.

Similar to the results of the S&P and SEI studies, Callan's annual publication further confirms the fallacy of chasing prior year's winners. For example, as illustrated in Figure 7.2, the top-ranking asset class for a given year fell to the bottom half the subsequent year six out of nine times. In fact, four of the six times the top ranking asset class not only landed in the bottom half the following year, but also was the worst performing asset class that year. Given the seemingly-random patchwork of asset class performance rankings from one year to the next, Callan's periodic table of investment returns is sometimes referred to as a quilt chart.

Figure 7.2. The Callan Periodic Table of Investment Returns – Annual returns for key indices ranked in order of performance (2007–2016)

2007	2008	2009	2010	2011	2012	2013	2014	2015	2016
MSCI Emerging Markets 39.78%	Bloomberg Barclays Agg 5.24%	MSCI Emerging Markets 79.02%	Russell 2000 Growth 29.09%	Bloomberg Barclays Agg 7.84%	MSCI Emerging Markets 18.63%	Russell 2000 Growth 43.30%	S&P 500 Growth 14.89%	S&P 500 Growth 5.52%	Russell 2000 Value 31.74%
MSCI EAFE 11.17%	Bloomberg Barclays High Yield -26.16%	Bloomberg Barclays High Yield 58.21%	Russell 2000 26.85%	Bloomberg Barclays High Yield 4.98%	Russell 2000 Value 18.05%	Russell 2000 38.82%	S&P 500 13.69%	S&P 500 1.38%	Russell 2000 21.31%
S&P 500 Growth 9.13%	Russell 2000 Value -28.92%	Russell 2000 Growth 34.47%	Russell 2000 Value 24.50%	S&P 500 Growth 4.65%	S&P 500 Value 17.68%	Russell 2000 Value 34.52%	S&P 500 Value 12.36%	Bloomberg Barclays Agg 0.55%	S&P 500 Value 17.40%
Russell 2000 Growth 7.05%	Russell 2000 -33.79%	MSCI EAFE 31.78%	MSCI Emerging Markets 19.20%	S&P 500 2.11%	MSCI EAFE 17.32%	S&P 500 Growth 32.75%	Bloomberg Barclays Agg 5.97%	MSCI EAFE -0.81%	Bloomberg Barclays High Yield -4.47%
Bloomberg Barclays Agg 6.97%	S&P 500 Growth -34.92%	S&P 500 Growth 31.57%	Bloomberg Barclays High Yield 15.12%	S&P 500 Value -0.48%	Russell 2000 16.35%	S&P 500 32.39%	Russell 2000 Growth 5.60%	Russell 2000 Growth -1.38%	S&P 500 11.96%
S&P 500 5.49%	S&P 500 -37.00%	Russell 2000 27.17%	S&P 500 Value 15.10%	Russell 2000 Growth -2.91%	S&P 500 16.00%	S&P 500 31.99%	Russell 2000 4.89%	S&P 500 Value -3.13%	MSCI Emerging Markets 11.60%
S&P 500 Value 1.99%	Russell 2000 Growth -38.54%	S&P 500 26.47%	S&P 500 15.06%	Russell 2000 -4.81%	Bloomberg Barclays High Yield 15.81%	MSCI EAFE 22.78%	Russell 2000 Value 4.22%	Russell 2000 -4.41%	Russell 2000 Growth 11.32%
Bloomberg Barclays High Yield 1.87%	S&P 500 Value -39.22%	S&P 500 Value 21.17%	S&P 500 Growth 15.05%	Russell 2000 Value -5.50%	S&P 500 Growth 14.61%	Bloomberg Barclays High Yield 7.44%	Bloomberg Barclays High Yield 2.45%	Bloomberg Barclays High Yield -4.47%	S&P 500 Growth 6.89%
Russell 2000 -1.57%	MSCI EAFE -43.38%	Russell 2000 Value 20.58%	MSCI EAFE 7.75%	MSCI EAFE -12.14%	Russell 2000 Growth 14.59%	Bloomberg Barclays Agg -2.02%	MSCI Emerging Markets -1.82%	Russell 2000 Value -7.47%	Bloomberg Barclays Agg 2.65%
Russell 2000 Value -9.78%	MSCI Emerging Markets -53.18%	Bloomberg Barclays Agg 5.93%	Bloomberg Barclays Agg 6.54%	MSCI Emerging Markets -18.17%	Bloomberg Barclays Agg 4.21%	MSCI Emerging Markets -2.27%	MSCI EAFE -4.90%	MSCI Emerging Markets -14.60%	MSCI EAFE 1.00%

Source: adapted from 'The Callan Periodic Table of Investment Returns' (2017).

This year-by-year rotation of leaders and laggards reinforces several key principles of investing:

- Past performance does not predict future performance.

- Diversification across asset classes helps reduce portfolio volatility as compared to a concentrated strategy of only owing a few asset classes.

- Asset classes express mean reversion characteristics, with large variations over shorter periods typically becoming more stable when viewed over the long term.

More evidence of the dangers with chasing returns

In case these three studies have not provided you with sufficient proof that focusing on past performance is hazardous to investor wealth, consider these statistics from Barry Ritholtz – American author, wealth management veteran, and industry commentator – in his presentation 'Romancing Alpha, Forsaking Beta' given at Harvard University's Kennedy School in 2013:

- Only one-in-five investment managers outperform their benchmark in a given year.

- Within that quintile, only one-in-ten outperform in two of the next three years.

- Over five years, only 1-in-33 stay in the top 20% over five years.

- Once costs and fees are included, fewer than 1-in-100 outperform on a net basis.

These shocking statistics beg the question – is it rational for investors and financial advisors to focus a majority of their efforts on manager selection when odds of sustainable success are less than 1-in-100?[51]

Failing to heed past performance warnings

Despite the SEC's disclaimer warnings and many studies suggesting investing based on past performance is suboptimal, both investors and financial advisors continue to commonly make this mistake.

Investors too often chase performance

In the absence of a financial plan designed to meet specific goals, investors tend to build their portfolios by collecting funds piecemeal rather than holistically evaluating investments. Such investors typically evaluate funds on a standalone basis without consideration for how they may fit within their broader portfolio allocation. A common way investors compare and pick funds is the use of Morningstar ratings. Unfortunately, this approach lends itself to performance chasing.

Morningstar launched its mutual fund star rating system in 1985. Investors and advisors quickly adopted this assessment tool as a convenient and easy way to evaluate funds. Also, the ratings became popular among fund companies as a means of touting their top performing funds. Morningstar ratings bring

---

[51]   Barry Ritholtz, 'Romancing Alpha, Forsaking Beta', Trustee Leadership Forum for Retirement Security Kennedy School, Harvard University (June 10–11, 2013).

together returns, risks, and fund expense adjustments into a single metric and are based on a bell curve distribution. If a fund scores in the top 10% of its category, it receives five stars; in the next 22.5%, four stars; in the middle 35%, three stars; in the next 22.5%, two stars; and in the bottom 10%, one star. The overall rating is a weighted average of the available three-, five-, and ten-year ratings.

Brokerage firms that cater to do-it-yourself investors – including Fidelity, E-Trade, TD Ameritrade, Scottrade, and T. Rowe Price – provide fund screening tools using Morningstar ratings and other metrics to help investors choose funds to buy and sell. Even FINRA, the US regulatory agency governing brokerage firms, includes a mutual fund analyzer on its website that highlights the star ratings as important information investors should know about.[52]

Based on research conducted by Vanguard, Morningstar ratings significantly influence fund flows. The study found that one-, three-, and five-year fund flows as of December 31, 2015 were positive for four- and five-star rated funds, but negative for funds rated three stars or less. In other words, investors have tended to flock to Morningstar's top-rated funds, while dumping their lower-rated investments. However, as Figure 7.3 shows, Morningstar's highly-rated funds are the most likely to underperform after receiving a four- or five-star rating.

Figure 7.3 demonstrates that, if anything, Morningstar ratings are inversely related to future performance – meaning the lower the rating, the better the chance of higher relative future returns. This is probably not a disclosure that an investor will ever see beneath a fund advertisement showcasing a five-star Morningstar rating. Furthermore, the Vanguard study revealed that investors have less than a 50% chance of picking a fund that outperforms in the future, regardless of its Morningstar rating at the time of fund selection.

Quantitatively-based rating systems such as Morningstar's ratings generally provide little assistance in predicting future winners. In spite of these shortcomings, investors continue to use metrics like these to make fund selections, as evidenced by strong fund flows into top-rated investments. This mistake exposes investors to a high probability that the funds they choose will likely underperform in the future. When investors focus on chasing past returns and funds with the highest star ratings, they overlook other ways to manage their wealth that ultimately give them a better chance of reaching their long-term goals.[53]

[52]   Maxime Rieman, 'Do Morningstar Ratings Help You Find the Best Mutual Funds?', www.nerdwallet.com (March 6, 2013).

[53]   Christopher B. Philips and Francis M. Kinniry Jr., 'Mutual fund ratings and future performance', www.vanguard.com (June 2010).

Figure 7.3. Highly rated funds have not led to future outperformance

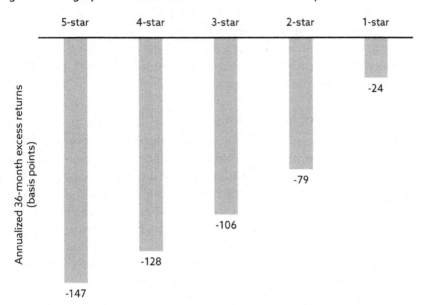

Source: Vanguard calculations using data provided by Morningstar, Inc., as of December 31, 2015.

Advisors also tend to focus on past returns

Not only do investors make the mistake of investing based on past performance, financial advisors commonly succumb to this hazard, too. Focusing on past returns within advisory practices manifests itself in several ways, including performance-based selling and performance-centric investment reviews. This focus tends to create lower client retention rates than practices that operate using a goals-based investing framework.

Performance-based selling

When attempting to win new client relationships, financial advisors commonly generate an investment proposal that lists a recommended asset allocation, underlying investments, and historical performance. Often investments are selected based on strong historical track records, as advisors want to show a portfolio of winners to prospective clients. Plus, this approach has the added benefit of hindsight.

Unfortunately, this practice sets the expectation that an advisor has the ability to outperform the market. For example, if a comparative benchmark returned

6% annually over the prior five-year period, the advisor is likely to show a portfolio comprised of cherry-picked funds that previously outperformed this mark, indirectly implying advisor skill. However, since past performance is not a great predictor of future returns, there is a reasonable chance that this proposed portfolio will experience lower relative returns going forward, providing a disappointing experience for the new client.

Performance-centric investment reviews

Another way past performance influences frequently permeate advisory practices is through the typical investment review process. For instance, advisors generally meet with clients on a periodic basis – such as quarterly, semi-annually, or annually. Traditionally, these client meetings have centered around an assessment of the economy and markets and a portfolio review that includes a performance report. Investment returns are discussed, usually with commentary on what worked and what did not for the reported periods. These meetings often end up being performance-focused. As a result, clients typically perceive the value of the advisory relationship primarily tied to investment performance instead of an assessment of the client's progress toward goal attainment.

Client retention risk when advisors focus on past performance

Advisors who focus on past performance are more prone to client retention risks. Although generating excess returns above the markets is possible, the data suggests the odds of doing so over the long run are low among asset classes marked by efficiency and high liquidity. Thus, when advisors construct investor portfolios with past winners that are substantially different from the market benchmarks, clients become exposed to potentially large performance variations from market returns.

Behavioral finance suggests investors experience more pain from loss than pleasure from gains. This asymmetric trade-off – especially when paired with the low probability that past top performing strategies will likely not persist as winners – creates greater client retention risks for advisors who fill client portfolios with past winners. Given this dynamic, even if outperformance is realized with such strategies, advisors have less to gain from this than they would lose if portfolios were to underperform.

Does it make sense for advisors to have their client performance (as well as their revenue stream) exposed to wide swings in relative returns? When these swings turn into significant underperformance, the odds that clients will leave their advisors for performance reasons substantially increase. All else being equal, this seems like a bad bet – especially knowing that the majority of clients would rather have their advisors help them achieve their long-term goals than outperform the markets.[54]

A better way to reach financial goals than looking in the rear-view mirror

"See, when you drive home today, you've got a big windshield on the front of your car. And you've got a little bitty rear-view mirror. And the reason the windshield is so large and the rear-view mirror is so small is because what's happened in your past is not near as important as what's in your future." This quote by Joel Osteen is in stark contrast to the chapter's opening quote suggesting we typically "drive into the future using only our rear-view mirror."

Investors and advisors are better served when keeping Osteen's forward-looking quote in mind instead of making investment decisions by looking backwards. Goals-based investing provides a better way to manage wealth than rear-view-mirror investing. It focuses investors and advisors on the future, not the past. And goals-based investing properly aligns energies spent on managing controllable factors that lead to more persistent, sustainable results.

Forward focus

Spending time evaluating historical investment performance may crowd out advisor activities that can lead to better investor outcomes. Such distractions blur focus. A friend of mine had a formative experience that highlights this reality.

Phillip grew up on a farm. His first foray into plowing a field was a disaster, as his rows were anything but straight. Phillip's dad noticed he was looking around while atop the tractor. A plane flew by and Phillip looked up. A rabbit scurried underfoot, and he watched the cottontail bound away.

Phillip's dad stopped him after observing the meandering results. My friend was instructed by his father to focus his eyes on a post at the opposite end of the field and remain locked on this view as he plowed. The result was a nearly perfectly plowed row!

Advisors who focus on the distractions of chasing past returns or star ratings tend to produce haphazard client outcomes similar to Phillip's poorly plowed

---

[54] Francis M. Kinniry Jr., Colleen M. Jaconetti, Michael A. DiJoseph, Yan Zilbering and Donald G. Bennyhoff, 'Putting a value on your value: Quantifying Vanguard Advisor's Alpha®', www.advisors.vanguard.com (September 2016).

field. To be truly effective, practitioners must fix their vision forward on clearly defined investor goals and priorities, filtering out all other diversions.

Manage what can be controlled

Not only should financial advisors have forward-looking focus, they also should prioritize their time around activities that are controllable and that demonstrate a high likelihood of persistence. Actions that meet these criteria include identification of low-cost investment strategies and tax-smart investing.

Low-cost investments

Despite its deficiencies, Morningstar's star rating system is widely used by advisors and investors to select funds, as noted in this chapter. However, Morningstar's own director of mutual fund research, Russel Kinnel, published a study that shows selecting funds based on their underlying expense ratio may be a more effective way to choose investments. He found that funds with low expense ratios tend to consistently produce favorable relative returns. These findings are consistent with a number of other similar studies.

Kinnel wrote, "If there's anything in the whole world of mutual funds that you can take to the bank, it's that expense ratios help you make a better decision. In every single time period and data point tested, low-cost funds beat high-cost funds."[55]

Identifying low-cost investments is a prudent strategy to help clients attain the outcomes they desire. Markets are not controllable or predictable. However, investment expenses are a known factor. By keeping an eye toward minimizing these costs, advisors are able to increase the probability of client success.

Tax-smart investing

Like managing investment expenses, tax-smart investing is an activity that can be controlled and normally results in a strategy that consistently adds value. The cause of this outperformance is clear – client tax liabilities are lessened. And when overall portfolio returns are increased by lower relative tax bills, assets can grow more quickly, allowing clients to build up larger funds.

Furthermore, the added value from tax-smart investing seems likely to persist. It is almost certain that there will continue to be taxes in the future. It also is highly likely that different investment returns and account types will continue

[55] Russel Kinnel, 'How Expense Ratios and Star Ratings Predict Success', www.morningstar.com (August 9, 2010).

being taxed differently. Accordingly, advisors and investors can reasonably expect this benefit from tax-efficient investing to continue.[56]

By focusing forward and managing controllable elements through a goals-based approach, advisors can deliver more reliable client outcomes. In turn, practitioners increase the likelihood of clients realizing long-term financial goals, while simultaneously reducing client retention risks. In chapter 14, advisory strategies are outlined that show how goal progress reporting and other tools can help clients focus on what really matters to their long-term financial success – instead of falling prey to the dangerous hazard of performance chasing.

---

[56] Dan Egan, 'When is past performance predictive?', www.dpegan.com (October 17, 2016).

PART 2

Improving Investor Outcomes

— with —

Goals-Based Investing

The purpose of Part 2 is to illustrate how goals-based investing provides a better pathway to investor success than traditional investing.

Part 2 begins with chapter 8, which provides an overview of goals-based investing and introduces the six components of the goals-based investing process. This chapter also reveals how goals-based investing helps overcome the first hazard of traditional investing – reacting to external factors. By linking to this universal hazard, chapter 8 establishes the framework for how advisors can deliver more value to their clients and sidestep this common pitfall through the adoption of goals-based investing. The subsequent chapters in Part 2 unpack each of the six components of goals-based investment in more detail and similarly link to the remaining six hazards of traditional investing found in Part 1.

Drawing from professional experiences of practitioners, true stories of advisors and investors are showcased that relate to the primary concept of each chapter. Goals-based methodologies are then explained. Research and easy-to-understand graphs show how the particular components of goals-based investing help improve investor outcomes. Each chapter concludes with specific actions financial advisors can take to embrace goals-based investing within their practices.

The following table provides a summary of the hazards of Part 1 and the solutions presented in Part 2.

Investing hazard	How advisors can address the hazard
Reacting to external factors	Adopt goals-based investing
Failing to plan	Identify and prioritize client goals
Quarantining portfolios	Manage client wealth holistically
Mismanaging risks	Assess risk comprehensively
Relying on alluring stories	Determine optimal mix of assets and construct portfolios intelligently
Ignoring taxes	Utilize tax-smart investment strategies
Focusing on past performance	Track goal progress

8

Goals-Based Investing

Bypassing the hazard of reactionary behavior

As explained in chapter 1, a pervasive danger that misleads financial advisors and investors is reactionary behavior. Cognitive biases, such as loss aversion and herding, induce counterproductive investment actions that result in a behavioral gap – the difference between potential and actual returns realized by investors.

This chapter shows how smart financial advisors can help clients sidestep the hazard of reactionary behavior through the adoption of goals-based investing. Herein, the core elements of goals-based investing are explained, and best practices for implementing this holistic approach are highlighted. Furthermore, strategies for identifying client resources, funding sources, and financial goals are explored, including the development of client roadmaps. The goals-based practices outlined in this chapter will position advisors to achieve better client outcomes than the suboptimal results achieved by emotion-based investing.

Heeding a guide's advice

A friend of mine went to Alaska to fish for king salmon a few summers' ago. His guide mentioned they would be fishing in bear country and noted a few rules to follow if they encountered a bear. The advice was straightforward: stay calm, do not run, and leave the area slowly.

The advanced instructions proved useful. While hiking alongside a riverbank, they wandered upon an unsuspecting brown bear. The 1000+ pound beast noticed them and turned aggressive. Fortunately, they escaped unharmed. So did the bear.

My friend hired the Alaskan guide primarily to find him fish. As it turns out, the guide's most valuable service was keeping him alive. The experienced angler knew the importance of sharing survival tips with my friend before they entered bear country and encountered a life-threatening situation.

Similarly, clients usually engage their advisors to find promising investment opportunities. Yet, the greatest value from an advisory relationship often is forged amid periods of crisis. Smart financial advisors prepare their clients beforehand through goals-based planning, and they build portfolios to weather market storms. Seasoned financial professionals provide behavioral coaching when market fears tempt investors to abandon their plans. And they find opportunities for their clients (like harvesting losses and tax-smart rebalancing) when market sell-offs occur.

These proactive and disciplined strategies are core components to goals-based investing and are explained in more detail below.

A primer on goals-based investing

Redefining priorities and success

Traditional wealth management emphasizes the means of accomplishing outcomes more than the outcomes themselves. For example, conventional advisors often focus conversations with existing and prospective clients on investment products and their related performance. Yet, investment vehicles are merely the means of achieving client goals. Because traditional investment approaches place so much emphasis around products and performance, discussions about client goals – the intended outcomes of managing wealth – are merely afterthoughts or get completely overlooked.

Goals-based investing changes these priorities. Advisors spend more time understanding clients' goals, assessing the probability of achieving these outcomes, and tracking progress of goal attainment. Within the framework of goals-based investing, advisors usually still reference investment solutions and performance with clients for accountability and transparency purposes, but these components are not the focal point of the client experience or primary drivers of advisory value.

Goals-based investing also redefines success. Conventional investment methodologies – centered on products versus client goals – not surprisingly quantify client success by comparing investment returns to market indices. Alternatively, goals-based investing measures success by evaluating how investments are helping to achieve client goals. This holistic perspective enables advisors to reframe the advisor-client relationship in relatable and meaningful terms. Clients may not comprehend alphas, betas, Sharpe ratios, and risk-adjusted returns. But most investors can understand how they are progressing toward their goals.

Furthermore, measuring goal progress is more relevant to achieving client outcomes than basing success on product performance. Beating the market is a notable objective, but it has little connection to whether or not a client will have sufficient assets to retire comfortably.

The differences between conventional wealth management and goals-based investing, including how advisors prioritize their activities and how success gets measured, are substantial. Figure 8.1 further contrasts these two methods.

Figure 8.1. Comparison of traditional investment approaches to goals-based investing

Traditional investment approach	Goals-based investing
Beating a benchmark	Helping attain client goals
Discussing risk relative to a benchmark	Discussing risk in terms of underfunded goals and the likelihood of not achieving desired outcomes
Offering the newest or hottest products and services	Constructing portfolio solutions that are aligned with client goals
Conducting annual investment reviews; focusing on account performance compared to market indices	Delivering a collaborative, interactive client experience; evaluating ways to increase the probability of client success

Source: John D. Anderson, 'Goals Based Investing: How can you overcome irrational client behavior? Goals based investing changes the conversation'.

Ultimately, goals-based investing helps advisors answer clients' most fundamental questions about their money: Do I have enough? What else can I do?

By clearly addressing these questions and designing plans that align with client goals, advisors are able to offer clients greater peace of mind. In turn, this collaborative, proactive process gives clients the fortitude and reassurance to stay on course, even when markets are highly volatile.[57]

57 'An Introduction To Goals Driven Investing', www.northerntrust.com (2015) and Susan Hoover, 'Ashvin B. Chhabra: Understanding Goals Is the Value Proposition', www. blogs.cfainstitute.org (August 5, 2015).

Evolution and adoption of goals-based investing

Clearly, goals-based investing offers advantages over traditional approaches to investing. Yet, it has been slow to gain widespread adoption among advisors until recently. According to research by the Money Management Institute and Dover Financial Research, goals-based investing is predicted to experience roughly a fourfold increase in adoption from 2015 to 2020.[58]

Hockey-stick growth – slow, extended periods of adoption followed by rapid industry acceptance – is not unique to goals-based investing. Many other sound investment theories have taken years to become widely adopted among investment practitioners. For example, Harry Markowitz pioneered modern portfolio theory in the early 1950s. However, it was not until 1990 that Dr. Markowitz received a Nobel Prize in Economics for his seminal work. Today, Markowtiz's concepts on risk, return, correlation, and diversification are considered foundations of modern finance.

In a similar, unhurried acceptance pattern, goals-based investing finally appears positioned to become the new industry norm in managing wealth. According to Craig Pfeiffer, president and CEO of the Money Management Institute:

> "the past decade has seen the beginning of a fundamental change in the delivery of financial advice – a shift toward measuring the achievement of client goals based on personalized performance and outcomes instead of against arbitrary market benchmarks. (Our research) clearly demonstrate that many large financial services organizations are already making significant investments in the infrastructure required to support the delivery of customized, goals-based guidance."

Figure 8.2 illustrates the evolution of investment theories, including Markowitz's Modern Portfolio Theory and the emergence of goals-based investing and behavioral finance theories developed by Drs. Kahneman and Tversky. The graph also conceptually shows how each new portfolio theory has provided increased value to investors.

[58] 'MMI Industry Guide Survey Finds Significant Commitment to and Progress on the Adoption of Goals-Based Wealth Management', www.mminst.org (November 11, 2015).

Figure 8.2. The evolution of portfolio management theory

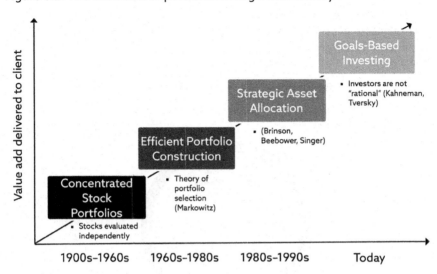

Source: John D. Anderson, 'Goals Based Investing: How can you overcome irrational client behavior? Goals based investing changes the conversation'.

Six components of the goals-based investing process

As goals-based investing gains traction among advisors and the wealth management industry, various methods of its implementation are emerging. For example, some models are built around granular client goals like saving for vacations, automobiles, or future medical costs. Other methods center more on comprehensive client goals such as maintaining a certain lifestyle in retirement or being able to gift to heirs or charities upon death.

Notwithstanding these differences, goals-based practices normally are built on a few key components, including the identification of client goals, resources, and risk, and the construction and monitoring of investment strategies designed with client objectives in mind. Nearly all approaches require advisors to understand an investor's life situation and goal priorities. They also entail advisors helping investors make informed decisions when goals conflict and financial circumstances change. Other common ground among goals-based models is the manner in which client success is measured – in terms of goal progress rather than relative investment performance.

In this book, the execution of goals-based investing is centered on a six-step process as shown in Figure 8.3. This includes defining goals, identifying assets, assessing risk, optimizing allocation, implementing solutions intelligently, and reviewing progress. The process is iterative, so as circumstances change, adjustments may be necessary to increase the likelihood of attaining client goals. Because life is ever changing, continued client engagement throughout this process is important.

Figure 8.3. Six components of the goals-based investing process

The six components of this process are summarized below.

Component 1. Define goals

The first step in the process of goals-based investing is to define client goals.

Investors have many different and unique goals. However, investor goals can generally be grouped into three main categories:

1. Needs – basic necessities for living.

2. Wants – significant extraordinary expenditures, such as a second home, boat, or travel.

3. Wishes – legacy gifts to family and charities, during and after a client's lifetime.

By identifying essential client needs, advisors can ascertain if clients have sufficient assets to maintain basic lifestyle goals. From there, advisors can assess if clients have excess resources to do more, such as funding extraordinary expenditures or aspirational desires.

Chapter 9 explores determining and prioritizing client goals in more detail.

Component 2. Identify assets

The second element in goals-based investing is identifying client resources.

Traditional investment approaches require an advisor to know about the assets the client is engaging the advisor to manage. Goals-based investing extends this knowledge to a client's entire spectrum of wealth – not just a specific account. To gain comprehensive understanding, advisors need to develop client balance sheets. This requires a collaborative effort between advisors and clients to gather and compile financial statements into a consolidated report that lists client assets, liabilities, and net worth. Aggregation technology can help facilitate this initial and ongoing effort.

From there, advisors can construct client life balance sheets. This forward-looking, personal financial statement accounts for both current and implied assets and liabilities. Examples of implied assets include a client's future stream of savings discounted to a present value and future pension income. Implied liabilities include the present value of future expected spending and essentially represent a client's future financial goals. When current assets and liabilities are combined with implied assets and liabilities, advisors are able to determine if existing resources and future savings are likely sufficient to meet a client's long-term goals.

Chapter 10 takes a deeper dive into ways advisors can identify client assets, develop balance sheets, and apply this knowledge to better match assets to desired client outcomes.

Component 3. Assess risk

Once client goals and resources are identified, advisors can then assess client risk, the third step in the goals-based investing process.

Traditional investing defines risk in terms of a client's risk tolerance and an investment's relative and absolute variations in returns. For example, conventional approaches generally use a questionnaire to identify a client's risk tolerance score that corresponds to an appropriate portfolio. Once assets are invested, advisors then assess a client's portfolio risk in terms of standard deviation (absolute risk) and tracking error (relative risk to a benchmark).

Goals-based investing redefines risk. Advisors adopting this approach evaluate client risk primarily as the probability of missing a goal. Rather than merely asking a client how much market risk he or she can withstand without panicking, goals-based investing balances risk willingness, capacity, and necessity in determining the likelihood of achieving a goal.

Risk willingness – essentially the same measure of risk assessed in a traditional client questionnaire – considers a client's behavioral risk. In other words, willingness is how a client will likely respond under various market and financial conditions. *Risk capacity* is the measure of a client's ability to take on risk relative to their financial assets. For instance, risk capacity calculates the portion of assets a client can afford to put into risky assets (such as equities) without jeopardizing goal achievement. And *risk necessity* is the amount of risk required for an investor to assume in order to achieve his or her goals.

The intersection of risk willingness, capacity, and necessity within a goals-based framework gives advisors a more complete picture of a client's risk than traditional measures relying primarily on risk tolerance questionnaires. Accordingly, advisors are able to better manage client risk factors to increase the odds of goal attainment.

Methods for assessing client risk are examined more closely in chapter 11.

Component 4. Define optimal asset mix

The fourth element in goals-based investing is determining the optimal household asset allocation. This step includes calculating the weights of equities (growth assets), bonds (income and stabilizing assets), and alternatives (diversifying assets) across a client's entire asset base.

In conventional investment approaches, asset allocation decisions are made on an account-by-account basis. In contrast, the recommended combination of assets within a goals-based framework are based holistically at the household level. For example, client goals, resources, and risk are collectively used to derive an appropriate household asset allocation. This process includes running multiple allocation scenarios using Monte Carlo simulations. With this information, advisors can determine the mix of assets that yield the highest probability of client success.

It is important that advisors use realistic return assumptions when running a scenario analysis, otherwise selected asset mixes may have too much or too little exposure to risky assets. A best practice in optimizing allocations is to use capital market projections based on expected returns rather than historical performance, as past returns may not best reflect the market environment going forward.

These concepts are explained in more detail in chapter 12.

Component 5. Implement intelligently

A fifth element of goals-based investing is implementing portfolio solutions in an intelligent manner to maximize client success.

Once an optimal household allocation is determined, advisors can then construct portfolios at the account level. One approach to portfolio construction is to bucket strategies that align with client needs, wants, and wishes. For instance, one portfolio may have higher liquidity and lower risk assets to meet basic client needs, while another portfolio may include more growth-oriented assets that align with the long-term nature of a client's legacy goals.

An alternative approach to portfolio construction locates assets across account types to benefit from the relative tax efficiencies of the accounts, while maintaining the targeted client allocation at the household level. The bucket approach may be easier for clients to understand because of the direct linkage between an account and a specific goal. However, asset location typically provides better after-tax returns by locating less tax-efficient assets in tax-deferred and tax-free accounts and more tax-efficient assets in taxable accounts.

Additionally, intelligent portfolio implementation entails using tax-smart withdrawal strategies to extend longevity of client assets. These income-maximizing strategies require advisors to make intelligent choices about the sequence of withdrawals from taxable, tax deferred, and tax-free accounts. Traditionally, best practices in generating retirement income suggest withdrawing assets in the following order: required minimum distributions (RMDs) from tax-advantaged accounts (if any), then from taxable accounts, next from tax-deferred accounts, and finally from tax-free accounts. But wealth advisors trying to optimize income for their retired clients may deviate from this exact ordering to balance reducing the current tax liability with minimizing taxes over the entire retirement period.

Another intelligent portfolio implementation method used by advisors is tax-smart equity management. This strategy builds upon asset location by minimizing the tax drag of equities located inside taxable accounts. Historically, tax-aware wealth advisors minimized taxes by harvesting losses to offset gains at year end. A more effective approach leverages tax-smart trading technology, enabling advisors to maximize the after-tax return of equity assets, while closely tracking the pre-tax performance of the underlying equity strategy. Such systems support advisors by daily automating the harvesting of losses, deferring the realization of capital gains, minimizing trading costs, and avoiding wash sales.

Chapter 13 takes a closer look at how portfolios can be intelligently implemented, including a more thorough examination of tax-smart strategies that help clients keep more of their returns and extend the longevity of their resources.

Component 6. Review progress

After asset allocation is determined and portfolios are implemented intelligently, the final component within the goals-based investing process is to review progress and make adjustments when necessary.

As previously explained, goals-based investing provides a more relevant way of evaluating client progress than the traditional approach. Rather than comparing portfolio returns to market indices, the goals-based approach measures success by how well a client is progressing towards specified goals.

Smarter investment decisions result by structuring advisor-client accountability around goal progress than from basing decisions on relative portfolio performance, which has minimal connection to goal attainment. For example, if goal probability decreases due to a client's overspending or lower savings than expected, a preset, goals-based trigger can alert the advisor to take action and help get the client back on track. At the other extreme, a dynamic trigger may indicate a client's goals are overfunded. Accordingly, the advisor might suggest the client take on less portfolio risk or consider adding more aspirational goals.

Methods for reviewing goal progress and making strategy adjustments are further explored in chapter 14.

How goals-based investing helps overcome behavioral biases

Each of the six components of the goals-based process are meant to seamlessly work together with the shared purpose of client goal attainment. When this holistic process is assimilated into an advisory practice, advisors are equipped to help clients sidestep the hazard of reactionary behavior.

For example, prior to tumultuous market environments, smart advisors use the goals-based investing process to proactively identify client goals, resources, and risk factors to build and implement all-weather portfolios aligned with desired client outcomes. As a result, this process gives clients the confidence to stick to their strategies instead of succumbing to their emotional responses when markets are spiraling downward.

Figure 8.4 lists the five behavioral biases from chapter 1 that trigger reactionary responses and explains how goals-based investing can help advisors and clients overcome these wealth-eroding behaviors.

Figure 8.4. How goals-based investing can help prevent behavioral bias responses among investors

Behavioral bias	How goals-based investing can help
Loss aversion – Regretting losses more than comparable gains are enjoyed.	The fear of loss is circumvented by contrasting the prescribed plan's probability of success to the negative impact of overreacting. Also, smart tax-management provides a strategic approach to taking losses versus a reactionary response induced by loss aversion. Accordingly, harmful withdrawal behavior is significantly curtailed.
Confirmation bias – Selectively seeking evidence to support an opinion while dismissing contradictory evidence.	Investment decisions are based on multiple factors, including client goals, resources, and risk willingness, capacity, and necessity. This evidenced-based approach evaluates various scenarios to test optimal portfolio allocations rather than making decisions using opinion-based rationale that is easily influenced by a person's confirmation bias.
Herding – Blindly following popular trends, believing crowds must have reasonable justification for their actions.	The collaborative advisor-client process of goals-based investing provides clarity and transparency with respect to investment decisions. Furthermore, solutions are designed specifically to achieve client goals rather than based on latest investment fads. As a result, clients have more confidence in the process and are less likely to be swayed by public opinion.
Anchoring – Overweighting the importance of psychological benchmarks, rules-of-thumb, or baseline numbers when making decisions, resulting in reluctance to revise opinions amid new and contradicting information.	Decisions are based on maximizing the likelihood of goal attainment. Accordingly, clients are more willing to relinquish their strong opinions knowing that, right or wrong, the most relevant and important thing is achieving their long-term financial goals.
Recency bias – Forming opinions and making subsequent decisions that are heavily influenced by recent events or experiences; extrapolating the latest circumstances into the future.	Recent investment experiences tend not to alter client goals. By taking a long-term view and designing solutions with the end in mind, advisors and clients are less apt to make the mistake of basing investment decisions on current events.

Source: Peter Brooks, Greg B. Davies and Robert E. D. Smith, 'A Behavioral Perspective on Goal-Based Investing', www.researchgate.net (January 2, 2016).

Clients prefer advisors who focus on goal attainment

Not only does goals-based investing help overcome cognitive biases, this holistic process also tends to be preferred by clients over traditional approaches to managing wealth. A primary reason for this preference is that investors understand and identify with goals more than they do with market benchmarks.

Research validates that the majority of investors favor financial advisors who focus on reaching client goals over those whose primary objective is to beat market benchmarks. According to Natixis' 2016 Global Survey of Individual Investors, 75% of investors indicated they are willing to set a goal that is independent of overall market returns, and virtually the same number also responded that they would be happy if they achieved their investment goals, even if they underperformed the market in a given year. This percentage was even higher for US investors, with 84% of the respondents indicating they would be more satisfied achieving investment goals than outperforming the market over a one-year period.[59]

Similarly, a 2013 study by Phoenix Marketing International revealed this strong, goals-based preference among investors. The study found that approximately nine-in-ten investors – across all affluent tiers – are satisfied with their financial advisor as long as they are able to meet their financial goals. Specifically, these approval ratings were 91% for mass affluent investors with wealth below $1 million, 87% for millionaires, and 94% for penta-millionaires.[60]

Financial advisor actions to move toward a better approach

As highlighted in this chapter, the objectives of goals-based investing – namely meeting client financial goals – differ from traditional investing that focuses on products and their relative performance. Since goals-based solutions are structured to achieve well-defined, personalized objectives rather than tracking irrelevant market indices, clients are more likely to avoid behavioral traps and experience better outcomes. Hence, investors tend to be more satisfied with financial professionals using goals-based investing processes than conventional advisors.

---

[59] Natixis Global Asset Management, 'Help Wanted: How investor behavior is rewriting the job description for financial professionals' (2016); and Natixis Global Asset Management, '2014 Global Survey of Individual Investors', www.fundresearch.de.
[60] John D. Anderson, 'Goals Based Investing: How can you overcome irrational client behavior? Goals based investing changes the conversation'.

Given these facts, it is not surprising that the benefits of goals-based investing are increasingly being recognized by the wealth management industry. Nor is it unexpected that advisor adoption of this client-centric approach is becoming more prevalent.

If you are among the group of advisors yet to embrace goals-based investing, below is an easy, first step you can take to begin incorporating this holistic processes into your practice: creating a wealth roadmap.

Create a wealth roadmap

A wealth roadmap is a document that summarizes a client's goals, resources, and time horizons. The primary purposes of this document are to capture a client's goals-based profile and to use this information to build solutions that align with client priorities and desired outcomes. Once a wealth roadmap has been created for an investor, it can serve as a dynamic tool for an advisor to review and update from time to time with the client.

Figure 8.5 is an example of a wealth roadmap. This example is completed for a hypothetical husband and wife client with multiple goals.

As Figure 8.5 illustrates, client goals are prioritized into three tiers – needs, wants, and wishes. For each goal, funding sources are identified and the time horizon for a given goal is specified. For example, note the retirement income goal under 'Needs'. Multiple funding sources, including Social Security, pension income, and investment accounts are listed. Also, the goal's time horizon is identified as a current need lasting throughout the husband's and wife's lifespans. The wealth roadmap also notes the client's other advisors, including tax and estate planning professionals.

Using this example as a reference, build a wealth roadmap for yourself. Identify and prioritize your financial goals into needs, wants, and wishes. Then, list funding sources and time horizon for each of your goals. Inputting this information into a document is simple. Determining the content may not be as easy, since goals may conflict and household priorities may differ.

After you have built your personal wealth roadmap, you may want to consider introducing this concept to a few clients, assuming you have legal and compliance permission to do so. This tool can serve as a starting point for moving towards a goals-based approach with clients, as it is easy to implement and essentially free to create.

A wealth roadmap also is a simple way to remind clients about the purpose of their investments. And it is a means for helping clients keep focused on their goals when markets turn volatile and behavioral influences tempt overreaction.

Figure 8.5. Sample wealth roadmap

Wealth Roadmap – Joe and Betty Client

	Client Goals	*Funding Sources*	*Time Horizon & Other Considerations*
Needs *Maintain current lifestyle*	• Generate $100,000 in after-tax, inflation-adjusted retirement income	• Social Security • Pension income • INTRUST IMAs • INTRUST IRAs • Company 401(k) • Held-away IMA	• Current requirement through the remainder of Joe and Betty's lifetimes
Wants *Maintain current lifestyle*	• Generate $25,000 in after-tax, inflation-adjusted excess retirement income for travel	• Same as above	• Current requirement through 2030
	• Generate $25,000 in after-tax, inflation-adjusted excess income every two years for a new vehicle	• Same as above	• Current requirement through 2030
Wishes *Legacy planning*	• Generate $4,000 in after-tax, inflation-adjusted excess income to fund 529 College Savings Plans for grandchildren	• Any remaining assets	• Recurring annually through 2025
	• Begin considering legacy planning	• Any remaining assets	• At Joe and Betty's direction, we may want to meet and begin establishing relationships with their children

Source: INTRUST Wealth

9

Determining and Prioritizing Client Goals

Sidestepping the hazard of directionless investing

FAILING TO PLAN is a hazard that commonly plagues investors and financial professionals. As revealed in chapter 2, empirical studies have found that fewer than 40% of investors have a written financial plan. And surprisingly only half of advisors have specified financial plans for themselves. Without specific plans in place, investing lacks direction and focus. As a result, long-term financial goals become exceedingly difficult to attain – like buying a home, paying for education, or maintaining a comfortable lifestyle throughout retirement.

Determining and prioritizing goals enables financial advisors to help clients and themselves avoid the hazard of failing to plan for the future. By starting with the end in mind, smart advisors are able to develop goals-based plans and investment strategies that align with their clients' desired outcomes. When financial goals are unknown or vague, investing is directionless, and planning becomes nearly impossible.

The process of developing financial goals begins with advisors collaborating with clients to identify long-term client goals and quantify accumulation and spending targets. It also entails advisors working with clients to evaluate the trade-offs associated with competing goals. By focusing on these important activities, advisors and their clients create the basis for well-designed, goals-based plans that position investors for long-term success.

In the previous chapter, six components of goals-based investing were introduced, including the first step – defining client goals. In this chapter, we explore this first, essential component in more detail. Financial goal hierarchy, beginning with basic needs and ending with aspirational wishes, is initially explained. Then, methods for identifying and prioritizing goals through advisor-client interactions and fintech solutions are introduced. From there, several simple methods for quantifying goals are shown. This chapter concludes by providing evidence of the benefits of financial preparation and highlighting practical steps advisors can take to begin incorporating goal-focused processes into their practices.

To gift or not to gift, that is the question

William Shakespeare's oft-quoted line from Hamlet – "to be or not to be, that is the question" – contemplates the struggle of making life-altering decisions when the impact of an action is both significant and uncertain. Hamlet's quandary reminds me of a situation involving spouses attempting to identify and prioritize goals.

The family in question had significant means and no concerns about sustaining their lifestyle throughout retirement. However, the husband and wife shared different perspectives on what to do with their surplus wealth. One spouse wanted to begin making large, equal gifts to their three adult children, while the other spouse wished to delay substantial gifting until later in life, ultimately leaving less to their children and more to philanthropic causes.

A heated exchange unfolded regarding the *obligation* to help the kids now – while they're raising families of their own – versus the fear that too much wealth might destroy the moral fabric of their children. The decisions surrounding the responsibility and stewardship of their resources weighed heavily on the husband and wife. These choices were further compounded by the knowledge that the outcomes of their decisions were unknown, yet likely very significant. Ultimately, the conversation ended amicably, and a middle ground was agreed upon. A moderate amount of current gifting to the three children was balanced with plans to pass remaining portions of their estate to family and multiple charities upon death.

As this story illustrates, financial goal setting can be a taxing endeavor. Advisors who understand and can explain the hierarchy of financial goals are able to help clients navigate these crucial planning conversations. For example, mentally segmenting financial objectives into three primary categories – basic needs, wants, and aspirational wishes – provides investors with a relatable framework for clearer goal identification and prioritization. This framework is discussed below.

Hierarchy of financial goals

As a freshman in college, I studied Maslow's hierarchy of needs theory in an Introduction to Psychology class. This psychological model attempts to explain human motivation. As a visual learner, the image of the multi-tiered pyramid shape used to portray Maslow's theory stuck in my memory. The most fundamental level of human needs – such as food, shelter, and clothing, as well as personal and financial security – are located at the base of this pyramid. Self-actualization and self-transcendence – realizing a person's full potential and finding fulfillment through altruism and spirituality – are located at the top.

With some adaptation, Maslow's hierarchy of needs provides a framework for classifying investors' financial goals. For example, foundational goals such as meeting basic lifestyle needs are represented at the base of a pyramid, while more altruistic financial goals like philanthropic giving are symbolized as the triangle's peak. In between, goals such as major purchases, college funding, or travel are denoted as the middle tier of investor wants and desires. Figure 9.1 illustrates this adaption.

Figure 9.1. Hierarchy of financial goals

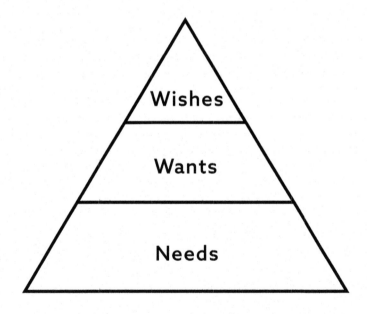

Needs

As illustrated in Figure 9.1, the base tier of financial goal hierarchy is needs. This goal category encompasses essential lifestyle expenditures such as housing and other basic necessities of daily living. In essence, financial goals in this tier answer the question – what does a client need for immediate safety? Without these things in place, an individual's wellbeing is compromised.

Wealthy households are unlikely to struggle meeting basic necessity goals. Nevertheless, it is important for financial advisors to understand how high net worth clients interpret and quantify their essential needs. This knowledge helps advisors assess the feasibility of clients attaining desired and aspirational goals.

For example, consider two 50-year-old investors both with $5 million in assets and the same life expectancy. One investor believes $75,000 per year is sufficient to fund basic needs, while the other, less frugal investor requires more than $300,000 a year for their necessities. Without this clarification, an advisor would not know the clients' resources available to fund other goals, and thus would not be able to correctly assess the viability of their remaining goals.

Wants

The middle tier of the hierarchy of financial goals is wants. These goals are comprised of client desires that go beyond the necessities of daily living. Wants represent the goals that investors hope to fulfill, but could live without. In other words, if wants go unrealized, client wellness is not upended.

Financial goals in this tier answer the question – what does a client desire to reasonably attain beyond life's basic needs? Examples of wants include purchasing a second home, funding college education for children or grandchildren, budgeting for a child's wedding, or setting aside amounts for extraordinary vacations.

Wishes

In addition to needs and wants, the final tier of the financial goal hierarchy is wishes. This last goal category is comprised of an investor's aspirational desires. These are goals that an investor would like to fund, but would not be too dissatisfied if they were not attained.

Financial goals in this final tier answer the question of what clients dream of accomplishing in their lifetimes or beyond. Like the other goal categories, aspirational wishes are unique to each client. Some common examples include starting a business, leaving an inheritance to surviving family members, and making significant philanthropic gifts.

Identifying and prioritizing goals

Effectively determining and ranking client needs, wants, and wishes requires collaboration between advisors and clients. This interactive process includes specifying the main financial goals of clients. Included in this detail are a goal's specific time horizon. Also, forecasts of outgoing and incoming cash flows associated with a goal need to be identified. Furthermore, determining the importance of attaining each client goal aids in establishing priorities among goals.[61]

For instance, consider an advisor who is engaged by a client in his 50s. To determine the client's goals and priorities, the advisor collaborates with the client to specify financial goals. In this dialogue, the client identifies the goal to retire in ten years as his highest priority. Together, the advisor and client identify the annual retirement income associated with this primary goal and estimate the client's life expectancy. This process is repeated for the client's other goals – each remaining goal is specified and its cash flows and time horizon are estimated.

Various methods exist to assist advisors in the identification and prioritization of clients' needs, wants, and wishes. Traditional approaches use face-to-face meetings to facilitate the completion of client goal questionnaires. Newer tactics leverage fintech solutions and gamification to engage clients in the goal setting process.

In-person meetings

Meeting face-to-face with clients is a preferred means for many advisors to establish and rank client goals. Skilled advisors are adept at getting clients to verbalize their desired financial outcomes and reading nonverbal cues during these conversations. For instance, one spouse may dominate the in-person discussion. By observing the other spouse's nonverbal reactions, smart advisors are able to redirect the conversation and use leading questions to draw out both spouses' points of view.

Fortunately, I had the benefit of learning how to run productive goal meetings with clients from a highly successful colleague. My friend and mentor had nearly 45 years of advisory experience before retiring at the age of 70 a few years ago. He taught me effective, old-school methods of discovering client goals, such as completing data gathering questionnaires with clients during in-person meetings. He used stories and examples from his professional experience to engage clients in this process. Additionally, he explained in advance to his clients

---

[61] Investment Management Consultants Association, 'Focus on Goals Based Investing Part 1', www.onefpa.org (November/December 2015).

the importance of coming prepared to discuss their financial needs, wants, and wishes at this goal-setting meeting. I continue to find these strategies productive when meeting with clients about their goals.

An example of a page from a data gathering questionnaire is illustrated in Figure 9.2. This particular page would be used by an advisor to identify a client's retirement goal. It also would be used to prioritize the retirement goal's relative importance by having the client rank it as a need, want, or wish with a score ranging from 10 as the highest priority to 1 as the lowest.

Fintech solutions

Newer fintech solutions can be used to complement in-person meetings for client goal development. One example is myMoneyGuide®, an online goals-based planning tool developed by MoneyGuidePro, a market-leading, goals-based planning software for financial professionals. This interactive, web-based experience allows clients to identify their goals by specifying their needs, wants, and wishes. It also allows clients to explore the possibilities of trade-offs, such as spending less, saving more, retiring later, or changing investment asset mixes. This dynamic process helps clients prioritize goals. The online tool is designed for client results to be shared with their advisor.

In addition to myMoneyGuide®, other financial planning software firms have introduced interactive web-based solutions for clients. Examples include emX developed by eMoney (www.emoneyadvisor.com) and WealthStation owned by Fidelity Information Systems (www.empower.fisglobal.com/ WealthStationOnDemand). Both of these tools engage clients through web-based portals and offer goals-based planning components.

Gamification

An emerging technique to identify and prioritize client goals is gamification. As this name implies, gamification applies concepts and techniques used in games to influence behaviors. Historically, educators have used gamification to help students learn a concept or change behavior by rewarding positive outcomes through a gaming experience. People – whether young or old – tend to respond better to positive motivation through rewards than to negative penalties associated with making mistakes.

In the context of financial advice, gamification creates a safe and fun environment for clients to evaluate and prioritize their financial goals. The intent of using gamification with clients is not to make light of the importance of planning. Rather, the primary purpose of this technique is to encourage clients to change certain behaviors, positioning them for better long-term success.

Figure 9.2. Example page from a client data gathering questionnaire

My Financial Goals

Retirement Goal:

Goal Importance (*circle one*)

10	9	8	7	6	5	4	3	2	1
Needs				Wants				Wishes	

Age to retire:

_____ Client   _____ Co-Client

Life expectancy:

_____ Client   _____ Co-Client

Retirement Living Expenses *Enter living expenses for the following retirement periods:*

Expense Period 1 -- Client retired/Co-Client working $ _____ per _____ ☐ Month ☐ Year

Expense Period 2 -- Client And Co-Client retired $ _____ per _____ ☐ Month ☐ Year

Expense Period 3 -- Client or Co-Client alone $ _____ per _____ ☐ Month ☐ Year

Expenses that end during retirement (*e.g. mortgage, loan*):

Description	Ending Year	Amount (Current Dollars)	Inflate
		$ _____ ☐ Mth ☐ Yr	☐ Yes ☐ No

Will this amount inflate? ☐ No ☐ Yes, Base Inflation Rate ☐ Yes, Base Inflation Rate +/– _____ %

Source: adapted from MoneyGuidePro, Detailed Questionnaire, p. 3

For example, both MoneyGuidePro and eMoney have game-like scenarios incorporated into their technology. These planning tools enable advisors and clients to instantaneously evaluate goal-attainment probability. Clients are able to interactively change inputs such as savings rates, retirement dates, longevity, and investment risk and see the impact of their changes. Positive results are reinforced with graphical representations using probability of success meters.

Another gamification technique is to use playing cards with images of various goals like retirement, saving for college, purchasing a vacation home, gifting to kids, budgeting for travel, and charitable giving. Household members separately rank their financial goals by ordering the cards according to their personal preferences. Differences in priorities between household members are discussed with the advisor. The ultimate goal of this process is to derive a combined card ranking that represents the household's mutually agreed upon goal priorities.

Additional insights regarding collaborative applications of fintech solutions and gamification are explored in Part 3 of this book.

Quantifying goals

Besides identifying and prioritizing client financial goals, advisors also must quantify them. This process entails estimating the dollar value of each goal.

To illustrate how to quantify client goals, this section focuses on the most common goal – retirement. According to a recent Gallup poll, 94% of investors with a written financial plan include retirement as a key goal. Given the prevalence of this goal and the retirement savings crisis in America as detailed in chapter 2, understanding how to estimate a retirement goal for clients is an essential advisor skill. Two quick and easy methods for calculating a client's retirement goal – using a savings factor and retirement benchmarks – are reviewed below. The next chapter explains a more advanced method of calculating goal values as implied liabilities within the framework of a client's life balance sheet.[62]

Using a savings factor to estimate a retirement goal

One method for quantifying a client's retirement goal is to use a savings factor. This simple approach estimates a client's required retirement savings by multiplying the client's current income by the savings factor associated with a given retirement age. Fidelity Investment's savings factors are shown in Figure 9.3.

---

[62] Jeffrey M. Jones, 'More Nonretired U.S. Investors Have a Written Financial Plan', www.gallup.com (July 31, 2015).

Figure 9.3. Retirement savings target as a multiple of current income

Desired retirement age	Savings factor
65	12x
67	10x
70	8x

Source: 'How much do I need to save for retirement?', www.fidelity.com (June 5, 2017).

Using the savings factor in Figure 9.3, the retirement savings goal for an investor earning $100,000 income is $1,000,000 assuming a retirement age of 67. If the desired retirement age is decreased to 65, the savings target increases to $1,200,000.

Fidelity's savings factor guidelines are based on some key assumptions. These include the investor living to the age of 93, 15% of income saved annually starting at age 25, at least 50% of savings invested in stocks on average over the investor's lifetime, and pre-retirement lifestyle is maintained by the investor throughout retirement.

Savings factors, such as Fidelity's guidelines, are rule-of-thumb multipliers and are not based on detailed projections of a household's specific retirement income needs. Each investor's circumstances will differ. For instance, individuals may live beyond 93, or die earlier. They may start saving at different ages than assumed, and annual savings rates may vary from the 15% assumption. Also, an investor may have lifestyle expectations more or less in retirement than preretirement. Furthermore, they may have a substantial pension. Each of these variables will impact an investor's savings factors. Accordingly, investors and advisors should keep these limitations in mind and recognize that the use of savings factors is broadly suggestive rather than a definitive measure of retirement readiness.

Fidelity also offers a web-based, interactive calculator for estimating retirement accumulation and income goals using savings factors. This online tool can be found at:

www.fidelity.com/products/retirement/widget/xfactor/retire_xfactor.html

Using retirement benchmarks to estimate retirement goals

Another simple method to estimate retirement goals is to use retirement benchmarks. Current interest rates, inflation, mortality tables, and other data are used to calculate these daily indices matched to an investor's age. To calculate an annual retirement income estimate using a retirement benchmark, divide an investor's current savings by the most recent retirement index level corresponding to the investor's age. This calculation can also be reversed to determine an investor's total retirement savings goal based on a specified annual, inflation-adjusted income.

An example of a retirement benchmark series is BlackRock's CoRI™ Retirement Indexes. CoRI indexes estimate the cost for each dollar of retirement income based on when an individual turns 65. This estimated cost per dollar of retirement income allows an investor to quickly calculate the retirement income that a given amount of savings could provide. It can also estimate how much money needs to be saved in order to fund a desired level of retirement income. One downside to CoRI indexes is that they are published for a limited age range – investors between 55 to 74 years old.

CoRI indexes assume an individual invests conservatively from his or her current age until retirement at age 65, and then buys an inflation-adjusted immediate annuity to generate retirement income for life. Each age-based index is updated daily to reflect current bond rates and annuity purchase rates.

Figure 9.4. Recent CoRI index values

Current age	Index level
64	$21.11
63	$20.48
62	$19.77
61	$19.09
60	$18.41
59	$17.77
58	$17.20
57	$16.63
56	$15.87
55	$15.23

Source: Chip Castille, 'Working to take longevity risk off the table', www.blackrock. com (June 6, 2016).

Using the information in Figure 9.4, consider a 55-year-old investor with $1,000,000 in retirement savings. Divide accumulated savings ($1,000,000) by the CoRI index level corresponding to the investor's age ($15.23). This results in $65,660, and represents the estimated amount of annual, inflation-adjusted retirement income starting at age 65 and maintained for life.

To forecast how much money an investor should save to reach a specific retirement income goal, the calculations just need to be reversed. For instance, if the 55-year-old investor wants $80,000 in annual income starting at age 65 instead of the approximate $65,000 estimated in the example above, then simply multiply this amount by the applicable CoRI index to estimate the total retirement savings goal ($80,000 x $15.23 = $1,218,400). This calculation indicates an additional $218,400 in retirement savings may be required in order to attain the desired retirement income target at age 65.

BlackRock offers an online, interactive tool based on their retirement indexes for use by advisors and investors. This free web-based retirement calculator can be found at:

www.blackrock.com/cori-retirement-income-planning?cid=vanity:cori:coritool

Both savings factors and retirement benchmarks are simple and quick ways to estimate retirement goals. When used together, these tools may offer a broad perspective of a client's potential retirement income and savings targets.

However, savings factors and retirement benchmarks have their drawbacks. They are based on a number of assumptions that may not be relevant to a given client and are limited to assessing retirement goals. The next chapter explains how to calculate a client's implied liabilities, which are a client's future financial goals expressed in today's dollars. This approach incorporates more investor-specific factors and can be used to estimate future retirement goals as well as other financial goals.

Goals help investors save more and increase their financial confidence

Intuition suggests the establishment of financial goals should help improve investor outcomes. Research also supports this belief.

According to the Employee Benefit Research Institute's 2016 Retirement Confidence Survey, pre-retirees who have done a retirement savings needs calculation tend to report higher savings goals than those who have not done the calculation. For example, 31% of pre-retirees who have calculated their retirement savings goal estimated they need to save at least $1 million for retirement. In comparison, only 18% of pre-retirees who have not calculated their retirement savings needs believe they should accumulate at least $1 million for retirement. At the other extreme, fewer pre-retirees who calculated retirement goals than those had not felt that $250,000 or less in savings would be sufficient for retirement (21% vs. 31%).

Despite higher savings goals, pre-retirees who have estimated retirement savings needs are more than twice as likely than those who have not done a goal calculation to report being very confident about their ability to afford a comfortable retirement (30% vs. 13%). These tendencies of saving more and increased retirement confidence also held true in each of the prior years the Employee Benefit Research Institute's survey was conducted.[63]

Financial advisor action – quantify your retirement savings goal

If the ideas and methods outlined in this chapter are new to you, you may want to consider practicing the concepts on yourself before introducing to clients. An easy, yet beneficial step in this direction is to calculate your retirement savings and income goals through the Fidelity and BlackRock websites as cited earlier in this chapter. After doing these goal calculations, compare the results and determine what factors contribute to the differences. Reading the fine print and disclosures associated with these online tools may help you better understand your results and variances.

Identifying and prioritizing financial goals are foundational steps for advisors to take when implementing goals-based investing with clients. Through the goal hierarchy of needs, wants, and wishes, advisors are able to group and prioritize unique client goals into an easy to understand framework. Furthermore, focused in-person meetings as well as fintech solutions and gamification can aid the goal setting process. By adopting these initial elements of the goals-based investing process, advisors enable clients and themselves to circumvent the hazard of failing to plan that results in directionless investing.

---

[63]   Ruth Helman, Craig Copeland and Jack VanDerhei, 'The 2016 Retirement Confidence Survey: Worker Confidence Stable, Retiree Confidence Continues to Increase', www.ebri. org (March 2016).

10

Managing Client Wealth Holistically

Avoiding the hazard of quarantining portfolios

A S EXPLAINED IN chapter 3, a hazard that ensnares financial advisors and investors is quarantining portfolios.

Assets managed in isolation limit the view of a client's total wealth, and often result in clients paying more in fees and taxes than they would under a coordinated approach. Moreover, this hazardous approach may produce mismatched strategies, whereby total investor wealth becomes misaligned with household goals. As a result, investor success is restricted.

This chapter demonstrates how smart financial advisors can sidestep the hazard of quarantining portfolios. Strategies based on managing client assets holistically are explained, including how to develop client balance sheets for a complete view of client wealth. Also, advisory solutions that match investor assets to liabilities are reviewed. These goals-based practices enable smart financial advisors to achieve better outcomes for their clients than the outcomes achieved by advisors managing client wealth in isolation.

"What's your best investment tip?"

A number of years ago, I recall having lunch with a client who asked me, "What's your best investment tip?" My answer clearly disappointed him.

The client was expecting a promising stock tip, just as his other financial advisors had peddled to him. He was hoping that I, too, would reveal to him an undiscovered company on the verge of a major breakthrough. My client envisioned a scenario of a sleepy company's stock coming to life and skyrocketing shortly after he invested. By garnering his advisors' best tips, he would surely see his wealth soar. He yawned with disinterest when I revealed my advice. In fact, he almost looked disgusted at me.

Without hesitation when asked the question, I responded that my top recommendation was for him to engage a personal chief financial officer (CFO). My client had a CFO for his family business. Surely, he did not need another one for himself? Yet, I confidently knew this was the best advice for my client.

He had amassed significant wealth through his business. Before long, he intended to stop leading the day-to-day operations of his company and hand the reins over to his kids. His cavalier style had enabled him to build a successful business. But I felt this act-first, think-later approach that had worked for him in the past would likely compromise his wealth in the future. I had seen entrepreneurial fortunes lost this way before.

At our lunch meeting, my client wanted an enticing story, not a goals-oriented strategy. What he needed much more than a stock tip was an advisor who would help him manage his wealth holistically. Effectively, this boring but prudent advice is what I meant when I recommended that he engage a personal CFO.

My client left the lunch dissatisfied with my response. He clearly wanted to keep his financial advisors isolated from each other. The idea of sharing his complete financial picture with one or all of his advisors made no sense to him. From his perspective, advisory value was limited to investment tips, not coordinated, goals-based advice.

Developing client balance sheets

Smart financial advisors understand their best investment tips are based on client-centric advice, rather than product-oriented pitches. Not all investors will recognize the value and benefits of a coordinated approach. However, investors that do recognize this will benefit immensely.

Client-centric advisors embrace the concept of serving as their clients' personal CFO. Similar to corporate chief financial officers who manage the financial health of their firms, top-performing advisors help their clients achieve financial wellness by holistically managing client wealth. These advisors develop customized, whole-picture strategies, enabling their clients to reach financial goals.

Understanding an investor's complete financial picture is an essential element in this approach. A financial advisor should create personal balance sheets that encompass the entirety of a client's assets, liabilities, and net worth. Without this baseline information, accurately assessing client financial wellness and the likelihood of goal attainment are virtually impossible.

Client net worth statements

Net worth is the difference between the assets and liabilities of a person or company. Client net worth statements are point-in-time, balance sheet reports that summarize client total wealth net of any liabilities. These statements give advisors accurate depictions of their clients' financial situations and are essential in setting realistic financial goals.

To compile a personal balance sheet and net worth statement, the financial advisor should request current copies of the client's financial records. Alternatively, financial advisors can use aggregation technology to efficiently generate client balance sheets and net worth statements. Examples of advisor-friendly aggregation solutions include Wealth Access (www.wealthaccess.com), Quovo (www.quovo.com) and Yodlee (www.yodlee.com).

Current bank account balances along with investment holdings and valuations should be provided by the client. Values of residential property and business interests also should be estimated. Other asset details to collect may include resale value of automobiles, personal property estimates, and any other financial and tangible assets owned by the client. The sum of all of these values is the total value of the investor's assets.

On the other side of the balance sheet are liabilities and net worth. To calculate total liabilities, the financial advisor should ask the client to list everything he or she owes. Common liabilities include: residential mortgages, auto loans, lines of credit balance, credit card debt, student loans, and other personal loans or guarantees.

The difference between the client's assets and liabilities is the client's net worth. Advisors should work with investors to update their balance sheets and net worth statements at least twice per year, to help validate progress toward client financial goals.

An example of a net worth statement is shown in Figure 10.1.

A point-in-time net worth statement like this provides a traditional means of measuring a client's net worth. An alternative method in assessing a client's financial wellbeing is to calculate an investor's life balance sheet.

Figure 10.1. Example of a client net worth statement

Net Worth Statement		Date: 9/30/2017
Assets	Amount	Total
Banking		
Checking Account	$10,000	
Savings Account	$40,000	
Total:		$50,000
Total for Banking		**$50,000**
Investments		
Taxable Investment a/c 1	$150,000	
Taxable Investment a/c 2	$250,000	
Taxable Revocable Trust	$100,000	
Employer 401(k) a/c	$750,000	
Individual Retirement a/c	$250,000	
Total:		$1,500,000
Total for Investments		**$1,500,000**
Real Estate		
Primary Residence	$435,000	
Total:		$435,000
Total for Real Estate		**$435,000**
Personal Property		
Automobiles	$55,000	
Total:		$55,000
Total for Personal Property		**$55,000**
Total Assets		**$2,040,000**

Total Net Worth

Net Worth Statement

Date: 9/30/2017

Liabilities	Amount	Total
Personal Loan		
Auto Loan	$15,000	
	Total:	$15,000
Total for Personal Loan		$15,000
Mortgage		
Mortgage on Primary Residence	$125,000	
	Total:	$125,000
Total for Mortgage		$125,000

Total Liabilities		**$140,000**
		$1,900,000

Life balance sheet

A life balance sheet accounts for both current and implied assets and liabilities. This forward-looking approach helps advisors determine if sufficient assets are available to meet a client's long-term goals.

Implied assets

The most common implied asset is an investor's future stream of savings discounted to a present value. For example, consider a 30-year-old investor with nearly 40 more years of anticipated employment income. Some of this future income will be consumed. The remainder is future savings. The forecasted string of annual savings of this 30-year-old, after discounting to today's dollars, is an implied asset – sometimes referred to as human capital.

Likely, the current value of future savings represents a significant portion of this young investor's total assets. As clients age and have fewer years to accumulate additional savings from working, the value of this implied asset decreases.

Another example of an implied asset is future pension income. This may include estimated Social Security benefits and income from a company-sponsored pension. These future cash flows represent implied assets and can be valued in present value terms on a client's implied balance sheet.

Implied liabilities

The other side of a life balance sheet includes current liabilities, such as mortgages and car loans, as well as implied liabilities – the present value of future expected spending. Essentially, implied liabilities are a client's future financial goals. These goals may include desired retirement income, college education funding, charitable bequests, etc.

Calculating implied assets and liabilities

Implied assets and liabilities are anticipated future cash flows discounted to a present value. To calculate these estimates, several items are required.

First, the cash flow amounts and duration of these cash flows need to be estimated. For instance, implied assets may include future savings of employment income, comprised of the year-by-year annual savings amounts. Implied liabilities may include annual retirement income requirements for the client's lifespan. Estimated cash flows for both assets and liabilities should factor in inflation.

Second, to calculate the value of implied assets and liabilities in today's dollars, an appropriate discount rate must be determined. One approach is to use the current intermediate-term yield of investment grade bonds as the discount rate.

If the cash flow estimates are highly uncertain, a higher discount rate should be used to adjust for this risk.

The equation for the present value of future cash flows is as follows:

present value $= F_0 / (1 + i)^0 + F_1 / (1 + i)^1 + F_2 / (1 + i)^2 + \ldots + F_n / (1 + i)^n$

Where:

F = future cash flows including projected inflation

i = discount rate

n = number of years

Advisors can use Excel or online tools to calculate the present value of implied assets and liabilities.

For example, consider a 60-year-old investor who intends to retire in five years with current assets and liabilities as shown in Figure 10.2. Over the next five years, the client intends to save an additional $25,000 per year in today's dollars. At retirement, the client wants to generate $100,000 in pre-tax, inflation-adjusted income through the remainder of his life. The advisor assumes the investor will live to the age of 90 and uses a discount rate of 5% and an inflation assumption of 3%.

Figure 10.2. Example showing calculations of future savings, future retirement expenses, and net present value calculations using Excel

Client Age	Future Savings (Including projected inflation at 3%)	Future Retirement Expenses (Including projected inflation at 3%)	Net Present Value of Future Savings (Discounted at 5%)	Net Present Value of Future Retirement Expenses (Discounted at 5%)
60	$25,000	$ —	$114,598	$1,787,026
61	$25,750	$ —	Formula=NPV(0.05, Cash Flows)	
62	$26,523	$ —		
63	$27,318	$ —		
64	$27,138	$ —		
65	$ —	$115,927		
66	$ —	$119,405		
67	$ —	$122,987		
68	$ —	$126,677		
69	$ —	$130,477		
70	$ —	$134,392		
90	$ —	$242,726		

Using Excel's net present value function, the advisor calculates the client's implied assets to be $114,598 (representing his future savings in present value terms) and the client's implied liabilities to be $1,787,026 (comprised of his future spending requirement in retirement in expressed in today's dollars). Figure 10.2 shows how an advisor would input the information from this example into Excel to calculate implied assets and liabilities.

Once a client's implied assets and liabilities are calculated, advisors can then compile a client's life balance sheet.

A client's net worth in a life balance sheet framework

Besides current and future liabilities, the right-hand side of a life balance sheet also lists a client's net worth or residual wealth. Similar to the traditional balance sheet, net worth within the framework of a life balance sheet is the difference between total assets and total liabilities. In other words, a client's net worth in this context is a client's excess wealth or surplus after accounting for current liabilities and the present value of future goal expenditures.

Figure 10.3. Graphical representation of a life balance sheet

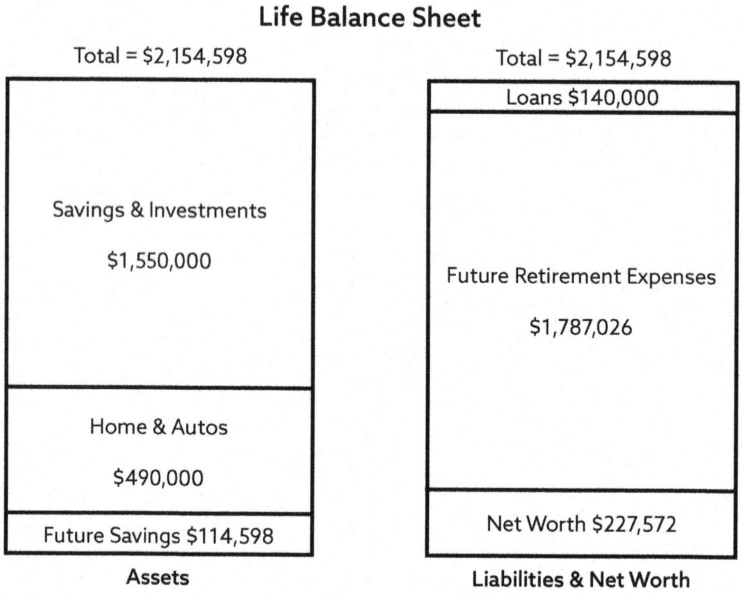

Life Balance Sheet

Total = $2,154,598   Total = $2,154,598

Assets:
- Savings & Investments $1,550,000
- Home & Autos $490,000
- Future Savings $114,598

Liabilities & Net Worth:
- Loans $140,000
- Future Retirement Expenses $1,787,026
- Net Worth $227,572

H. Evensky, S. M. Horan and T. R. Robinson, *The New Wealth Management: The Financial Advisor's Guide to Managing and Investing Client Assets* (John Wiley & Sons, 2011); and J. Wilcox, J. Horvitz and D. diBartolomeo, 'Investment Management for Taxable Private Investors', www.cfapubs.org (January 2006, corrected April 2016).

A graphical representation of a life balance sheet using the data from the 60-year-old-client example above is shown in Figure 10.3.

As we see in Figure 10.3, this client's total assets amount to more than $2 million, including current assets such as investments and property as well as the present value of future savings. The client's liabilities include current loan obligations and the present value of future retirement expenses. The difference between the client's total assets and liabilities is a positive net worth, indicating the client has surplus wealth after funding both current liabilities and future retirement expenses. How advisors can use this information with clients is explained in more detail below.

Matching client assets and liabilities

Life balance sheets allow financial advisors to determine if a client's current assets and future savings are sufficient to fund the client's current liabilities and future financial goals. Pension plans use a similar approach, known as liability-driven investing. This whole-picture method attempts to appropriately match a pension fund's assets to the plan's future obligations.

Financial advisors who adopt goals-based investing also attempt to match their clients' assets and liabilities. The primary objective of this approach is to help clients have sufficient assets to fund all of their liabilities – both current spending goals and amounts needed in the future.

Two ways for assessing if an investor's assets will adequately fund liabilities are the use of funded ratios and probability forecasting using Monte Carlo simulations. These methods are explained below.

Determining a client's funded ratio

The funded ratio is a measurement typically used by pension funds to calculate if pension assets will sufficiently cover the payments the plan will eventually have to make. The ratio helps test if a pension is fully funded or not.

Similarly, an investor's funded ratio is the ratio of assets to liabilities in present-value terms. This ratio helps financial advisors measure the relative size of a client's assets and future savings to a client's current obligations and anticipated spending requirements. This quick calculation also enables advisors to determine the feasibility of a client attaining their future financial goals.

The funded ratio uses asset and liability data from a client's life balance sheet and is calculated as:

funded ratio =
(current assets + implied assets) / (current liabilities + implied liabilities)

A funded ratio above 1 suggests a client may be able to meet future spending goals. A ratio below 1 reflects a situation where the client may not be able to fund all future liabilities and goals.

Funded ratio example

Following is an example with various funded ratio results using three different annual retirement income projections for the 60-year-old investor referenced earlier in this chapter.

As illustrated in the life balance sheet (Figure 10.3), the investor has current assets of $2,040,000 and implied future savings of $114,598. This example assumes the client has an annual, pre-tax retirement income goal of $100,000 in today's dollars, and the advisor uses a 3% inflation rate and a 5% discount rate.

Initially, the advisor estimates the investor will live to 90. Based on these assumptions, the present value of the client's future retirement savings liability is $1,787,026. Combined with the client's current liabilities of $140,000, total liabilities are $1,927,026.

In this scenario, the investor's funded ratio is 1.12. The ratio is calculated by dividing the client's current and implied assets of $2,154,598 by the client's current and implied liabilities of $1,927,026. The funded ratio of 1.12 implies the client's retirement income goal is 112% funded. Accordingly, this ratio suggests the client's total assets may be sufficient to cover the client's retirement income goal with potential surplus beyond this goal.

How do the results change if different income assumptions are used?

If the investor's annual retirement income goal increases by $25,000 per year to $125,000 in pre-tax, inflation-adjusted income and all other factors are held constant, the present value of the client's retirement income liability increases to $2,233,778. Hence, the client's funded ratio decreases to 0.91. This revised funded ratio implies the client's retirement income goal is only 91% funded, and thus the client may need to delay retirement, save more, and/or reduce the income goal.

Holding all else equal, a reduction in the investor's income goal to $75,000 per year results in a funded ratio of 1.45. This number implies the client's retirement income goal is fully funded and a relatively large surplus of the client's wealth may be available to fund other goals.

As these scenarios illustrate, varying only one factor – such as the amount of a retirement income goal – can significantly change an investor's funded ratio. Discount rate, life expectancy, and implied liabilities changes are inversely related to the funded ratio. For example, if any one of these inputs *increases* and all other assumptions remain constant, a client's funded ratio will *decrease*.

Running multiple funded-ratio scenarios with clients is a good practice. This iterative approach helps clients understand the impact and risks associated with changes to return assumptions, life expectancy, and spending goals.

However, advisors should use the funded ratio cautiously. Assumptions may not play out as anticipated, impacting an investor's true funding status. For instance, if an advisor underestimates a client's life expectancy then the client may run out of money – even though the previously-calculated funded status suggested otherwise. Also, if an investor underestimates future spending needs, the funded status will appear stronger than it really is. Given the funded ratio's sensitivity to the underlying assumptions, advisors should not only run multiple scenarios, but also periodically recalculate a client's funded status.[64]

When a client is underfunded

If the funded ratio is less than 1, a client's assets are underfunded relative to his or her long-term goals. In such cases, a client may not be able to attain 100% of planned expenditures in the future. This is especially true if investment returns turn out to be below expectations and a client's longevity is more than forecasted.

When the funding ratio is below 1, investors may have several options to help improve the likelihood of goal attainment. If an underfunded client has not yet retired, then he or she may need to work longer and save more. If a client is in retirement and working more is not an option, then this client may need to cut back on spending. Another option may include adjusting the mix of assets the investor holds to seek improvement in portfolio returns – but in turn, the investor most likely assumes more portfolio risk.

None of these choices will be easy for clients to make. However, financial advisors who learn to navigate these challenging conversations provide immeasurable value to their clients facing tough life decisions. Furthermore, the use of the

---

[64] S. Pittman, 'Use Your Client's Funded Ratio to Simplify and Improve Retirement Planning Decisions', *The Journal of Retirement* 3:2 (2015); and T. Noonan and M. Smith, *Someday Rich: Planning for Sustainable Tomorrows Today* (John Wiley & Sons, 2011).

funded ratio enables financial advisors to shift the focus of client interactions away from account-specific performance toward more holistic planning. Thus, advisors are able to coach and advise clients on matters that have substantive impact on their clients' long-term outcomes.

For example, advisors using the funded ratio can illustrate to investors the impact of taking early retirement versus delaying retirement. They also can show investors the importance of sticking to a budget, and how overspending may dramatically affect one's ability to fund long-term goals. Accordingly, these types of coaching conversations enable advisors to go beyond reviewing near-term investment results with clients and redirect the focus of client interactions towards the evaluation of life decisions that can improve the likelihood of goal attainment.

When a client is overfunded

If the funded ratio is more than 1, an investor's assets are fully funded relative to his or her long-term goals. However, a funded ratio above 1 does not guarantee a client's assets will be sufficient to fund all future goals. Lower-than-expected investment returns and increased longevity could easily turn a funded plan into one that is not. Because of this uncertainty, retired investors who have funded ratios only slightly above 1 should remain cautious about increasing their spending.

A funded ratio in excess of 1.25 suggests a client's assets cover more than 125% of his or her future liabilities. In these circumstances, high net worth individuals may be able to consider doing additional things with their excess discretionary wealth. Legacy goals such as gifting to charity and leaving money to heirs are options that advisors may wish to discuss with their well-funded clients.

Other techniques: Monte Carlo simulation

Another method used by advisors to determine if assets adequately match an investor's goals is Monte Carlo simulation, a type of probability analysis. This technique uses hundreds or thousands of simulations with randomly-generated values to produce a distribution of possible outcomes. A number of financial planning systems and other software applications, some of which are highlighted in Chapter 16, enable advisors to quickly run these simulations.

Monte Carlo simulation allows financial advisors to assess the likelihood of a client achieving his or her goals under a wide array of scenarios. Randomly generated annual returns are applied to a client's assets based on underlying return and standard deviation expectations. This technique yields the percentage of trials resulting in successful goal attainment for a client.[65]

For example, an advisor runs a Monte Carlo simulation for the 60-year-old investor previously referenced in this chapter. To run this analysis, the advisor inputs the client's age, assets, future savings, income goals, and life expectancy into the planning system. Additionally, the advisor inputs estimates for inflation, the discount rate, investment returns, and portfolio risk.

The software then automatically generates 1000 scenarios with a different return sequence for each trial. The simulation estimates a 62% probability of success. These results suggest that the client's goals are fully funded 620 times out of 1000 scenarios. The remaining 380 trials result in a failure to fully fund the client's goals. Based on these results, the advisor may want to rerun the simulation with higher future savings or lower income goals to increase the investor's probability of success.

Figure 10.4. Example of a Monte Carlo simulation output

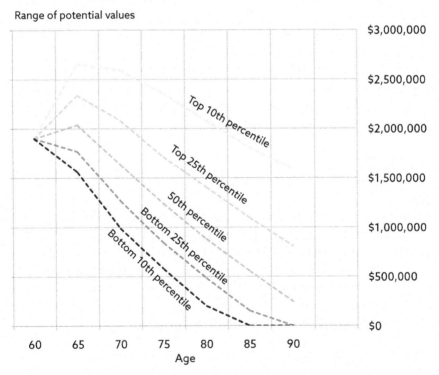

Figure 10.4 is an example of the output from a Monte Carlo simulation. The dotted lines represent a sampling of the different Monte Carlo trials, ranging from the bottom tenth percentile of return sequences to the top tenth percentile.[66]

Achieving a 100% probability of success is not necessary for clients to have confidence that their assets will adequately fund their future financial liabilities. Very high success rates suggest a client may be overfunded. In most circumstances, a probability level of 75% to 85% is acceptable.[67]

A weakness of Monte Carlo simulation is its dependency on projected market returns, inflation estimates, and risk assumptions. As these variables change, the resulting probability of success may be significantly impacted. For instance, if historical returns are used in the analysis, but actual returns are substantially lower, a client's plan may appear sufficiently funded when in reality, it is not.

Therefore, like funded ratios, financial advisors should use Monte Carlo simulation cautiously. The results are merely estimates of future outcomes and should not be viewed with complete certainty. However, the analysis does provide another way for advisors to assess if investor assets are reasonably matched to their goals. And when Monte Carlo simulation is used in tandem with the funded ratio, advisors are able to get a firmer picture of an investor's funded status. For example, if a client's funded ratio is in excess of 1.25 and the probability of success is greater than 75% using Monte Carlo analysis, the combined results suggest the client's assets may adequately align with the client's goals, thus providing the client with more confidence and peace of mind.[68]

Better client outcomes by managing the whole picture

As illustrated in this chapter, smart financial advisors manage their clients' assets holistically, avoiding the hazard and corresponding dangers of quarantining portfolios. They develop whole pictures of client wealth that enable them to maintain the right focus on goal achievement for their clients. Additionally, advisors who manage client portfolios holistically reduce client taxes and fees, align investment strategies with long-term client goals, and may reduce regulatory risk.

---

[66] 'How is the Monte Carlo Probability of Success calculated?', MoneyGuidePro Support.

[67] Sue Stevens, 'Monte Carlo Explained', www.morningstar.com (December 29, 2005).

[68] P. Sullivan, 'Tips to Manage Spending in Retirement', www.nytimes.com (April 11, 2014).

Clear views

Part 1 of this book explained that one danger of quarantining portfolios is blocked views. To overcome this risk, advisors collaborate with clients to help create net worth statements and life balance sheets. Together, these reports not only show the whole picture of current client wealth, but they also capture the present value of a client's future savings and long-term goals. With full knowledge of an investor's financial circumstances, advisors are able to provide comprehensive planning services that lead to better investor outcomes than managing wealth in isolation.

Lower taxes and fees

Clients are more inclined to consolidate assets with advisors offering whole-picture advice than advisors focused on product sales. Numerous studies show that fee-based advisory practices with holistic planning services consistently manage a greater percentage of their clients' total assets than commission-based firms. For example, Corporate Insights, a Canadian research firm, collected information from over 50,000 clients of large broker dealers, financial planning firms, and private banks. Their research found that offering holistic advice was the single factor that most increased consolidation of client assets with a primary advisor.[69]

Not only do advisors benefit when they manage client assets holistically; so do their clients. Investments spread across multiple advisors tend to cost investors more in fees than when assets are consolidated with a primary advisor. This is true because asset-based fees are commonly discounted by advisors as a client's assets increase. Lower fees reduce headwinds for investors, leaving more wealth available to reach their goals.

Furthermore, when more assets are consolidated with a primary advisor, tax-smart strategies are easier for advisors to execute. Distributions and withdrawals can be coordinated across portfolios. And gains and losses between accounts can be synchronized to minimize the tax impact for clients. Lower tax liabilities allow investors to keep more of their wealth, giving investors increased likelihood of achieving their desired outcomes. Chapter 13 provides additional details on tax-smart strategies and ways advisors can implement these ideas.

---

[69] S. Schmitt, 'What Top Performing Advisors and Teams Have In Common', IMCA Annual Conference 2013, www.imca.org (April/May 2013); and D. Richards, 'A proven path to gaining client assets', www.advisoranalyst.com (October 26, 2011).

Aligned strategies

Total client views enable advisors to align client wealth to their goals. Life balance sheets and asset-liability matching help advisors determine a client's funded status with funded ratios and probability of goal attainment through Monte Carlo simulations. These assessments expose whether or not an investor is underfunded. They also reveal if an investor's goals are too lofty relative to his or her assets and future savings rates. In such cases, advisors will want to discuss with the client about scaling back overly-ambitious goals. With these tools, advisors can adjust investment strategies to better line up with a client's desired outcomes than when operating with blocked views.

Complete pictures also give advisors supporting evidence to coach their clients facing life decisions, such as when to retire and how much to leave heirs. These collaborative discussions provide the foundation for developing financial plans that appropriately match client resources and goals. And once well-designed plans are in place, higher investor confidence results, increased client engagement occurs, and better outcomes are ultimately achieved.

Regulatory compliance

As outlined in Part 1, quarantining portfolios may jeopardize an advisor's ability to meet the fiduciary standard, creating unnecessary regulatory risk. To truly comply with the fiduciary standard, advisors should have a complete understanding of a client's financial situation. Advisors who adopt the whole-picture practices outlined in this chapter better position themselves and their practices to meet fiduciary regulations, and thus reduce the likelihood of incurring the high penalties associated with noncompliance.

Whole-picture action steps for financial advisors

This chapter has provided smart ideas for managing client wealth holistically. Some advisors may already be deploying these strategies. Many others likely are not.

Below are five action steps for advisors wanting to incorporate whole-picture methods into their practices. The first few steps involve you trying out the ideas from this chapter on yourself.

Step 1 – Develop your net worth statement

Start by developing your own balance sheet and net worth statement. Gather all the necessary asset and liability information and input the data into Excel or an online aggregation tool. The difference between your assets and liabilities is your net worth. Once this information is inputted and your net worth determined, print or save your net worth statement. At the top of the report, add the current date for future reference.

Step 2 – Create your life balance sheet

Next, determine your implied assets and liabilities to create a life balance sheet. To calculate your implied assets, enter your year-by-year anticipated savings, future Social Security and pension benefits, and any other future asset like an inheritance into a spreadsheet. These amounts should factor in an assumed inflation rate. Discount these values to today's dollars using the current yield on investment grade intermediate-term bonds, such as the yield on the Barclays US Aggregate Bond Index. If these future cash flows are highly uncertain, you may want to increase your discount rate.

To calculate your implied liabilities, list your year-by-year future income requirements in retirement and other future spending goals like a home purchase or legacy gifts. Determine the timing and length of these expenses. Make any necessary inflation adjustments and discount the future annual expenditures with an appropriate discount rate.

Add your implied assets and liabilities to the current values of your net worth statement from Step 1. The difference between your total assets (both current and implied assets) and total liabilities (both current and implied liabilities) is your net worth or surplus wealth. Together, these items comprise your life balance sheet.

Step 3 – Determine your funded ratio

Using your life balance sheet, calculate your funded ratio by dividing your total assets by your total liabilities.

Step 4 – Assess your goal progress

Is your funded ratio as calculated in Step 3 higher than 1? If not, your discretionary wealth is negative and you may need to increase your annual savings, work longer and/or decrease your future spending goals. If your funded ratio is above 1, your current assets and future savings may be sufficient to fully fund your goals.

Remember, however, that a funded ratio above 1 does not assure goal attainment, as many assumptions are factored into this calculation and expectations may not occur as anticipated. Despite these limitations, the funded ratio provides a quick assessment of your overall goal progress.

Step 5 – Rollout to clients

After you have tested these concepts on yourself, you may want to begin using them with a select group of clients – assuming you have legal and compliance approval to do so.

If your clients are accustomed to having performance-based discussions, then you may need to provide them with the rationale for why holistic-based strategies improve upon traditional approaches. These conversations may not be easy. Changing behaviors and expectations can be hard. So, be patient with clients as you begin asking them to open up their complete financial picture to you.

You may find clients to be more receptive to taking small steps toward holistic advice than immediately embracing all the tools and concepts outlined in this chapter. For example, consider introducing a simplified version of the life balance sheet. In this approach, the client initially does not provide you with statements from held-away asset and liability accounts. Instead, at the beginning, you merely ask the client to estimate balances from these accounts and identify a few long-term goals such as retirement income. With this information, you are able to quickly generate a basic life balance sheet and estimate the client's funded ratio.

As the client experiences the value of these initial conversations around holistic planning, he or she may be more inclined to disclose complete financial details to you down the road. This go-slow approach helps clients build trust in a goals-oriented process and often paves the way for you to have more collaborate relationships with your clients in the future.

Not every investor, though, will embrace a whole-picture approach. Remember my client who simply wanted a hot stock tip? Unfortunately, he had no appetite for goals-based advice.

When situations like this occur, do not give up. Keep introducing these concepts to your clients and prospects. Likely, you will find that a number of investors desire holistic planning. These clients will recognize that your best investment tips are based on their complete financial view rather than product-oriented pitches. They also will value how your whole-picture approach better positions them to reach their financial goals. As a result, you may garner more of your clients' assets. And your client outcomes will likely improve.

11

Comprehensive Risk Assessment

Dodging the hazard of badly managed risk

A N EVER-PRESENT DANGER that can unexpectedly entangle financial advisors and the clients they serve is the mismanagement of investor risks. In chapter 4, the high costs associated with misperceiving, partially assessing, and improperly balancing client risks were evidenced. Examples of these costs include delayed retirements and unmet client needs, wants, and wishes.

Three types of risks were introduced earlier in Part 1 – investment risks including market and specific risks, behavioral risks such as emotional and cognitive biases, and goal risks that may lead to goal failure. Traditional investment approaches commonly ignore or gloss over the third risk type – goal risk. When advisors and investors mistakenly overlook goal risk, portfolios may become impaired and financial destinations left unreached. This all-too-familiar reality parallels a story a friend of mine told me.

"Dad, help – I'm stranded!"

These were the panic-stricken words my friend heard when taking a call from his 17-year-old son. The teenager recently had gotten his driver's license and was driving home from his part-time job when the car broke down. Stranded roadside, the young driver had no clue what to do or why steam was pouring from underneath the car's hood. The dad calmed his son down, called for roadside assistance and went to pick him up.

After getting the car towed, my friend asked his son to recall what happened as they drove home. The teenager remembered driving within the speed limit. He also remembered seeing the RPMs on the car's tachometer were not racing too high. And then, he told his dad that the car just began spewing steam from beneath the hood. Not knowing what else to do, the teenager smartly pulled over, stopped the vehicle, and called for help. The dad asked if the temperature gauge had indicated the car was overheating. A blank stare was the only response received back from his son.

As my friend recounted this story to me, he said his son knew to watch his driving speed and the engine's revolutions. But apparently the 17-year-old had slept through the driver's education lesson about a car's temperature gauge and the importance of paying attention to it.

This story unfortunately reminds me of how some advisors and investors approach monitoring risk. They watch two risk gauges, but ignore a third. Most pay attention to investment risks such as market exposure and too much concentration in a single security. This is akin to having a portfolio structured to stay within a certain risk speed limit. And some advisors and investors are aware of behavioral risks and the importance of watching that emotional responses do not run too high when encountering market volatility. But many forget, ignore, or do not know to watch out for goal risk.

Smart financial advisors, on the other hand, recognize the importance of assessing client risk in a comprehensive manner. Such advisors evaluate client risk principally as the probability of missing a goal. Instead of simply asking a client how much market risk he or she can withstand without panicking, goals-based investing balances and takes into consideration each of a client's risk drivers when determining the most appropriate strategy for achieving client goals.

To help advisors and investors understand how this smart approach to managing risks is put into practice, this chapter first reviews the three risk types and explains how these risks can each be managed. From there, the three drivers of investor risks are described, and methods to balance them when constructing goals-based investment solutions are introduced. Also, various fintech tools that help assess client risk in a comprehensive manner are mentioned. The chapter concludes by highlighting practical ways advisors can incorporate a balanced risk-scoring process into a goals-based framework.

Risk management strategies for the three types of investor risks

The three types of investor risks described in chapter 4 – investment risks, behavioral risks, and goal risks – can cause investor goals to be compromised if mismanaged. Yet, when controlled, these risks can help achieve clients' desired outcomes. For instance, a certain level of investment risk (when adequately diversified) helps provide the necessary growth potential in a portfolio to realistically achieve an investor's long-term financial goals.

Figure 11.1 provides examples of the three types of risks and lists ways these risks can each be managed.

Figure 11.1. Risk management strategies for investment, behavioral, and goal risks

Risk type	Examples	Risk management strategies
Investment risks	Market risks including interest rate, inflation, currency, and macro risks; and diversifiable risks including credit, liquidity, and company-specific risks	Construct well-diversified portfolios that significantly reduce or eliminate unsystematic risks
Behavioral risks	Cognitive biases such as loss aversion and herding that induce poor investment decisions resulting in actual investor returns being substantially lower than potential returns	Use an intelligently-designed risk tolerance questionnaire to assess a client's willingness to assume risk; constrain portfolio optimization to the client's determined behavioral risk threshold
Goal risks	Low probability of attaining a financial goal relative to a client's current and implied assets	Increase savings, decrease goal expenditures, or assume more portfolio risk

Determining a client's willingness, capacity, and necessity to assume risk

Once client goals and resources are identified, advisors should then assess client risk – the third step in the goals-based investing process. However, since investor risk is multidimensional, the task of risk assessment is complex. Accordingly, evaluating a single risk dimension, such as behavioral risk, is not sufficient by itself. Determining a client's preference toward each type of investor risk is essential to effectively assess client risk in a comprehensive manner.

This holistic assessment of investor risk begins by understanding the three drivers of risk – willingness, capacity, and necessity to assume risk. These risk drivers are explained below.

Willingness

One driver of risk is the willingness of an investor to assume risk. This is closely linked to an investor's behavioral risks and views toward investment risks. Willingness, sometimes referred to as risk appetite or risk tolerance, is the amount of investment risk that a person has the fortitude to assume in pursuit of potential gains. For example, investors with high willingness toward risk generally focus on the potential for significant investment returns and have sufficient tolerance to stomach the possibility of large losses. In contrast, investors with low willingness to assume risk are very sensitive to losses and tend to prioritize preservation of capital over portfolio growth.[70]

The degree of willingness to accept risk is unique to each investor. Thus, it is crucial for advisors to understand if each of their clients has the emotional discipline to stick with a recommended investment strategy when markets become turbulent. Having a clear understanding of willingness as a driver of risk enables advisors to better predict how clients will likely respond under different market environments. However, if this understanding is not attained, investors are more prone to make poor investment decisions.

To illustrate this reality, consider the following example. An advisor unknowingly recommends that a client assume more investment risk than she is willing to withstand. When the market comes under extreme duress, the client abandons her investment strategy – doing so at one of the most inopportune times.

Because all investing involves some exposure to risks, attaining successful investor outcomes is dependent on an investor's willingness to withstand periods of volatility. Behavioral biases often emerge during bear markets and must be effectively managed to achieve long-term financial goals. Figure 11.2, developed by Larry Swedroe, author of *The Only Guide You'll Ever Need for the Right Financial Plan*, provides guidelines for advisors to assess a client's willingness to assume investment risk.

An alternative method to express the maximum tolerable loss is to convert these percentage guidelines to a client-specific dollar amount potentially at risk, or to define the possible loss in terms of a reduction in a client's net worth. Some clients are better able to indicate their risk tolerance when maximum loss potential is expressed in actual dollars rather than as a percentage.

The most common advisory method of assessing an investor's willingness to take risk is the use of risk tolerance questionnaires. This traditional approach asks clients to answer a series of questions, typically including questions about

---

70   Michael Pompian, 'Risk Profiling Through A Behavioral Finance Lens', www.cfapubs. org (February 2016).

their time horizon, investing experience, appetite to take on risk, and comfort level of staying invested amid market declines.

Figure 11.2. Guidelines for assessing an investor's willingness to assume downside risk

Maximum tolerable loss	Maximum equity exposure
−5%	20%
−10%	30%
−15%	40%
−20%	50%
−25%	60%
−30%	70%
−35%	80%
−40%	90%
−50%	100%

Source: Larry E. Swedroe, Kevin Grogan and Tiya Lim, *The Only Guide You'll Ever Need for the Right Financial Plan: Managing Your Wealth, Risk, and Investments* (Bloomberg Press, 2010).

The answers are then scored by the advisor. More points are given to responses indicating long investment time horizons and higher degrees of willingness to withstand market volatility. Fewer or no points are allocated to responses suggesting a low tolerance for risk. The client's combined final score gets mapped to one of the advisor's risk-based portfolios. Low scores place investors in a conservative portfolio, middle-of-the-road scores tie investors to a moderate portfolio, and high scores get mapped to an aggressive portfolio. Generally, more than three portfolio mapping options exist, with variations of an advisor's risk-based models ranging from conservative allocations to aggressive, high-growth asset mixes.

A number of web-based risk tolerance questionnaires exist, helping advisors gauge clients' willingness to take risk. These tools usually allow advisors to map client responses to their own model portfolios. One of the longest-standing risk tolerance assessment tools is FinaMetrica (www.riskprofiling.com). This online solution uses a psychometrically-designed risk tolerance questionnaire consisting of 25 questions – notably more than the typical 10 to 15 questions. FinaMetrica's use of more questions is designed to improve the reliability of the outputs and to gain more behavioral-based information that help advisors understand their clients' emotional responses to risk. A more recent, notable competitor in this space is Riskalyze (www.riskalyze.com). This web-based tool similarly asks a series of questions to help advisors understand their clients' willingness to assume investment risk.[71]

Capacity

Another risk driver is an investor's capacity to take on risk. Essentially, capacity for risk is the measure of an investor's ability to assume investment risk relative to their financial resources. For example, one way advisors measure risk capacity is to calculate the portion of a client's total assets that can be invested in risky assets, such as equities, without unnecessarily compromising the client's ability to achieve their financial goals.

In practice, clients will have different risk capacities. Unlike the risk driver of willingness, capacity for risk does not depend on a client's tolerance to endure a market decline. Instead, a client's financial capacity for risk depends on his or her accumulated savings, stability of earned income, ability for additional savings, time horizon, and flexibility to adapt if expected returns are not achieved.[72]

An investor with a low risk capacity cannot afford to experience large portfolio drawdowns without significantly reducing the likelihood of goal attainment. A low capacity for risk may be caused by high, current liquidity needs and/or limited resources to fund planned expenditures. In contrast, an investor with a high risk capacity has plenty of financial resources to fund current and future goals, and these goals likely are not jeopardized if markets tumble. Another reason an investor's capacity for risk may be high is that savings are not needed for decades, making near-term market corrections less impactful.

Normally, the lower an investor's risk capacity, the more conservative the investment mix needs to be. When capacity for risk is low, investing a portfolio conservatively is important because an investor cannot financially afford to lose much money. Another reason to invest conservatively when risk capacity is low is because an investor may need the assets right away to fund an upcoming goal. Investors with higher risk capacities are financially able to own riskier investments, such as equities and high-yield bonds, while being able to withstand market downturns without seriously impairing their goals.[73]

---

[71]   Michael Kitces, 'Adopting A Two-Dimensional Risk Tolerance Assessment Process', www.kitces.com (January 25, 2017).

[72]   Kerry Pechter, 'The Essence of Goal-Based Investing', www.retirementincomejournal.com (September 7, 2016).

[73]   'How much investment risk can you really take on?', www.merrilledge.com.

Advisors are able to calculate a client's risk capacity by using goals-based planning software to do scenario analysis. (See chapter 16 for a listing of fintech solutions in this space.) Scenario analysis may involve Monte Carlo simulation or another type of stochastic modeling. When scenario analysis is used, risk capacity is measured by the probability of success, whereby low probabilities (<50%) indicate reduced capacity for risk and higher probabilities (>75%) may suggest greater capacity to assume risk.

If an advisor does not have access to these simulation tools, risk capacity can be assessed by simply running through potential worst-case scenarios. This approach involves an advisor stress testing the financial capacity of a client under difficult market environments and evaluating the resulting impact to client goals.

For example, if a client's household asset mix is expected to generate an average return of 7% per year, the advisor could assume a much lower average return, such as 3% annually, and calculate the impact of the lower returns on the client's future wealth totals. This process can be repeated using different return expectations.

When this method is used, practitioners should assess risk capacity by measuring the extent to which excess funds, if any, are expected to be available after meeting client goals under the lower return assumptions. If shortfalls exist, risk capacity is low. If excess funds are anticipated after goals are fully funded in challenging environments, capacity for risk is higher.

Necessity

A third risk driver is the necessity for risk. This risk driver relates to the amount of risk that needs to be assumed in order to achieve the client's goals. A high necessity for risk means an investor needs a high rate of return, or his or her goals will likely be unattainable. Since seeking excess return itself is risky, that ultimately means high necessity goals are inherently risky goals. Conversely, a low necessity for risk means an investor is not dependent on high returns to satisfy his or her financial goals.

For example, if a goal requires a high expected return in order to reasonably attain it, the client needs to take on more risk than someone whose required return for goal realization is lower. Higher degrees of required risk are assumed by investing in portfolios with more exposure to risky assets (e.g. equities). By investing aggressively, investors anticipate that the additional assumption of risk will result in a higher return. In contrast, once a client has accumulated substantial surplus wealth, taking more risk than is necessary may be imprudent.

In such cases, the value of additional gains pales in comparison to the potential pain of steep losses and severe reductions in net worth.

An important factor when evaluating an investor's necessity for risk is to differentiate between authentic needs and desired wants or aspirational wishes. These distinctions are unique to each investor's personal preferences. However, advisors and investors should recognize that as more goals are deemed to be true needs, the requirement for more risk increases. On the other hand, fewer needs translate to a lower necessity for risk. Thus, clients should not haphazardly approach the task of assigning priorities to their financial goals. Rather, they should carefully evaluate that their identified needs are really essential to their financial wellbeing – otherwise, clients may assume unnecessary risk to meet expectations of higher required returns.

Conflicting goal priorities sometimes surface with couples, as highlighted in chapter 9. Examples include conflicts over providing support to adult children and grandchildren, or spending for their own lifestyle and other goals. When differences of opinion about goals and their necessity occur, advisors should listen to the concerns of the couple, explain the impact of their choices on necessity for risk, and ultimately help them find common ground in finalizing goal priorities.[74]

Calculating a client's necessity for risk is similar to how advisors determine client risk capacity by using goals-based planning software. Projection capabilities of planning tools like MoneyGuidePro (www.moneyguidepro.com) or eMoney (www.emoney.com) are commonly used by advisors to estimate the returns required to achieve client goals given their available resources. A certain level of risk is associated with the required return – this is the risk needed. With a client's requirement for risk determined, advisors are able to evaluate investment strategy options that have comparable levels of risk.[75]

Other methods of assessing risk necessity include calculating a client's funded ratio. As explained in the previous chapter, when a client's funded ratio is below 1, the client is underfunded. Thus, necessity for risk is high. In contrast, funded ratios above 1 imply the client is fully funded and necessity for risk is lower.

---

74 Larry E. Swedroe, Kevin Grogan and Tiya *Lim, The Only Guide You'll Ever Need for the Right Financial Plan: Managing Your Wealth, Risk, and Investments* (Bloomberg Press, 2010).
75 Geoff Davey and Paul Resnik, 'Risk Profiling Art and Science', www.riskprofiling.com (June 2012).

Balancing between willingness, capacity and necessity

Once client willingness, capacity, and necessity to take risk are known, a comprehensive picture of client risk emerges. Accordingly, advisors who are armed with this holistic perspective are able to gauge if any one of a client's risk drivers are imbalanced or in conflict with another, potentially jeopardizing goal attainment.

Quite frequently, such imbalances and conflicts between willingness, capacity, and necessity occur. In a research paper titled 'Risk Profiling Art and Science' by the cofounders of FinaMetrica, the authors found that in about 60% of investor plans, there is no portfolio able to achieve client goals (within risk capacity constraints) where the investment risk is consistent with risk willingness. This scenario requires investors to make compromises, such as lowering goal expenditures, in order to have reasonable chances of realizing their goals.

Figure 11.3. Optimal level of client risk for goal success – the intersection of willingness, capacity, and necessity

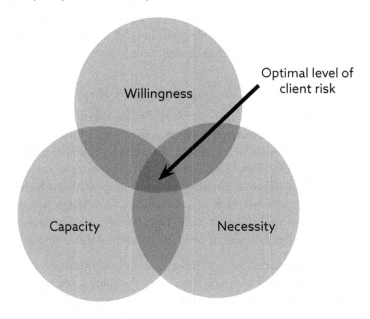

In another 30% of investor plans, the authors found that risk willingness, risk capacity, and risk necessity are more or less aligned. In the remaining 10% of plans, the risk necessary to achieve the client's goals (within risk capacity constraints) is less than risk willingness. This least-common imbalance offers investors the most flexibility, allowing them the opportunity to add more goals, increase current spending, or lower investment risk.[76]

When risk imbalances arise, it is imperative that advisors work with clients to make the necessary adjustments to align client risk drivers with one another. Figure 11.3 conceptually illustrates the ideal location of client risk, where willingness, capacity, and necessity intersect.

When willingness is less than necessity

One type of risk imbalance is when willingness to assume risk is less than the necessity for risk. This mismatch can occur when available investor resources are insufficient to fund goals given a lower tolerance for taking investment risk. In such cases, risk necessity can be reduced by lowering or delaying goals, increasing savings, or converting personal use assets to investment assets – such as downsizing one's home and investing the difference.

Another way to resolve this imbalance may be for the client to assume more risk, as long as the client's risk tolerance is not stretched so far that a market downturn induces a panicked sale of assets. If clients are unwilling to make any of these compromises, advisors need to ensure clients clearly understand that portfolio underperformance will most likely result in goals not fully being attained in the desired timeframe and/or the necessity to forgo lower priority goals.[77]

When risk necessity is less than risk willingness

Another type of risk imbalance is when the risk necessary for goal attainment (within risk capacity constraints) is less than risk willingness. For example, consider a client with a high tolerance for risk who is willing to hold up to 80% of her wealth in riskier assets such as equities. This client also has ample financial resources to fully fund all of her goals, indicating she has a high capacity for risk. Moreover, scenario analysis using Monte Carlo simulation suggests this client has a 95%+ probability of success in achieving all of her needs, wants, and wishes. This analysis shows her necessity to assume risk is very low.

The resulting mismatch in risk willingness and risk necessity affords investors like this example client with a high degree of flexibility when selecting household portfolio allocations. More often than not, advisors will recommend clients with this type of risk imbalance to lean more toward conservative investment mixes – since these clients have accumulated more than enough resources to fund their goals, and taking on excess risk could result in the reversal of this good fortune.

---

76   Ibid.
77   Ibid.

Figure 11.4 is an example report similar to ones generated from goals-based planning applications, illustrating a case where risk necessity is less than risk willingness. The arrow on the far left column of the report indicates the client has a moderately aggressive risk tolerance, and the rows with light gray shading indicate each portfolio option at or below this risk willingness level. The calculated probabilities of success are listed in the middle column for a series of model portfolios ranging from ultra conservative to ultra aggressive.

Notably, in this example, the probability of success remains quite high regardless of which portfolio option is selected (87%–98%). This result occurs when a client has surplus wealth relative to his or her goals. Given the low necessity for risk in this example, a model portfolio with less risk than the client is fully willing to assume could be selected, while providing a higher probability of goal attainment.

Figure 11.4. Example planning report showing an investor with risk necessity less than risk willingness

Risk tolerance	Portfolio options	Results		Bear market loss	
		Probability of success	Safety margin (current dollars)	Great Recession return	Bond bear market return
	Ultra Conservative	97%	$1,971,453	9%	–7%
	Conservative	98%	$2,377,151	3%	–2%
	Moderate Conservative	98%	$3,001,624	–4%	1%
	Balanced	94%	$4,321,120	–17%	5%
→	Moderate Aggressive	91%	$6,098,481	–31%	10%
	Aggressive	89%	$7,083,145	–37%	13%
	Ultra Aggressive	87%	$8,517,454	–47%	16%

Source: adapted from a MoneyGuidePro report.

Incorporating a balanced risk scoring process into your advisory practice

Perhaps, you are already among the group of advisors who are comprehensively assessing client risk. If that is the case, the risk management concepts explained in this chapter – such as balancing between risk willingness, capacity, and necessity – are likely not new ideas to you. However, if find yourself among the set of advisors relying on traditional risk assessment methods – including the use of simple risk tolerance questionnaires or relying on intuition and gut feelings, I encourage you to consider adopting a more thorough approach to managing client risks.

One way to move in this direction is to separate the measurement of risk willingness from risk capacity and necessity. This separation prevents unknowingly blending the risk drivers together that can result in recommending a portfolio with too much risk when a client has a low willingness or capacity for risk. For instance, when client risk drivers are separately assessed, advisors are able to factor in a client's low risk willingness or capacity as a constraint in the determination of an appropriate portfolio mix.

There are a number of web-based solutions specifically designed to independently assess a client's risk willingness, including two solutions mentioned earlier in this chapter – FinaMetrica and Riskalyze. Furthermore, a number of relatively inexpensive goals-based planning tools are available that enable advisors to separately measure risk capacity and necessity. Examples previously mentioned include MoneyGuidePro, eMoney, and FIS WealthStation. These planning applications use Monte Carlo simulations to assess probabilities of success and failure related to goal risk. Another fintech option advisors may want to consider for holistically assessing risk is Tolerisk (www.tolerisk.com). This solution allows advisors to use a single tool to separately gather information about a client's risk willingness and risk capacity.[78] Additional fintech options are listed in chapter 16.

When advisors and investors mistakenly overlook risk as multidimensional, portfolios may become impaired and financial goals left unattained. In contrast, smart advisors take time to discover client risk drivers, using well-designed risk tolerance questionnaires to assess risk willingness and goals-based planning tools to determine risk capacity and necessity. They also seek to identify the presence of imbalances between the drivers of client risk.

When risk imbalances exist, advisor best practices include reviewing possible alternatives, providing illustrations that explain the trade-offs, and guiding clients to find optimal solutions based on their preferences. By helping clients through this process, advisors are able to provide substantial value to their clients. Also, investors who engage throughout this holistic risk assessment process are more likely to remain committed to their advisors as well as to their goals-based plans.

---

[78] Michael Kitces, 'Adopting A Two-Dimensional Risk Tolerance Assessment Process', www.kitces.com (January 25, 2017).

12

Asset Allocation and Portfolio Construction

Avoiding the hazard of investing based on alluring stories

INVESTMENT STORIES CAN be captivating, but they rarely help clients achieve their financial goals. As highlighted in chapter 5, investing prompted by storytelling generally does not have happy endings. It should be avoided by investors and advisors alike.

Stories ensnare investors by misdirecting focus towards products and markets rather than investor goals. They entice a reliance on intuition instead of evidence and distort the true merits of an opportunity. Advisors are harmed by storytelling, because an overreliance on investment tales limits their effectiveness with clients. For example, when an advisor's primary role is relegated to a storyteller selling hot product ideas or market timing strategies, the opportunity to deliver comprehensive advice is missed.

This chapter outlines a more constructive way for advisors to manage wealth as opposed to storytelling, pitching products, and relying on salesmanship. This approach applies the fourth element of the goals-based investing process – determining the optimal asset allocation for clients. It leverages merit, evidence, and best practices of modern finance to drive client success.

A seminal paper on asset allocation titled 'Determinants of Portfolio Performance' asserts that a portfolio's asset mix accounts for more than 90% of a portfolio's return variability, with security selection and market timing playing only minor roles. Based on these conclusions and similar findings from other research, creating well-designed asset allocation strategies is a smart method for building investor portfolios.[79]

Asset allocation involves dividing investments among different types of assets, such as equities (growth assets), bonds (income and stabilizing assets), and alternatives (diversifying assets). This investment methodology relies on the premise that returns of different asset classes tend not to move in tandem with one another. By optimally diversifying across asset classes that are not perfectly correlated, financial advisors are able to maximize expected return for a given level of client risk.

Methods for deriving the ideal asset mix for clients are explained in this chapter. The first step entails specifying the asset classes and determining realistic capital market assumptions for these investment categories. Next, approaches to calculating the optimal asset mix for various levels of risk, including the use of passive and active strategies as well as alternative investments, are considered.

The third step – scenario analysis via Monte Carlo simulations – is further explored as a means of assessing asset allocation options for clients. This process involves projecting asset mix returns and wealth forecasts to determine the allocation providing the highest probability of success within an investor's constraints. Also, the rationale is given for the importance of identifying an optimal household allocation before determining account-level asset mixes. The chapter concludes by highlighting ways advisors can intelligently deploy asset allocation and portfolio construction strategies within their practices.

Using realistic capital market assumptions

The first step to create optimized asset allocation models is to determine realistic capital market assumptions. For taxable investors, this initial step also requires making after-tax adjustments to the estimated asset class returns.

Estimating asset class returns

A familiar investment disclosure is "past performance is no guarantee of future results." This perspective is especially relevant when determining asset class returns for goals-based investing. Simply using historical returns for capital market assumptions may result in overweighting previous asset class winners and underweighting historically lower-returning assets. Also, using historical returns in financial planning software can lead to overconfidence in estimated goal attainment – especially if returns from the past 30 years are likely higher

---

79 Gary Brinson, Randolph Hood and Gilbert Beebower, 'Determinants of Portfolio Performance', *Financial Analysts Journal* (July–August 1986), pp. 39–44.

than future returns over the next decade, as many investment professionals currently believe.

Accordingly, a best practice in optimizing allocations is to use capital market projections based on expected returns rather than historical performance. A common approach for determining expected returns for stocks, bonds, and other asset classes is to use a form of risk layering – sometimes referred to as the building block approach. Figure 12.1 provides a visual representation of this risk layering or building block approach to estimating capital market returns.

Figure 12.1. Sample capital market assumptions using risk layering methodology

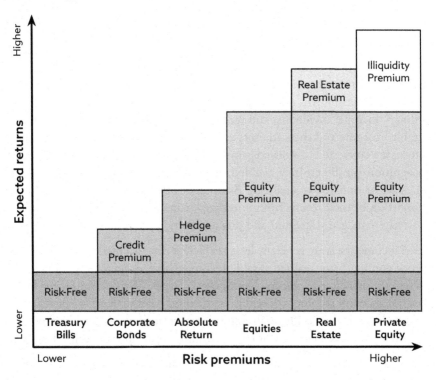

This method begins by estimating the return on a risk-free asset such as a treasury bill or note. Once a forecasted risk-free rate is determined, successive layers of risk premium are added based on the riskiness of an asset class. For instance, corporate bonds are generally less risky than equities, and thus should have a lower risk premium. In other words, the estimated long-term return of corporate bonds (derived by combining the risk-free rate plus the risk premium of the corporate bond asset class) is likely to be lower than the forecasted long-term return of equities.

Rather than estimate future asset class returns themselves, some financial advisors rely on estimates generated by other industry experts. A number of large asset management firms like Goldman Sachs and JPMorgan make their return assumptions publically available.

Adjusting return assumptions for taxes

Once pre-tax returns are estimated, practitioners who advise taxable clients should adjust their capital market assumptions based on the tax impact on various asset classes. Pre-tax return is comprised of two components – unrealized gains and the realized portion, including ordinary income, dividends, and realized short-term and long-term capital gains.

Asset classes that have a higher proportion of their pre-tax return from unrealized gains are considered more tax-efficient and require a lower reduction to their after-tax returns than asset classes that derive more of their return from ordinary income, dividends, and realized gains. This difference exists because taxable investors and their advisors can control the timing of when unrealized returns are converted to realized gains. In some circumstances, this taxable gain recognition can be entirely avoided, such as when assets are passed through an estate or donated to charities. Asset classes that tend to generate a higher proportion of their return from unrealized gains include equities (particularly passively-managed strategies) and private equity.

Fixed income assets are generally less tax efficient due to a higher portion of their return coming from realized taxable income; these assets require a bigger tax haircut to their after-tax return assumptions. The exception is municipal bonds (munis), as muni income is generally tax exempt. Another less tax-efficient asset class includes hedge funds or absolute return strategies, since a larger portion of their return often comes from realized short-term gains or realized income.

Figure 12.2 provides an example of pre-tax capital return assumptions, asset class tax haircuts, and resulting long-term, after-tax return estimates for a range of asset classes.

Figure 12.2. Sample forecasted asset class returns and tax adjustments

Asset class	Pre-tax return	Tax haircut	After-tax return
Cash – risk-free	1.5%	−0.5%	1.0%
Bonds	2.5%	−1.0%	1.5%
Absolute return	3.0%	−1.0%	2.0%
Equity – active	8.0%	−2.0%	6.0%
Equity – indexed	8.0%	−0.5%	7.5%
Real estate	10.0%	−1.5%	8.5%
Private equity	12.0%	−1.0%	11.0%

Source: Adapted from Patrick Geddes, Lisa R. Goldberg and Stephen W. Bianchi, 'What Would Yale Do If It Were Taxable?', www.cfapubs.org.

Constructing optimized asset allocation models

After asset class assumptions are determined and adjusted for taxes, advisors are then able to calculate the optimal asset mix for various levels of risk. This process entails the use of an optimization algorithm known as mean-variance optimization (MVO).

Mean-variance optimization and the efficient frontier

Nobel Prize-winning economist Harry Markowitz first introduced the concept of asset class optimization using MVO in 1952. This work became the foundation of Modern Portfolio Theory. It concludes that diversifying a portfolio with low-correlation investments can reduce overall portfolio risk. For more than half a century, MVO has been the standard approach for constructing asset class models.[80]

Minimizing portfolio risk helps preserve and build wealth over the long run. A portfolio with lower risk typically will not decline as much when markets retreat; thus, it does not require as high a return to recover compared to portfolios that suffer significant declines. For example, a portfolio that loses 25% of its value must subsequently return 33% to return to breakeven. But a portfolio that falls by 10% only needs to generate a 11% return to fully recover its loss.

When running a MVO calculation, forecasted asset class return assumptions along with standard deviation and correlations are used to derive the optimal mix

[80]   Harry Markowitz, 'Portfolio Selection', *Journal of Finance* (March 1952).

of assets for a given level of risk. Although forward-looking return estimates are preferred over historical returns, using historical averages for standard deviation and correlation is an acceptable practice, as these inputs can be more difficult to estimate. A number of technology tools are available to aid advisors in running optimizations, including solutions by Morningstar Direct (www.morningstar. com/company/direct), Zephyr's AllocationADVISOR (www.styleadvisor.com), and WealthStation's Allocation Master (www.allocationmaster.wealthstation. sungard.com). Also, Excel has an embedded Solver function that enables advanced users to run asset allocation optimizations.

The set of optimal asset allocation portfolios ranging from low risk to high risk for a given set of asset classes and corresponding assumptions comprise what is known as the efficient frontier. The aforementioned software applications facilitate the creation of efficient frontiers based on inputted assumptions and constraints by an advisor. Asset mixes that fall below the efficient frontier are suboptimal, as they do not offer sufficient return for the level of risk. Figure 12.3 illustrates a hypothetical efficient frontier, two optimized allocation models, and a suboptimal portfolio.

Changes to optimized allocations when using after-tax return assumptions

A groundbreaking research paper published in the *Financial Analysts Journal* in 2016 highlights the differences between pre-tax and after-tax optimized allocations by deconstructing Yale's endowment portfolio as if it were a taxable entity. The paper introduces the readers to David Swensen, the longstanding chief investment officer at Yale. Swensen pioneered the endowment model – an approach that now is widely adopted by institutional investors and a growing number of financial advisors.

This model incorporates a broad array of assets, including absolute return, real assets, and private equity strategies rather than investing exclusively in traditional assets like stocks and bonds. During Swensen's tenure at the university, he has consistently outperformed the market. As of June 30, 2016, the Yale endowment was valued at $25.4 billion, averaging an annual return of 8.1% for the prior ten years. In comparison, the average return for college and university endowments for the same period was a substantially-lower 5.1%.[81]

A growing number of financial advisors are attempting to emulate Yale's success through the incorporation of more asset classes such as absolute return strategies into private client portfolios. The intent driving this trend

[81]   Geraldine Fabrikant, 'Yale Endowment Earned 3.4% in a Year When Many Peers Lost', www.nytimes.com (September 23, 2016).

is to generate more efficient portfolios with the potential for higher returns and less risk than traditional asset mixes like a portfolio comprised of 60% equities and 40% bonds. However, since Yale is a tax-exempt entity, Swensen's investment methodology ignores the tax impact on portfolio decisions – making this approach not directly applicable to high net worth investors with taxable portfolios. Although Swensen has not specifically shown how to apply his endowment model in a taxable environment, his writings and reports provide suggestions as to how this might be done.

Figure 12.3. Example of a hypothetical efficient frontier

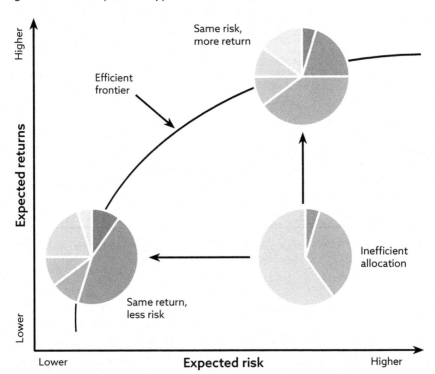

So, how might Yale invest if it were a taxable investor? The authors of the paper attempt to answer this question. They do so by describing how to derive implied pre-tax returns from an endowment like Yale's and how to convert pre-tax returns for equities, hedge funds, real assets, private equity, and other asset classes into after-tax returns. Once these adjustments are made, the paper outlines how to create a new asset allocation mix for taxable investors using MVO.

According to this research, the resulting allocation – when factoring the impact of taxes – looks very different from the asset class weightings when taxes are ignored. Generally, the after-tax optimized asset mixes have lower allocations to tax-inefficient asset classes and higher allocations to tax-efficient strategies. This is shown in Figure 12.4.

Figure 12.4. Comparing pre-tax allocations to after-tax allocations using active equity, indexed equity, and tax-efficient equity exposures

Asset class	Pre-tax weight	After-tax weight: active equity	After-tax weight: indexed equity	After-tax weight: tax-aware equity
Cash – risk-free	1.5%	0.0%	0.0%	0.0%
Bonds	4.9%	35.0%	25.8%	14.5%
Absolute return	17.8%	0.0%	0.0%	11.9%
Equity – active	15.7%	0.0%	0.0%	0.0%
Equity – indexed	0.0%	0.0%	45.6%	0.0%
Equity – tax-aware	0.0%	0.0%	0.0%	26.4%
Natural resources	7.9%	12.2%	0.0%	5.2%
Real estate	20.2%	13.9%	9.0%	2.8%
Private equity	32.0%	38.9%	19.6%	39.1%

Source: Adapted from Patrick Geddes, Lisa R. Goldberg and Stephen W. Bianchi, 'What Would Yale Do If It Were Taxable?', www.cfapubs.org.

As illustrated in Figure 12.4, the resulting equity exposure in the after-tax optimized allocations depends heavily on the tax efficiency of the underlying equity strategies. Actively-managed equity strategies are normally less tax efficient than equity index funds and tax-managed equity strategies. Surprisingly, the optimized asset mix has no equity exposure when using actively-managed equities ('After-tax weight: active equity' column). However, when equity index funds (with less tax impact from reduced trading) are substituted as the equity component, the resulting allocation looks very similar to a traditional 60%/40% stock-bond mix ('After-tax weight: indexed equity' column). When using a tax-efficient strategy for the equity exposure, less tax-efficient assets like absolute return strategies get included into the mix, taking advantage of their diversification benefits while offsetting some of the tax drag ('After-tax weight: tax-aware equity' column).

Another finding of the authors' research was that correlations become even more important in the presence of taxes. Absolute return strategies that are highly correlated to equity markets never get included in the re-optimized Yale portfolio once taxes are introduced. Only absolute strategies with low to negative correlations to stocks and bonds get allocations, since only then are the diversification benefits sufficient to overcome the tax drag of these alternative strategies. Furthermore, advisors should evaluate the appropriateness of high allocations to private equity when optimizing after-tax allocations. Given the illiquidity, investor qualifications, and long time horizons associated with this asset class, acceptable allocations to private equity may vary significantly from one client to the next.[82]

As previously highlighted, financial advisors who merely apply the same pre-tax allocation to taxable portfolios will likely create suboptimal allocations for their taxable investors. Despite this likelihood, very few advisors have adequately adapted their asset allocation techniques on an after-tax basis. In order to capture the endowment model's diversification benefits for taxable investors, advisors should adjust their asset class return assumptions for taxes, as Figure 12.2 illustrated earlier in this chapter. Once these return adjustments have been determined, advisors can input this information into optimization software like the applications previously noted to create more optimal asset allocation models and efficient frontiers for taxable investors.

Scenario analysis

After the optimal asset mix for different risk levels is determined, the third step in the asset allocation process is the use of scenario analysis. The purpose of this step is to assess the impact of various asset allocation options on client goal attainment. By using Monte Carlo analysis, simulations can be run for asset mix returns, future savings assumptions, and goal expenditures. The results suggest which allocation may provide a client with the highest probability of success given the client's constraints and risk preferences. Specifically, *probability of success* is a statistical measure of the percentage chance that a client will not run out of money before the end of his or her life.

Goals-based planning software such as MoneyGuidePro (www.moneyguidepro. com), eMoney (www.emoneyadvisor.com), and WealthStation (www.sungard. com/solutions/wealth/advisor-services/wealthstation) allow for the loading of firm and/or advisor asset allocation models into the simulator as well as capital

---

[82]   Patrick Geddes, Lisa R. Goldberg and Stephen W. Bianchi, 'What Would Yale Do If It Were Taxable?', www.cfapubs.org.

market assumptions. When working with planning software, it is important to understand the program's input expectations and what it does with them.

For example, advisors should determine if return inputs need to be based on arithmetic or geometric averages. If the wrong return type is entered, forecasted results may be over- or under-inflated, jeopardizing the reliability of the planning analysis. Accordingly, advisors should verify the results to confirm the average of the simulations closely matches the average returns initially inputted into the tool. Another consideration is whether return calculations are gross or net of inflation. Most planning tools will adjust for the impact of inflation on client results.[83]

After return and allocation assumptions are loaded into an advisor's planning system, advisors then are able to input client goals, resources, current allocations, and risk preferences. By using the software's simulation modules, advisors can test various asset allocation models against the client-specific inputs. This analysis indicates which asset mix yields the highest probability of achieving client goals.

The objective of scenario analysis is to find the most appropriate allocation model for an investor that falls within the investor constraints. If none of the asset allocation model simulations yield a high enough probability of success for an investor (e.g. above 70% confidence level), then the advisor should collaborate with the client to evaluate possible adjustments. Considerations may include reducing or delaying goal expenditures, increasing savings, or assuming more risk. The real-time analysis of the goals-based planning software programs allows for interactive discussions between advisors and clients. These dynamic conversations are useful when evaluating asset allocation choices, goal considerations, and the impact of risk preferences.

Determining household allocation

Thus far in this chapter, we have explored establishing realistic capital market return assumptions, adjusting these return forecasts for taxes, optimizing asset allocation models, and applying scenario analysis to determine appropriate client allocations. A final consideration is how to determine a client's household asset allocation within a goals-based investing framework.

Two primary methods exist. One approach is to determine appropriate allocations for each client goal by using scenario analysis to find the best fitting allocation per goal, in a *goal bucketing* strategy. The combination of these

---

[83]   Joe Tomlinson, 'Predicting Asset Class Returns: Recommendations for Financial Planners', www.advisorperspectives.com (January 29, 2013).

allocations rolls up to create the household allocation. The second approach is to derive a household allocation by holistically evaluating a client's goals, resources, and constraints by applying scenario analysis at the household level. These two methods are contrasted below.

As described in chapters 8 and 9, client financial goals can be categorized as layers of a pyramid comprised of needs, wants, and wishes. The bottom layer – needs – represents basic necessities of daily living. Goals associated with this category tend to be invested conservatively. The top layer of the goal hierarchy – wishes – is associated with aspirational and legacy goals. Given the nonessential nature of goals in this category, client asset allocations linked to wishes may be invested more aggressively. By segmenting allocations per goal or goal category, this approach creates a household portfolio of sub-portfolios. For example, this goal bucketing strategy may result in three distinct client allocations comprised of a liquidity portfolio, market portfolio, and aspirational portfolio tied to a client's needs, wants, and wishes goals, respectively. When these three portfolios are combined, the client's household allocation results by default.

The benefits of a goal-bucketing strategy for determining a household allocation is that it is easy for clients to understand, since each client goal or goal category is represented by a distinct asset allocation strategy. This methodology also accommodates the behavioral bias of mental accounting. A drawback to this approach is that it is suboptimal for implementing asset location – an asset allocation strategy that takes advantage of the tax structures of accounts, placing the least tax efficient assets in tax-free and tax-deferred accounts and the most tax-efficient assets in taxable accounts.[84]

An alternative approach to determining a client's household allocation in a goals-based framework is to do so holistically. This method was introduced by Fowler and de Vassal in a research paper published in 2006.[85] The authors described a holistic optimization of goals approach that derives a single asset allocation strategy that best meets the combination of client goals. Once this household allocation is set, client assets are then spread across different account locations based on relative tax efficiency. This asset allocation concept, which can extend the longevity of client assets and enhance after-tax returns, is described in more detail in the next chapter.

In contrast to the goal-bucketing approach, the primary benefit of this holistic method is its adaptability to deploy tax-advantaged asset location strategies.

[84]   David Blanchett, 'The Value of Goals-Based Financial Planning', *Journal of Financial Planning* 28:6 (2015), pp. 42–50.

[85]   Gordon B. Fowler and Vladimir de Vassal, *Journal of Wealth Management* 9:1 (Summer 2006), pp. 18–30.

However, several drawbacks exist. The holistic approach may be more difficult for clients to understand, especially when the subaccount allocations are implemented with vastly different allocations based on their tax efficiency rather than aligned with specific goals. Furthermore, this method makes individual goal progress reporting much more difficult, as the underlying portfolios are not specifically associated with a client's individual goals.

Five steps to implement smart asset allocation strategies with clients

The asset allocation concepts highlighted in this chapter move beyond storytelling, pitching products, and market timing as a means of delivering advice to clients. The merit-based and time-tested principles of modern finance explained herein take a more complete perspective of wealth and leverage goals-based investing technology to derive strategies best aligned to accomplish client goals.

As you continue to enhance your advisory practice, you should consider adopting the asset allocation concepts outlined herein. For one reason, your clients will appreciate it when you carefully evaluate their risk preferences and goals to provide an optimal household allocation and corresponding portfolios. These methods also tend to result in stickier client relationships, as your advisory value is viewed as more consultative in nature rather than being merely that of a product salesperson.

Below are five ways that you can begin deploying the concepts outlined in this chapter within your practice.

1. Stop using stories to sell

If you rely on product pitches and salesmanship to earn a living as an advisor, recognize there is a better way to manage client assets. This smarter approach relies on intelligent asset allocation and aligning investment strategies with client goals. By taking a merit-based approach, your advisory value extends beyond the investment performance you are able to generate and centers more on the successful attainment of client financial goals.

2. Build forward-looking return assumptions

Develop or review your long-term asset class return assumptions and evaluate if they are representative of future prospects of the capital markets. Adjust them for taxes if necessary. You may want to compare your forward-looking assumptions to those published by large asset management shops. Also, if your firm already produces assumptions, make sure you understand the rationale behind the forecasts.

3. Optimize your asset allocation strategies

Once capital market assumptions are determined, construct your asset allocation models for various risk levels by using a mean-variance optimizer tool. The resulting asset mixes should range from conservative allocations to aggressive allocations to accommodate a wide range of client goals and risk levels. Perhaps your firm centrally creates your allocation models, or you use a third-party strategist to construct these asset mixes. If this is the case, take the time to understand the inputs and assumptions used by these teams to create the models. With this understanding, you will be better able to communicate the value of this process to your clients.

4. Load your return assumption and asset mixes into your planning tool

After long-term capital market assumptions and allocation models are created, you or your team should load these inputs into your goals-based planning software. This will enable you to run client specific scenarios that incorporate your capital market perspectives and model portfolios.

5. Use scenario analysis to apply models to client household targets

With models and returns loaded into your planning tool, you are now able to run Monte Carlo scenario analysis for your clients. To do so, input the client's resources, goals, and risk preferences and run multiple simulations to test which allocation model achieves the highest probability of goal achievement within the client's constraints. Based on the results of this analysis, you and your client may need to make interactive adjustments via the planning software in order to achieve a satisfactory goal confidence level.

In closing, remember that investment products and their performance are the means to accomplish client goals – not the primary focus of successful goals-based advisory relationships. Also, keep in mind that intelligently-designed approaches to asset allocation and systematic methods of determining clients' asset mixes are key components for achieving the outcomes your clients desire. Moreover, mastery of these practices will help position you to retain and attract more clients in the future.

13

Tax-Smart Investment Strategies

Overcoming the hazard of unnecessary tax drag on investor wealth

As described in chapter 6, ignoring taxes is a common hazard that unnecessarily erodes investor wealth and limits the growth potential of advisory practices. High net worth investors and their advisors must deal with the complexities of managing taxable, tax-deferred, and tax-free accounts. Fully optimizing after-tax returns among these multiple account types requires expertise and technology that are absent from many advisory practices.

Unfortunately, investor returns are routinely cut when portfolios are not managed in a tax-efficient manner. Furthermore, investors regularly leave money on the table when locating assets inefficiently and sourcing retirement income suboptimally.

Overlooking taxes is a costly mistake for financial advisors, too. When practitioners fail to manage client wealth using tax-aware strategies, they miss opportunities to significantly grow their businesses. Over 80% of high net worth investors expect their advisors to maximize after-tax returns subject to their unique goals and risk constraints. Yet, less than one-in-five advisors attempt to implement the basic tax-smart strategy of harvesting losses. Even fewer take advantage of more advanced tax-aware techniques. At best, tax management is an afterthought for the majority of advisors. This mismatch between demand for tax-efficient investment services and the available supply of advisors with these capabilities represents untapped growth potential for financial professionals with proven tax-management expertise.[86]

---

[86] More Conversation Needed on Best Practices for Tax-Aware Portfolios', www.

This chapter shows how advisors can intelligently implement tax-smart investment solutions to increase the odds of client goal achievement and to differentiate and grow their practices. Picking up where the last chapter left off – the determination of an optimal household allocation – this chapter segues into best practices for constructing and managing portfolios at the account level.

First, strategies for enhancing after-tax returns by locating less tax-efficient assets in tax-deferred and tax-free accounts and more tax-efficient assets in taxable accounts are explained. Second, tax-smart withdrawal strategies are highlighted. In this section, conventional income sourcing methods are contrasted with other withdrawal sequencing techniques that help extend the longevity of client assets.

The third section explores tax-smart portfolio management strategies including harvesting losses, deferring the realization of capital gains, and avoiding wash sale violations as a means of minimizing tax drag. Each of these three tax-smart methods – asset location, intelligent withdrawal strategies, and tax-aware portfolio management – independently can enhance after-tax returns, and collectively they can provide 1%–2% or more of extra return on an after-tax basis. The chapter closes by outlining seven steps advisors can take to help investors keep more of what they earn.

An unexpected outcome of tax management – IRS audits?

Smartleaf (www.smartleaf.com) is a leading provider of automated portfolio rebalancing and tax optimization technology for financial advisory firms. The firm's co-founder and president, Gerard Michael, published an article about an unexpected outcome of well-executed tax management. He wrote:

> "We've heard from clients who are doing such a good job with tax management that... they're triggering IRS audits. We're not talking about complex tax shelters here, just simple gains deferral and loss harvesting – done consistently and well. While being audited is never a good thing in itself, we're pleased to report the investors in question viewed the audit as the ultimate endorsement of the manager's skill and value."

If basic tax management can trigger an IRS audit, this suggests effective implementation of tax-smart strategies is the exception, not the norm for the wealth management industry. Practitioners serving high net worth clients need to do more than merely give lip service to tax management. They should imbed tax efficiency into the fabric of their practices. To accomplish this objective,

lifehealth.com (August 5, 2015).

advisors must understand the principles of tax-smart investing and leverage fintech solutions to automate tax management across their books of business.

Hopefully, the wealth management industry will eventually adopt standard methods of documenting the value of tax management – helping investors distinguish between advisors who really do focus on enhancing after-tax returns and those who just talk about it.

Until then, Smartleaf's Gerard Michael "looks forward to hearing from wealth managers who become heroes in their clients' eyes – for getting them audited."[87]

Triggering an IRS audit is clearly not the goal of effective tax management. Improving client outcomes is. One method to increase odds of goal attainment by lessening the subtractive nature of taxes is intelligent asset location.

Asset location

It is common knowledge that the top three rules of real estate are location, location, location. Investors and advisors would be well served by applying similar advice when managing wealth. Asset location – the strategic placement of investments within taxable and tax-advantaged accounts – can improve after-tax returns over time, allowing investors to keep more of their wealth and have a better chance of reaching their financial goals. As noted in chapter 6, Vanguard research suggests the tax-smart strategy of using intelligent asset location has the potential of increasing after-tax returns by as much as 0.75% per year.[88]

The process of adding value by locating assets tax-efficiently focuses on what advisors can control instead of what they cannot. Matthew Kenigsberg, a senior vice president in Strategic Advisers, Inc., a Fidelity Investments company, conveyed this thought as follows: "You can't control market returns, and you can't control tax law, but you can control how you use accounts that offer tax advantages – and good decisions about their use can add significantly to your bottom line."[89]

Asset location involves two primary steps. First, investments should be ranked by their relative tax efficiency. The second step typically involves placing less tax efficient assets in tax-deferred and tax-free accounts and more tax efficient assets in taxable accounts, while keeping the investor's optimal household allocation intact. Although asset location can enhance after-tax returns in a

---

[87]   Gerard Michael, 'Our Kind of Audit', www.linkedin.com (February 3, 2017).

[88]   Francis M. Kinniry Jr., Colleen M. Jaconetti, Michael A. DiJoseph, Yan Zilbering and Donald G. Bennyhoff, 'Putting a value on your value: Quantifying Vanguard Advisor's Alpha®', www.advisors.vanguard.com (September 2016).

[89]   Fidelity Viewpoints 'Why asset location matters', www.fidelity.com (March 15, 2017).

variety of circumstances, the strategy is most effective when investors are in a high marginal tax bracket, their assets are evenly allocated between tax-efficient and less tax-efficient assets, and their taxable and tax-advantaged accounts are roughly equivalent in size.

Ranking the relative tax efficiency of investments

Generally, less tax efficient investments incur greater tax drag than more tax efficient assets when held in taxable accounts. Figure 13.1 shows the relative tax efficiency of various asset classes and the primary tax treatment of the asset classes' expected returns.

Figure 13.1. Relative tax efficiency of asset classes

	Asset class	Tax treatment of expected returns
Most tax efficient	Municipal bonds	Exempt
	Equity – tax-aware	Taxed primarily at long-term capital gains rates
	Equity – indexed	
	Private equity	
	Cash	Taxed primarily at ordinary income rates
	Real estate (REITS)	
	Equity – active	
	Commodities	
	Taxable bonds	
Least tax efficient	Absolute return	

For illustrative purposes only. Not meant as tax advice. Source: Adapted from LifeYield and EY, 'Improving After-Tax Returns, Retirement Income, and Bequests Through Tax-Smart Household Management' (October 2010); and Fidelity Viewpoints, 'How to invest tax efficiently', www.fidelity.com (March 1, 2017).

Absolute return and commodities strategies normally are considered highly tax inefficient, because they tend to generate most of their returns from short-term capital gains as a result of high frequency trading. These gains usually are taxed at higher ordinary income rates. Taxable bonds also are generally highly tax inefficient, because they generate interest income that is taxed at ordinary income rates. In the US, as of the 2016 tax year, capital gains on the sale of stocks held less than a year along with taxable interest income are currently taxed at a top federal rate of 43.4% (including the top marginal income tax rate of 39.6% and the 3.8% Medicare surtax on net investment income).

At the other end of the tax efficiency spectrum are municipal bonds, the most tax-efficient asset class due to their exemption from federal taxes (and state taxes in some cases). Also, individual equities managed tax efficiently and equity index funds are among the most tax-efficient investments, as the majority of their returns are typically taxed at the long-term capital gains rate. Qualified dividends and capital gains on the sale of stocks held a year or more are taxed at a top US federal rate of 23.8% (including the top long-term capital gain rate of 20% and the 3.8% Medicare surtax on net investment income) as of 2016.

Locating investments to maximize after-tax returns

Once an investor's household allocation is known and the tax efficiency of underlying assets is determined, the next step is to spread the investor's assets across different account locations based on their relative tax efficiency. This process entails locating investments in the most tax-efficient account types to minimize taxes while maintaining the overall household allocation target.

Each investor's situation is unique, and there is not a single approach that is universally appropriate for all circumstances. However, generally most tax-efficient assets should be placed in taxable accounts, and the least tax efficient in tax-deferred accounts such as a traditional IRA, 401(k), or deferred annuity, or in a tax-exempt account such as a Roth IRA. Figure 13.2 suggests potential locations for assets in these various account types.

Likely asset types for a tax-deferred account include high-yield bonds, real estate investment trusts, and any actively-traded strategies that generate numerous short-term gains. Low-turnover index funds or exchange-traded funds, tax-managed equity strategies, and municipal bonds are typically best suited for taxable accounts, as these assets typically generate low, or no, taxable distributions.

The asset location logic for taxable bonds implies these assets normally belong in tax-advantaged accounts, as a primary component of their return is interest income taxed at an investor's ordinary income. However, Michael E. Kitces, director of planning research at the Pinnacle Advisory Group, suggests an alternative consideration to this standard asset location advice. According to Mr. Kitces, this logic may be less important now than historically, given the current low interest rates on high-grade taxable bonds. "Focus on making sure your highest-returning and least-tax-efficient investment is inside your 401(k) or IRA, and your most tax-efficient investment is in your taxable account," he said. "And don't worry about everything else. Just get those two right and you've done yourself a ton of good."[90]

---

[90]   Carla Fried, 'Minimizing the Tax Drag on Your Investments', www.nytimes.com (February 7, 2014).

Figure 13.2. Potential placement of assets to help enhance after-tax returns

Asset class	Tax treatment of expected returns	Taxable	Tax deferred	Tax exempt
Municipal bonds	Exempt	+	–	–
Equity – tax-aware		+	o	o
Equity – indexed	Taxed primarily at long-term capital gains rates	+	o	o
Private equity		+	o	o
Cash		o	+	+
Real estate (REITS)		–	+	+
Equity – active	Taxed primarily at ordinary income rates	–	+	+
Commodities		–	+	+
Taxable bonds		–	+	+
Absolute return		–	+	+

+ Likely more appropriate   o May be appropriate   – Likely less appropriate

For illustrative purposes only. Not meant as tax advice. Source: Adapted from LifeYield and EY, 'Improving After-Tax Returns, Retirement Income, and Bequests Through Tax-Smart Household Management' (October 2010); and Fidelity Viewpoints, 'How to invest tax efficiently', www.fidelity.com (March 1, 2017).

In contrast to locating assets tax efficiently, traditional asset allocation methodologies typically determine an investor's optimal mix of assets at the household level and replicate this asset mix across each account type regardless of tax impact – perhaps with the exception of locating municipal and taxable bonds in a tax-aware manner. Another approach to account-level asset allocation is to bucket strategies in various accounts that align with investor goals. For example, one account may be positioned for liquidity, holding lower-risk assets to meet basic client needs, and a second account may contain more growth-oriented assets that align with the long-term nature of a client's legacy goals. A drawback to the traditional approach and the goal bucketing strategy is that both methods are typically less tax efficient than locating assets in a tax-smart manner.

To illustrate the mechanics of a tax-aware asset location strategy, consider an affluent client with two account types: a taxable account and a tax-deferred IRA. Also, this client's optimal asset allocation (based on her goals and total wealth) is a mix of 40% equities, 40% bonds, and 20% alternative investments. To minimize the tax drag, the more tax-efficient equities are placed in the client's taxable account, and the less tax-efficient bonds and alternative investments are located in her IRA. In contrast, the traditional method places the same mix of assets in both accounts, irrespective of the accounts' tax statuses. The result is shown in Figure 13.3.

Figure 13.3. Example contrasting the traditional method of allocating assets across accounts and a tax-smart asset location strategy

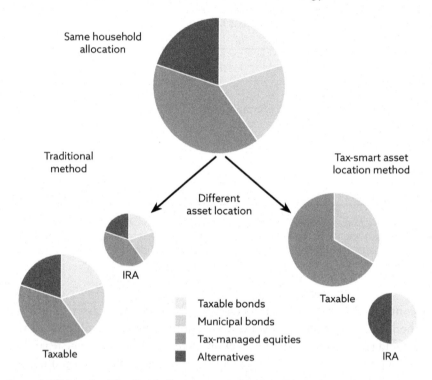

Source: Bill Martin, 'The Quest for Income Longevity: 5 Ways to Make Money Last', www.linkedin.com (April 23, 2015).

Optimizing asset location is not an easy endeavor for financial advisors. It can be done manually, but this approach requires substantial time to implement and sustain – time that might be better spent developing business or meeting with clients. Accordingly, advisory firms should consider leveraging fintech solutions to help automate tax-smart asset location services. Fintech providers such as Retiree Inc. (www.retireeincome.com) and LifeYield (www.lifeyield.com) can help automate this process. Practices that take advantage of such technology usually can justify the costs, as these solutions can drive meaningful increases in after-tax returns, improved client satisfaction, high retention rates, and increased wallet share of client wealth.[91]

Smart withdrawal strategies

Taking advantage of strategic asset location is a key component in preserving more of investor returns, but it is not the only method of reducing tax drag and intelligently implementing investment advice. Another core strategy is the use of smart withdrawal strategies to lower investor tax bills and to extend the longevity of their assets throughout retirement. Optimal income sourcing requires advisors to make intelligent choices about the sequence of withdrawals from taxable, tax-deferred, and tax-free accounts.

Conventional wisdom

Traditionally, best practices in generating retirement income suggest withdrawing assets in the following order:

1. Tax-advantaged accounts if the investor has required minimum distributions (RMDs).

2. Taxable accounts.

3. Tax-deferred accounts such as traditional IRAs and 401(k)s.

4. Tax-free accounts such as Roth IRAs and 401(k)s.

The logic of this conventional withdrawal sequencing is to preserve the funds in tax-free accounts for as long as possible, allowing these assets to continue growing tax free. This methodology is commonly recommended by industry publications, large mutual fund complexes, and major brokerage houses.

However, the conventional wisdom is often not the ideal sequencing strategy for sourcing retirement income. A primary goal of a smart withdrawal strategy should be to minimize the actual taxes paid. But the conventional approach effectively bypasses the details of this goal, relying instead on generalities that often fall short of accomplishing this objective. Prior best practices normally waited to liquidate tax-deferred account assets until taxable assets were drained. For some clients this traditional approach could push them into higher tax brackets in later years, as tax-deferred account distributions are taxed at higher ordinary income rates.

---

91 LifeYield and EY, 'Improving After-Tax Returns, Retirement Income, and Bequests Through Tax-Smart Household Management' (October 2010).

A smarter approach to income sourcing

Financial advisors looking to optimize income for their retired clients should consider deviating from this traditional ordering to balance reducing the current tax liability with minimizing taxes over the entire retirement period. By more evenly sourcing income between taxable and tax-advantaged accounts, an investor's overall tax liability may be reduced. Essentially, this strategy takes advantage of a retiree's low tax bracket years by not letting them go to waste.[92]

Professor Kirsten Cook, Professor William Reichenstein, CFA, and William Meyer explain this smarter approach to income sourcing in a research paper titled 'Tax Efficient Withdrawal Strategies'. They also compare the impact on asset longevity of this approach with several different retirement income strategies.

According to their research, in order to extend the life of investor assets, practitioners should identify opportunities to withdraw funds from an investor's tax-advantaged accounts when the retiree's tax rates are likely the lowest. Normally, this means sourcing withdrawals from taxable accounts first, but also taking withdrawals from tax-deferred accounts or executing Roth conversions – a taxable exchange of assets from a tax-deferred account to a tax-free account – during years in which the investor is in a lower federal tax bracket.

By sourcing income this way, lower tax brackets are filled up with taxable income from these withdrawals or conversions. The most opportune time to utilize this strategy is typically during the years before required minimum distributions from tax-deferred accounts begin, or when the investor has large tax deductions such as those from high medical expenses.[93]

Consider this example. A retiree has investments located in both taxable and tax-deferred accounts. Similar to the conventional approach, the advisor recommends that the retiree first sources income from her taxable accounts to pay for living expenses until these accounts are depleted. However, each year, the retiree reviews her expected taxable income for that year with her financial advisor and accountant. In the early years of retirement when she is in the 10% tax bracket, the advisor recommends she convert part of her tax-deferred account to tax-free Roth IRA until the retiree reaches the top of the 15% tax bracket. Accordingly, she is able to lock in low rates of taxation on these

---

92   Michael Kitces, 'Tax-Efficient Spending Strategies From Retirement Portfolios', www.kitces.com (June 22, 2016).
93   Kirsten A. Cook, William Meyer and William Reichenstein, 'Tax-Efficient Withdrawal Strategies', *Financial Analysts Journal* 71:2 (2015).

Roth conversions prior to hitting potentially higher tax bracket years when her required minimum distributions begin.[94]

Strategically withdrawing income in this manner can result in significant tax savings for high net worth investors – often exceeding tens of thousands, or hundreds of thousands, of dollars over an investor's lifetime. Furthermore, smart income sourcing can help assets last longer in retirement – commonly adding two or three years to the longevity of investor wealth compared to the conventional wisdom approach and as many as five years or more when compared to the most tax inefficient withdrawal strategy. Figure 13.4 illustrates how money can last longer when smart tax planning is effectively implemented.

Figure 13.4. Comparison of asset life under three withdrawal strategies

Source: Kirsten A. Cook, William Meyer and William Reichenstein, 'Tax-Efficient Withdrawal Strategies', *Financial Analysts Journal* 71:2 (2015).

Besides potentially extending the longevity of client assets, another reason financial advisors may deviate from conventional withdrawal ordering is to

94 Example adapted from Jonathan Duong, 'Tax-Efficient Withdrawal Strategies', *Financial Analysts Journal* (March/April 2015).

minimize estate taxes for their clients and heirs. For some clients, advisors may look to limit distributions from taxable accounts in order to take advantage of the step-up in cost basis associated with certain bequests. According to research conducted by Ernst & Young, tax-aware asset location and withdrawal strategies can increase income in retirement by as much as 33% and the remaining assets to pass on as a bequest by up to 45%.[95]

Similar to optimizing asset location, implementing tax-smart withdrawal strategies is not easy, especially when attempting to do this manually. This process can be incredibly time consuming and error prone. Consequently, advisors undertaking intelligent income sourcing practices should consider adopting technology solutions to aid in this process. Besides helping to facilitate asset location strategies, fintech providers Retiree Inc. and LifeYield can also help automate the recommendation, implementation, and management of tax-smart withdrawal strategies. Software applications like these enable advisors to highlight the benefits of tax-smart withdrawal strategies with clients and prospects as well as freeing up more time to deepen their advisory relationships.

Determining an optimal withdrawal strategy requires making assumptions, including estimating future tax rates as well as forecasting the investor's future income levels. Meeting with clients to evaluate these assumptions and reviewing with them various scenarios using tax-smart technology demonstrates a level of professional competency in an advisor. In turn, this approach to sourcing retirement income often increases clients' confidence in the advisor as well as giving clients more assurance in their ability to fund their goals through retirement and beyond.

Tax-smart portfolio management

In addition to strategic asset location and intelligent withdrawal sequencing, tax-efficient portfolio management within taxable accounts also helps to minimize the negative impact of taxes on investor wealth over time. Traditional approaches to managing accounts tax efficiently have focused on harvesting losses to offset gains at year end and using municipal bonds to generate tax-exempt income for high net worth investors. However, a more effective approach exists – one that leverages tax-smart rebalancing technology to daily monitor opportunities to reduce the tax drag on portfolio returns.

Fintech providers such as Smartleaf (www.smartleaf.com), InvestEdge/ Northfield (www.investedge.com), FolioDynamix (www.foliodynamix.com),

---

95   LifeYield and EY, 'Improving After-Tax Returns, Retirement Income, and Bequests Through Tax-Smart Household Management' (October 2010).

and Envestnet/Tamarac (www.tamaracinc.com) offer advanced tax-efficient portfolio management and rebalancing capabilities.

These systems typically utilize six primary tax-management strategies for US investors that either avoid or manage transactions to mitigate tax impact while minimizing drift to the target portfolio. The six strategies form the foundation for comprehensively managing taxes at the portfolio level and are explained below.

1. Defer the realization of gains

Investment gains are only taxed when an asset is sold. Accordingly, by deferring the realization of gains of appreciated assets in a portfolio, taxes on these assets are deferred, allowing the ongoing growth of the assets to continue compounding over time.

2. Manage the holding period

If an appreciated asset is sold within 12 months of its purchase, the realized value above the asset's purchase price is considered a short-term capital gain and taxed as ordinary income. Realized gains from appreciated investments held for more than a year are treated as long-term capital gains, and normally qualify for a lower tax rate. Also, dividends are taxed at the higher ordinary income rates, but may qualify for a lower tax rate if the underlying investment has been held for more than 61 days. Awareness and management of holding periods when selling assets or purchasing dividend-paying stocks can help prevent triggering higher taxes than necessary.

3. Harvest losses

When a security is sold for less than its cost basis (purchase price), a tax loss is realized. This harvested loss can be used to offset realized capital gains. As previously noted, the vast majority of advisors do not take advantage of this simple, tax-aware strategy. Moreover, many advisors and investors who do harvest losses, only do so once a year – typically in December. However, the benefit of tax-loss harvesting increases if it is done continuously, as the opportunity to take losses may present themselves throughout the year as security prices fluctuate. Additionally, losses can be indefinitely carried forward. Advisors and investors should keep in mind that tax-loss harvesting provides the most tax benefit in the presence of realized capital gains.

4. Pay attention to tax lots

Most tax-aware trading systems will default to highest in, first out (HIFO) tax-lot accounting whenever selling a security. This method of lot selection can reduce a realized gain or increase a realized loss compared to the tax impact of selling a lower cost-basis lot.

5. Avoid wash sales

When a security is sold at a loss and the same or similar security is repurchased within 30 days, a wash sale violation occurs. In such cases, part or all of the realized loss cannot be utilized at that time. Instead, the excess loss is added to the basis of the new purchase, postponing the realization of the loss. Thus, monitoring wash sales and avoiding these violations can be a valuable way to avoid diminishing the tax benefits of tax-loss harvesting.

6. Track closely to target portfolio

Deferring gains, managing holding periods, harvesting losses, and other tax-management strategies may cause portfolios to drift from their target strategy. This portfolio drift, if left unmanaged, may lead to substantial differences in risk and returns of an investor's tax-managed portfolio from its underlying model portfolio. Tax-smart rebalancing solutions help minimize this tracking error using optimization solvers embedded within their applications. As a result, these fintech solutions enable advisors to achieve the dual goals of maintaining performance integrity of tax-managed portfolios and executing effective tax management for clients.

Empirical evidence and research studies have shown that active tax management of portfolios – using the aforementioned six strategies – can meaningfully increase after-tax returns. In actual results of tax-managed core equity portfolios managed by Parametric Portfolio Associates over a 13-year period beginning in 1999, the firm added an average of 1.7% annually of value on an after-tax basis. The firm was able generate this tax benefit while closely tracking the strategy's target benchmark – the S&P 500 Index – with an average excess return of 0.2% per year.

Furthermore, other independent studies have consistently shown that tax-aware management can provide 1%–2% of extra return on an after-tax basis. These numbers may not seem significant. However, over time, this extra return can provide very meaningful growth in a portfolio.[96]

[96] David Stein, 'Tax-efficient Equity Investing: A Primer from Parametric', Parametric Portfolio Associates whitepaper (2013).

Seven steps advisors can take to help investors keep more of what they earn

When ignored, taxes are unnecessarily hazardous to the growth and preservation of investors' long-term wealth. However, as outlined in this chapter, techniques exist for financial advisors to lessen the detractive effects of taxes on their clients. Strategies such as intentional asset placement, intelligent retirement income sourcing, and tax-efficient portfolio management help increase the probability of investors realizing their financial goals. These tax-smart methods also enable advisors to differentiate and grow their practices by delivering more value to their clients.

Below are seven tax-aware actions that advisors can take to help investors keep more of what they earn.[97]

1. Incorporate investment-related tax planning discussions during your client review meetings, making sure clients are aware of your tax-management capabilities, the potential value these strategies can add over time, and how taxes may impair their goal progress if not properly managed.

2. Understand your clients' tax situations, specifically identifying their marginal tax rates and the presence of realized and potential capital gains and losses.

3. Assess how your clients' assets are allocated across all of their taxable, tax-deferred, and tax-free accounts, and determine if assets are appropriately placed to maximize after-tax returns.

4. For clients in or near retirement, determine if more optimal income sourcing methods exist; educate these clients on how Roth conversions may help take advantage of lower tax bracket years – potentially lowering their total tax liability throughout retirement.

5. Utilize tax-management in your clients' taxable portfolios, incorporating gain deferral, holding-period management, tax-loss harvesting, and wash-sale avoidance strategies.

6. Leverage fintech solutions to help automate asset location, income sourcing, and tax-smart portfolio management. If these applications are absent in your practice, consider doing vendor searches to identify appropriate technology that will maximize your firm's tax-management effectiveness, scalability, and efficiency.

---

[97]   Adapted from John Frownfelter, Stephen Dolce and Rey Santodomingo, 'The Keys to Building More Tax-efficient Portfolios', www.seic.com (2016).

7. Enhance value to your clients and practice by differentiating your service model. Focus on tax-management throughout your practice and utilize reporting solutions that clearly demonstrate the benefits of active-tax management. By doing so, clients will be able to see how your approach differs from most other advisors who continue to emphasize only pre-tax returns.

14

Tracking Goal Progress

Moving beyond the hazard of focusing on past performance

RELYING ON PAST performance is a constructive way to make many decisions. But this approach tends not to work well when investing. Chapter 7 exposed the foolishness of chasing returns, highlighting several studies that show past winners are often tomorrow's losers.

Despite this well documented reality, both investors and advisors habitually rely on past performance when choosing investments and measuring progress. For financial advisors, this misaligned focus typically results in client interactions that emphasize the means of wealth management – not its desired outcomes. Practitioners commonly dissect historical metrics of stocks, bonds, mutual funds, ETFs, and related performance results, but rarely make ongoing assessments of goal progress when meeting with clients.

Goals-based investing provides a better framework for managing wealth than traditional investing. This smarter approach redirects investors and advisors towards desired financial outcomes instead of historical returns. Advisors spend more time understanding clients' goals, assessing the probability of achieving these outcomes, and tracking progress of goal attainment. Investment solutions and performance are referenced for transparency, but are not the focal point of the client experience. Moreover, this forward-looking approach centers investment activities on managing controllable factors, thereby increasing the probability that investors will meet their long-term goals.

This chapter explains how to move beyond the hazardous practice of rear-view mirror investing by unpacking the final component of the goals-based investing process – reviewing progress and making adjustments when necessary.

First, traditional investment performance reporting is contrasted with goal progress reporting, a tool that enables advisors to redirect client focus away from past returns and towards probability of goal attainment. Next, ways to implement goal progress reporting are reviewed. The concept of dynamic triggers is then introduced. These real-time flags help uncover when a client's overspending, insufficient savings, or portfolio strategy may be impairing goal progress.

After illustrating how advisors can effectively use these tools with clients, a synopsis of various fintech options in this space is provided. The chapter finishes by noting specific actions advisors can take to deemphasize past performance, and leverage goal progress reports and dynamic triggers, within their practices.

Performance and progress reporting comparison

One of the few tangible things financial advisors have traditionally produced to prove they are earning their fees is the performance report. Investment results in these reports tend to be organized around the structure of client accounts, asset mixes, and past performance, but do not necessarily address how clients are progressing toward their goals. This disconnect results in missed opportunities for advisors to showcase a broader value proposition – one that centers around the achievement of client goals.

A new type of client report that addresses these shortcomings is becoming increasingly popular among advisors. Goal progress reporting fills these gaps by providing visual evidence of this enhanced level of advisory value. Such reports move beyond merely conveying investment performance to tracking how clients are progressing toward their long-term goals.

On the surface, performance reporting and progress reporting may seem very similar. Yet, they are quite different. The definitions of performance and progress provide clues to their nuances. According to the Merriam-Webster dictionary:

- *Performance* is the execution of an action.

- *Progress* is a forward or onward movement (as to an objective or to a goal).

Based on these definitions, performance looks backward, whereas progress points forward. This distinction is certainly true between the two report types. For example, consider how success is measured differently between investment performance reporting and goal progress reporting as noted below.

Measuring success with traditional reporting

Investment performance reporting calculates a portfolio's rate of return compared to a corresponding benchmark, typically a market index like the S&P 500. Relative returns of the portfolio and benchmark are reported for multiple time frames, such as the prior quarter, one-, three-, and five-year periods. Within the context of performance reporting, success is defined as the portfolio beating the benchmark for a given period of time. This backward-looking measure of success is directly linked to the portfolio's historical returns.

Measuring success with goal progress reporting

In contrast, goal progress reporting measures the funded status of a client's financial goal relative to his or her assets designated for this goal. Accordingly, the client's goal becomes the benchmark, not market indices. This personalized benchmark helps gauge whether or not a client has accumulated sufficient resources to adequately fund future needs, wants, and wishes. In turn, goal progress success is determined by whether the client is on track to fully fund the future goal, and risk is expressed in terms of falling short of funding forthcoming goal expenditures.

A useful metric to contextualize a client's current goal progress is the probability of success as determined by Monte Carlo analysis. By simulating thousands of potential return sequences and factoring in a client's current asset values, portfolio composition, future savings, and goals, probability of success estimates the likelihood that the client will reach a specific financial goal.

Figure 14.1 explains the key differences between traditional performance reporting and goal progress reporting.

Figure 14.1. Comparison of performance reporting and goal progress reporting

Traditional performance reporting	Goal progress reporting
Measures portfolio performance relative to a market benchmark.	Measures performance relative to an investor's financial goal.
Determines whether investment manager has investment selection skill.	Determines whether an investor is on track to meet his or her goal.
Provides relative measure of performance.	Provides absolute measure of performance.
Measures risk in terms of standard deviation.	Measures risk in terms of likelihood of not achieving goal.
Breaks down portfolio into components or parts.	Shows portfolio at the total fund level.

Source: Adapted from Marshall Smith, 'Does Goal Based Reporting Make Traditional Reporting Irrelevant?', www.firstrate.com (July 6, 2015).

Benefits of tracking goal progress

Progress reporting helps advisors and investors counteract common behavioral risks such as overreacting to short-term market downturns by focusing forward on long-term investor goals. Daniel Crosby, PhD, a behavioral finance expert, affirmed this benefit in *The Laws of Wealth*. He wrote, "Measuring performance against personal needs rather than an index has been shown to keep us invested during period of market volatility, enhance savings behavior, and help us maintain a long-term focus."[98]

To realize the benefits of progress reporting, a client's goals-based plan must first be developed. Yet, according to a CEB Wealth Technology report, nearly seven out of ten high net worth clients do not have a written financial plan. The CEB study also found that of the clients who did have a plan, the majority indicated they would prefer to see the progress of their wealth management against their goals versus traditional performance reporting metrics. These findings suggest the importance of goal-based reporting to clients and highlight the opportunity to increase advisor adoption of planning and progress reporting within advisory practices.

---

[98] Daniel Crosby, *The Laws of Wealth: Psychology and the secret to investing success* (Harriman House, 2016).

"As the industry accepts that more clients judge the success of their portfolios based on their life goals as opposed to just benchmarks, firms will need to adjust the way they demonstrate value," said Darrin Courtney, Research Director, CEB Tower Group. "Firms are aware of this however, as demonstrated by a recent survey of senior wealth executives about preferred features in a client reporting solution, where the vast majority chose the ability to tie performance to individual client goals as the most important requirement."[99]

Deploying goal progress reporting within an advisory practice

Smart financial advisors recognize the value of goal progress reporting and are increasingly deploying these solutions within their practices. As the CEB research indicated, high net worth clients want to know how they are progressing toward their financial objectives more than they desire reports that focus on past performance and detailed investment metrics.

However, in the absence of appropriate technology, advisors often find that implementing goal progress reporting can be difficult to efficiently scale. Furthermore, legacy custodial and portfolio accounting systems generally work well with traditional performance reporting solutions, but often do not interact as smoothly with goal progress reporting solutions without revisions to back-office and front-office technology.

Given these challenges, the following considerations should be addressed by advisors and their firms when implementing goal progress reporting:

- Client accounts and the underlying assets are not always mapped one-to-one with client goals. For example, advisors taking advantage of asset location strategies may place client assets in different account types to minimize taxes rather than segmenting account assets by goals. Also, assets within a single account may correspond to multiple goals, such as basic needs as well as aspirational wishes.

- Both account aggregation (to support the viewing of assets holistically) and disaggregation (to enable the mapping of holdings to specific goals) are important tools for goals-based reporting.

- Traditional account-level reporting likely still needs to be maintained to support compliance and tax requirements. Also, clients are used to

99 Emily Traxler, 'First Rate Changes the Way Wealth Managers Communicate with Goal Based Reporting' (February 18, 2015); and CEB TowerGroup Wealth Management, 'Shifting To The Center: Financial Planning Is The Hub Of Wealth Management', www.fisglobal.com (2014).

traditional performance reporting. Providing this view along with a goals-based view may continue to be an important requirement for clients.[100]

Figure 14.2 illustrates the disaggregation and remapping process, as well as the process of re-aggregating holdings for a household view. The busyness of this graphic demonstrates the reality that this reporting structure cannot be efficiently supported without appropriate technology.

Figure 14.2. Disaggregation, remapping, and aggregation for goals-based reporting

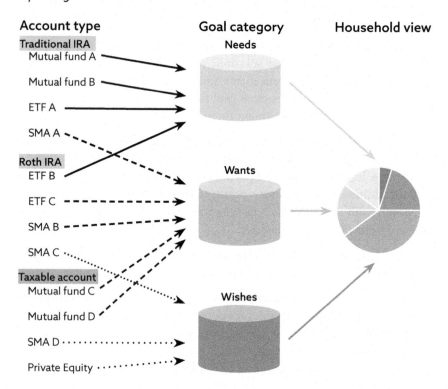

Source: Adapted from Scott Welch, 'Managing Client Relationships in a Goals-Based Framework', Investment Management Consultants Assocation, *Investments & Wealth Monitor* (November/December 2015).

In this example, the client has three accounts – a tax-deferred traditional IRA, a tax-free Roth IRA, and a taxable account. The assets were placed into the three accounts to maximize after-tax returns. However, the assets in each account

---

100   Paolo Sironi, 'FinTech Innovation: From Robo-Advisors to Goal Based Investing and Gamification', *The Wiley Finance Series* (September 26, 2016).

do not directly correspond to the client's three primary goals based on her needs, wants, and wishes. Conservative, highly liquid (marketable) assets are disaggregated from their respective tax-deferred and tax-free accounts and mapped to the client's basic needs goal bucket. Similarly, more aggressive, less liquid holdings such as private equity are mapped from the client's taxable account to her aspirational goal bucket.

This disaggregation and remapping process enables advisors to leverage the tax benefits of asset location, while representing goal progress in a way that mirrors a client's specific goals. Additionally, the process of re-aggregating assets associated with specific goals to a household view facilitates advisor-client discussions about the client's overall goal progress.

Once a client's long-term financial objectives have been agreed upon, generally the most important question to answer for the client is how is he or she doing relative to these goals. Practitioners too often complicate this straightforward question with detailed investment metrics that do very little to answer this overarching client question. As illustrated in Figure 14.3, goal progress reporting removes the unnecessary noise of in-depth performance reports, and presents information in a way that aligns with how clients think about their money.

The sample report in Figure 14.3 illustrates a client's progress toward a specified goal. The report was generated by separating the client's aggregated investments into goal categories and then reporting progress metrics for each goal on a separate report page – in this case, the client's lifestyle goal. The upper sections of this report indicate cumulative goal progress to date and the probability of success of reaching this specific goal in the future. Both of these metrics indicate that the client is on track to meet her lifestyle goal in 2020. The lower portion of the report recaps the client's goal criteria. It also highlights net cash flows associated with this goal and how the investment mix is allocated.

Progress reports, such as the one shown in Figure 14.3, are like a type of Rosetta Stone that decipher investment statistics into a report that shows the likelihood of funding long-term objectives via sound planning and intelligently-constructed investment strategies. By successfully translating investment data into understandable metrics, client reporting changes from a routine client expectation of nominal value to a mechanism that communicates what matters most to investors. Progress reporting also equips advisors and investors with the knowledge of when adjustments may be required to improve the chance of investor success.[101]

---

[101] Bob Dannhauser, 'Talk Your Walk: Client Reporting in a Goals-Based Framework', www.blogs.cfainstitute.org (March 21, 2013).

Figure 14.3. Sample progress report

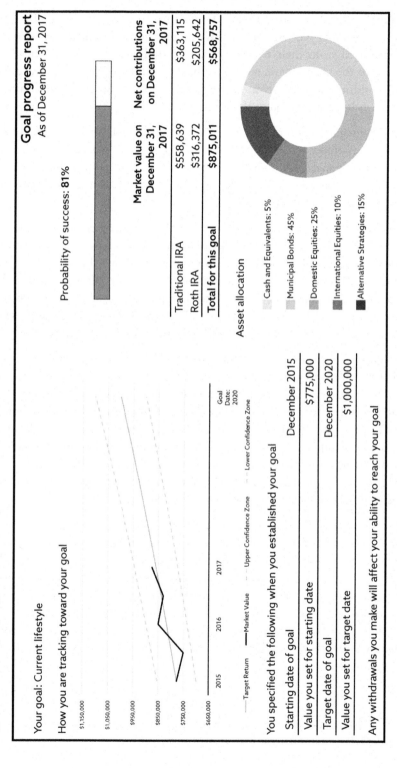

Your goal: Current lifestyle

How you are tracking toward your goal

$1,150,000

$1,050,000

$950,000

$850,000

$750,000

$650,000

2015   2016   2017   Goal Date: 2020

— Target Return   — Market Value   -- Upper Confidence Zone   -- Lower Confidence Zone

You specified the following when you established your goal

Starting date of goal	December 2015
Value you set for starting date	$775,000
Target date of goal	December 2020
Value you set for target date	$1,000,000

Any withdrawals you make will affect your ability to reach your goal

Goal progress report
As of December 31, 2017

Probability of success: **81%**

	Market value on December 31, 2017	Net contributions on December 31, 2017
Traditional IRA	$558,639	$363,115
Roth IRA	$316,372	$205,642
Total for this goal	**$875,011**	**$568,757**

Asset allocation

Cash and Equivalents: 5%

Municipal Bonds: 45%

Domestic Equities: 25%

International Equities: 10%

Alternative Strategies: 15%

Source: Adapted from Raef Lee, John D. Anderson and Michael Kitces, 'The Next Wave of Financial Planning', www.onefpa.org (2015)

Dynamic triggers and plan adjustments

When progress is measured in relation to investor goals, advisors are able to show if clients are ahead, behind, or on track to meet their long-term objectives. Probability of success ranges, sometimes referred to as confidence bands, serve as dynamic triggers that alert advisors and investors when action may need to be taken. Progress reports and dynamic triggers identify helpful course corrections for clients – such as saving more, spending less, increasing portfolio risk, decreasing risk, or re-evaluating goals altogether. Adjusting these controllable factors when necessary is normally a much more productive action for clients to take than overreacting to near-term market movements.

The following scenarios illustrate how dynamic triggers alert advisors when actions may be required to improve goal probability for clients. Also, these scenarios demonstrate how subsequent plan adjustments can help investors get back on track to meet their goals.

Suppose a financial advisor is working with a client who hopes to retire in ten years. The advisor develops a financial plan based on the client's retirement goal, assuming the client invests 15% of his income annually toward this goal until retirement. The plan also assumes the client's investments generate an average real return of 4% per year. Based on this plan, the advisor recommends that the client target a 70%–90% probability of success level for goal achievement. Using a goals-based monitoring and reporting system that aggregates all of a client's assets, the advisor sets dynamic triggers to automatically alert her if the client's probability of success falls outside of this targeted range.

Initially, the client's likelihood of success is 80%, meaning that 80% of the Monte Carlo simulations met or exceeded the goal and 20% of scenarios did not fully fund his retirement goal. A year later, the advisor is alerted by her system that the client's probability of success is below 70%. She sets a meeting with the client to review goal progress and to determine the cause of this downward drift in the client's success rate. At this meeting, the advisor learns the client not only failed to save the projected 15% of his salary, but also purchased a boat using proceeds from an investment account managed by another advisor. In this crucial conversation with the client, the advisor was able to show the impact of under-saving and overspending on the client's retirement goal. This discussion prompts the client to get back on track toward his retirement goal and to avoid making similar missteps in the future.

Next, consider a second client scenario with exactly the same retirement goal, time horizon, forecasted savings, portfolio return assumptions, and targeted probability range as noted above. Similar to the first scenario, the advisor receives an alert from her system that the client's probability of success is outside the targeted range. However, this alert was triggered by a likelihood of success above the upper threshold of 90%. Again, the advisor sets a meeting with this client to review goal progress and to determine what is driving the client's confidence level for success upward.

In this case, the client's success rate was increased by strong portfolio performance and an unexpected windfall of assets not yet invested. After reviewing the progress report, the advisor and client mutually agree to lessen the risk of the client's portfolio mix, as a higher level of risk is no longer necessary to achieve the client's retirement goal. Furthermore, in light of this proactive coaching and goals-based advice, the advisor is given the client's additional windfall of assets to manage.

As these two examples highlight, client-specific alerting based on predetermined goals often leads to more constructive responses than market-induced actions. Investors are less prone to abandon their financial plans when markets plummet (or assume too much risk during bull markets) if they have clearly defined goals and understand how their investments are structured to help achieve these objectives. Additionally, goal progress reporting and monitoring typically increase the frequency with which clients review their financial plans. In turn, clients better understand their overall financial picture and what actions they can take to improve their probability for success. Moreover, clients tend to set more realistic return expectations for their portfolios when focusing on goal progress.

Relevance of traditional reporting in a goals-based framework

Does goal progress reporting make traditional performance reporting irrelevant? The short answer is no. Both types of reporting can coexist, as they serve different purposes.

The central question clients typically want answered from their financial advisors is, "Am I on track to meet my goals?" Since goal progress reporting directly answers this question, this type of report should play the predominant reporting role under most circumstances. A secondary question clients tend to ask of their advisors is, "Is my portfolio performing as needed?" For this reason, traditional performance reporting may still play a role in client communications – albeit a lesser one.

Consider this analogy. When planning a road trip to a new destination, it is helpful to map the best route prior to hitting the road. Along the way, with the aid of an app like Google Maps or Ways, the traveler's progress is shown, as well as an estimated time of arrival. Also, a smart traveler will make sure his vehicle is adequately serviced before making the trek. And while en route, the vehicle's performance metrics – such as fuel efficiency and average speed – may be helpful for the traveler to monitor.

In a similar manner, a goals-based plan maps out the best path to a client's desired financial destination. Goal progress reporting shows how far along the client has traveled towards this end and if he or she is expected to arrive on time. Likewise, traditional performance reporting indicates if the client's investment vehicle is operating sufficiently. Ultimately, the financial plan, progress reporting, investment solution, and related performance are all relevant factors in helping investors attain their long-term goals.

Fintech considerations for goals progress reporting

As noted earlier in this chapter, generating goal progress reports is a complex endeavor. Attempting this manually consumes significant resources that could otherwise be used to help service existing clients and grow an advisor's practice. Therefore, advisors and their firms should leverage fintech solutions to help automate this important, but time-consuming function.

Just a few years ago, very few technology options for sourcing goal progress reporting existed. Today, and likely in the future, solutions to aid with these efforts are becoming more prevalent. Four categories of fintech providers are beginning to support goal progress reporting solutions, including:

- Traditional performance reporting vendors. (e.g. FirstRate and InvestEdge).

- Goals-based financial planning technology (e.g. eMoney, MoneyGuidePro and WealthStation).

- Integrated advisory platform solutions (e.g. Envestnet and SEI).

- Digital advice providers for advisors (e.g. Betterment, FutureAdvisor, Schwab).

When selecting a technology solution to support goal progress reporting, advisors should first understand the full capabilities of existing technology within their firms. It is possible that these solutions may provide some form of goal progress reporting that is not currently being utilized.

Another important consideration is how well the reporting solution integrates with other technologies within the firm. Options with little to no integration with other systems may not afford the desired efficiencies and scalability. A third factor to evaluate when selecting a progress reporting solution is the configurability of the client reports. Flexibility of reporting may be an important component to ensure that the system's reports adequately convey the intended goal-based messages to clients.

Six steps advisors can take to adopt goal progress reporting

Relying on past performance can be counterproductive for investors. It often leads to the dangerous activity of chasing returns. Unfortunately, the advisory practice of using performance reports as a primary client communications tool reinforces this reliance of looking to the past to make investment decisions for the future.

By focusing forward and managing controllable elements through a goals-based approach, advisors are able to increase the likelihood of clients attaining their goals. However, the missing element from many advisors' toolkits is the goal progress report. As this chapter explains, progress reporting shows clients how they are progressing toward their goals, thereby helping them remain focused on what matters most to their long-term financial success rather than being lured by past returns.

If you find yourself among the group of advisors presently not using goal progress reporting, hopefully you are now motivated to adopt this enhanced reporting with your clients. To move forward in this direction, consider the following six recommendations for implementing goal progress reporting within your practice:

1. Start by deemphasizing past performance

If traditional reporting is central to your existing client experience, begin lessening the focus on performance discussions with clients. In place of these conversations, increase dialogue with clients about their goals, the role their portfolio plays in accomplishing these goals, and their overall financial plan.

2. Evaluate technology options that provide goal progress reporting capabilities

Determine if existing systems support goal progress reporting. If they do not, evaluate if any providers integrate with your core technology. Also, you should consider the extent to which reporting customization is available from the different reporting solutions. You may want to receive proposals from several vendors to compare options, pricing, and compatibility with existing infrastructure.

3. Select fintech provider and implement solution

Once a vendor has been selected, develop a project implementation plan with the help of the solution provider. Branding, report configuration, and system integration testing are likely items that will be necessary prior to rolling out the reporting technology to clients.

4. Introduce and explain goal progress reporting with clients

When clients are accustomed to reviewing performance reports, it is important to communicate with them why you are refocusing reporting around their goals. Take time to make sure clients understand the core elements of the goal progress report and explain how it can be used to monitor their progress. Perhaps you still include traditional performance reporting, but make it less of a priority when conveying results with clients.

5. Monitor goal progress dynamically using alerting functionality

One of the most compelling benefits of progress reporting technology is alerting functionality that notifies you when clients may be off course to meet their goals. Make sure to utilize this functionality within your goals-based software. Also, you should have processes in place to proactively contact clients when adjustments to their plan may be required. Besides the reporting technologies noted in this chapter, additional information on progress reporting applications can be found in chapter 16.

6. Coach clients when course corrections are necessary

If a client gets off track, you should be prepared to have a potentially difficult coaching conversation with the client. This may involve a discussion about reducing their spending, saving more, changing their portfolio risk, or modifying their goal.

Financial advisors who adopt goal progress reporting create a client experience that centers on activities that truly matter to clients – attaining their long-term financial goals. By focusing client interactions on goal progress, practitioners move away from using market benchmarks as the measure of success and redefine positive outcomes in terms of a client's personal benchmark; one that is based on the client's unique financial desires and aspirations. In turn, clients are provided with a framework that promotes smarter investment, spending, and saving decisions.

PART 3

A Collaborative
Framework
— *for* —
Success

The purpose of Part 3 is to explain the importance of collaboration and engagement between advisors and investors in a goals-based framework. This section also demonstrates the significance of leveraging fintech solutions to enhance the advisor-investor relationship and position wealth management firms for sustainable growth.

Finally, Part 3 concludes by sharing two stories about goals-based investing and fintech put into action. The first narrative is about the experiences of an advisor transitioning from a traditional investment approach to a goals-based practice. The second is about an investor facing a difficult life choice and how goals-based investing brought clarity and confidence to the decision-making process.

Ultimately, Part 3 equips financial advisors with the knowledge and motivation to successfully adopt goals-based investing and collaborative fintech solutions within their practices.

15

The Advisor-Client Relationship in a Goals-Based Practice

Increasing engagement and improving outcomes through collaboration

> "The spirit of collaboration is penetrating every institution and all of our lives. So learning to collaborate is part of equipping yourself for effectiveness, problem solving, innovation, and life-long learning in an ever-changing networked economy."
>
> — Don Tapscott, digital strategist, author, and consultant

IS COLLABORATION AN essential skill for financial advisors to thrive in the future?

Although Tapscott's quote above is industry agnostic, it implies the answer is unequivocally yes. Indeed, advisors must learn to collaborate with clients or face eventual irrelevancy.

This bold claim runs counter to how most traditional advisory practices are structured, whereby advisors control nearly all functions of the advisor-client relationship. Conversely, extensive and ongoing collaboration between advisors and their clients is the lifeblood of goals-based advisory relationships. It is through this shared work and common purpose of goal achievement that client engagement flourishes and desired outcomes are more likely to be attained.

According to a study conducted by CEB's wealth management consulting group, today's wealth management clients desire to collaborate with advisory firms when planning for their financial future. Contemporary clients – unlike investors from just a decade ago – have access to an increasing amount of data, mobile devices, and social media apps, and they demand personalized advice from their advisors similar to their expectations of other service providers.

The study found that the majority of high net worth clients are no longer interested in merely comparing their portfolio returns to market indices. Instead, today's clients want to know if their investments are appropriately aligned to meet their long-term financial goals, and if adjustments are necessary to improve their likelihood of success. To succeed at these investor objectives, financial advisors can no longer remain stuck in the traditional approach. Collaboration, frequent client interactions, and a partnership-like approach with investors will be the hallmarks of the thriving advisory practice of the future.[102]

Within this chapter, the client experiences of the traditional and goals-based advisory models are contrasted, making the case for why advisors should pursue a collaborative relationship with their clients instead of maintaining the status quo mode of operation. Also, the six components of the goals-based investing process are recapped, and ways to increase collaboration within each component are explained. Since changing the nature of the advisory relationship can be difficult for both advisors and clients to initially embrace, the chapter concludes by offering five ideas for advisors to consider when making the transition to a more interactive client experience.

Differences between traditional and goals-based client experiences

The client experience of traditional investment-focused practices differs significantly to that of goals-based advisory firms. Two analogies that illustrate these differences are likening the role of a traditional advisor to that of a bartender and the responsibilities of a goals-based practitioner to that of a personal trainer.

For example, a bartender is a patron's friend who listens to problems and commiserates over the pathetic performance of the local sports franchise. But at the end of the day, a bartender is just there to sell another drink – or, in the context of a traditional advisory relationship, pitch a client another investment product.

---

[102]   CEB TowerGroup Wealth Management, 'Shifting To The Center: Financial Planning Is The Hub Of Wealth Management', www.fisglobal.com (2014).

On the other hand, goals-based advisors are more akin to personal trainers – those who urge clients on, letting them know when they are making bad decisions and influencing clients to make smart choices for the long run. In the advisory setting, this analogy translates to holistic, goal-focused financial professionals who are willing to coach their clients and have challenging conversations with them to better position them for long-term success. These advisors do not rely on selling investments to clients to make a living. Rather, they are highly qualified practitioners that count on the merits of their advice and planning to deliver value to their clients.[103]

These two advisory models and their contrasting client experiences are further examined below.

Advisor-client relationships within traditional practices

The traditional advisory model attempts to create value primarily through investment performance. This requires an asymmetric relationship between the advisor and the client, as investing normally is the advisor's domain of expertise, not the client's. Consequently, the client's role is limited to handing over assets to the advisor to manage and occasionally meeting the advisor to review results. Once discretion is given to the advisor, success of the advisory engagement – as measured by relative investment performance – rests entirely on the advisor's shoulders.

This traditional model demands very little collaboration between the two parties. As illustrated by Figure 15.1, the client's main objectives are to grow assets and limit losses. The advisor's primary roles are to pick investments and report performance periodically to the client.

Moreover, investors are commonly dissatisfied with comparing their returns to market indices, even though they are accustomed to this advisory approach. For example, when a diversified portfolio increases in value at a slower pace than a rally in equity markets, investors tend to be disappointed that they left money on the table. Similarly, when their portfolio loses value, but less than equity indices during a bear market, investors generally are still dissatisfied – as behavioral finance suggests that people feel more regret from losses than equivalent gains.[104]

And if the client perceives performance results to be disappointing, as often is the case, he or she really has only two choices – fire the advisor or remain as

103 Andrew Kent, 'Are Your Reps Bartenders or Personal Trainers?', www.cebglobal.com (August 31, 2010).
104 Jean Brunel, 'Does Goals-Based Investing Help Achieve Better Investor Outcomes?', www.onefpa.org (November/December 2015).

a dissatisfied client. Until recently, clients may have been inclined to stay put. But new technology advances are making it much easier for investors to move assets between advisors, thereby placing more competitive pressures on this old-school advisory model.

Figure 15.1. Advisor-client relationship – traditional model

Objective of traditional model:
To create value primarily through investment performance

Advisor-client relationships within goals-based practices

The roles of advisors and clients in practices focused on goals-based investing are much more interconnected than in the traditional advisory model. In fact, to be truly effective in attaining client goals, ongoing collaboration between the advisor and client is an absolute necessity in such practices. Advice, consultation, and coaching are the core services provided by goals-based advisors. And through collaborative interactions with clients, the mutual goal of the advisor-client relationship is to increase the probability of success – defined as the client attaining his or her long-term financial goals.

However, given the complexities of client circumstances, the uncertainties of their outcomes, and practical constraints on client resources, advisors likely will not have simple, straightforward solutions. This reality means clients must make trade-offs, and with the help of their advisors, consider and weigh the consequences associated with different courses of action.

For example, clients may face choices between saving more for their kids' college funding or retiring sooner. Other decisions may include saving more now for goals by cutting current spending, or delaying goals and maintaining existing lifestyle choices. Making these tough decisions, where there may not be right answers other than personal preferences, requires that clients understand the trade-offs and that they are engaged in the development of their goals-based plans. When this level of involvement and collaboration occurs, clients tend to have buy-in to their plans. In turn, they are better able to remain focused on goal attainment rather than the distractions of external factors such as market volatility.

Michael Kitces remarked, "The highest and best purpose of financial planners may not simply be to consult with and answer complicated questions, but to actually work collaboratively with clients utilizing technology to help them simulate the possibilities in real time, choose which goals to pursue, and then leverage the planner's knowledge and experience to craft a plan to get them there."[105]

SEI, a global provider of asset management, investment processing, and investment operations solutions for advisory practices, refers to this collaborative, technology-driven process as co-planning – that is the advisor and client create a goals-based plan together. The co-planning process eliminates static financial plans. Rather, co-planning involves the creation of a live, dynamic goals-focused plan, driven by the changing needs and circumstances of investors, as well as the markets. Accordingly, the advisor-client relationship in this co-planning model requires ongoing collaboration that involves reviewing, updating, and revising a client's goal-based plan in real time.

Furthermore, SEI states, "One of the most significant advantages of co-planning is deeper client engagement. As with any other activity, if someone plays an active role in the process he or she is more likely to be invested in the outcome."[106]

Figure 15.2 illustrates the increased level of collaboration between advisors and clients in a goals-based framework in contrast to the traditional advisory model.

In the goals-based model, the client has questions and concerns that cannot be fully solved by the advisor merely through an investment solution – the primary means of the traditional model. However, through a collaborative process, the advisor is able to gain a complete view of the client's resources and can then help derive a goals-based plan unique to the client's needs, wants, and aspirational wishes.

---

[105]   Michael Kitces, 'Real-Time Collaborative Financial Planning And The Evolving Role Of The Financial Advisor', www.kitces.com (October 29, 2014).
[106]   Adapted from Raef Lee, John D. Anderson and Michael Kitces, 'The Next Wave of Financial Planning', www.onefpa.org (2015).

Figure 15.2. Advisor-client relationship – goals-based model

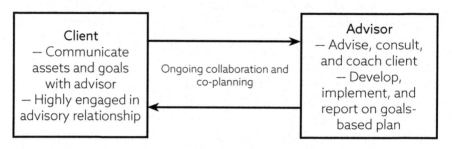

Objective of goals-based model:
To increase the client's probability of success in attaining his or her goals

With this knowledge, the advisor is able to leverage his or her investment management expertise to construct tax-smart investment strategies that are designed to align with the client's long-term goals and risk preferences. Moreover, through goal progress reporting and alerting, the advisor is able to monitor if the client is on track to meet the goals and if adjustments are necessary.

The advisor-client relationship within the six components of goals-based investing

As detailed in Part 2, the execution of goals-based investing is centered on a six-step process:

1. Define goals

2. Identify assets

3. Assess risk

4. Define optimal asset mix

5. Implement intelligently

6. Review progress

The process is iterative, so as circumstances change, fine tuning of a plan may be necessary to increase the likelihood of attaining client goals. Without regular advisor-client interactions, confidently knowing if a client is on track to meet his or her goals in a dynamic environment is difficult for advisors to accurately assess. Thus, ongoing client engagement throughout each of these six components of goals-based investing is vitally important.

Figure 15.3 lists the six components and describes the roles that advisors and clients play within each.

Figure 15.3. Advisor and client roles within the goals-based investing process

Component of goals-based investing	Role of the advisor	Role of the client
Define goals	Encourage the client to evaluate the purposes for his or her wealth. Goals-based questionnaires can help facilitate these conversations. Also, consider using gamification to aid in goal determination and prioritization.	Identify long-term financial goals and prioritize them as needs, wants, or wishes.
Identify assets	Aggregate the client's assets into a net worth statement and update periodically. Leverage aggregation technology if possible to help automate this process.	Provide investment statements and information about other assets to advisor. Notify advisor of any changes. If aggregation technology is offered by the advisor, utilize this tool to create a more efficient process for the advisor.
Assess risk	Determine intersection of client's willingness, capacity, and necessity to assume risk using advanced risk tolerance assessment tools and goals-based planning technology to stress test outcomes under various market scenarios.	Thoughtfully answer the advisor's risk tolerance questionnaire. Evaluate trade-offs between growth potential and downside risk associated with different investment strategies.
Define optimal asset mix	Establish capital market assumptions and use these inputs to create asset mixes that optimize risk-adjusted returns. At the household level, select the best fitting asset class mix for the client relative to his or her goals and risk preferences.	Understand the impact of the advisor's return estimates and how these might impact the goals-based plan.

Component of goals-based investing	Role of the advisor	Role of the client
Implement intelligently	Locate assets tax efficiently across taxable and tax-advantaged accounts. If client requires retirement income, evaluate and present options to client to optimize after-tax income. Manage taxable accounts in a tax-aware manner, by harvesting losses, deferring gains, and avoiding wash sales. Leverage technology to automate these tasks.	Communicate marginal tax rates and tax budget constraints to advisor. If in the withdrawal stage, consider income optimization strategies, including Roth conversions to maximize after-tax income.
Review progress	Communicate regularly with the client about how he or she is progressing toward identified goals. Utilize dynamic triggers within planning software to alert if plan adjustments may be necessary. When this is the case, proactively reach out to the client to discuss actions that may help get the client back on track for goal attainment.	Engage in the review process with the advisor. Communicate any changes in circumstances and be willing to make adjustments to spending, saving, and goal targets to improve probability of success.

Figure 15.3 highlights the importance of advisor and client mutual involvement within a goals-based investing framework. This model simply does not work if clients are not engaged throughout each component of this process.

However, as client involvement increases, the workload for advisors can equally increase. Coordinating a collaborative client experience can be incredibly taxing and time consuming for advisors, especially when technology is not fully utilized. For example, if goals-based plans are generated outside of a client meeting setting, the advisor has to guess in advance which "what if" scenarios the client wants to evaluate when they meet. Sometimes the advisor anticipates correctly, but more often than not the client asks for variations to the pre-run scenarios. The advisor then must go back to the office, rerun the analysis, and schedule another meeting to review the results. This cycle may repeat multiple times – leaving both the advisor and client frustrated by the lengthy, time-wasting process.

A more productive and engaging experience is for the advisor to facilitate collaborative, real-time planning and progress review meetings with the client, using goals-based technology displayed on a big flat screen TV or monitor. In this setting, the client is able to view various *what if* scenarios for their plan – such as evaluating different retirement ages, spending levels, or adding more goals. Some advisors even hand the controls over to the client, allowing the investor to move sliders or change inputs directly in the software.

The impact of plan changes is explored in real time, as the advisor guides the client through this collaborative process. Results are interpreted and a path forward is recommended by the advisor. As a result, the client is involved in the goals-based process. Furthermore, this dynamic, co-planning approach tends to increase the client's level of engagement as compared to less interactive methods.[107]

Effectively transitioning to a collaborative client experience

Change is rarely easy. It requires adaptation and a willingness to embrace a new perspective. Moving from a traditional investment-centric advisory model to a goals-based process is no exception. Without a doubt, this transition can be very hard – both for advisors and their clients.

To fully embrace a goals-based framework, investment-centric advisory practices will likely require modifying firm structure, training staff, and enhancing technology. For example, to properly align investment policies with distinct client goals, policy statements should be unique to each investor. This means firm structure, including trading and compliance practices, should be restructured to accommodate a systematic way of processing and monitoring individualized accounts. If these changes are not made, firm costs may spiral out of control.[108]

On the training front, advisors may need to learn a broader set of skills beyond knowing how to sell investments. For instance, a goals-based framework will require advisors to understand financial planning best practices and tax-smart management techniques and how to run supporting systems. Financial

---

107 Michael Kitces, 'Real-Time Collaborative Financial Planning And The Evolving Role Of The Financial Advisor', www.kitces.com (October 29, 2014).

108 Jean Brunel, 'Does Goals-Based Investing Help Achieve Better Investor Outcomes?', www.onefpa.org (November/December 2015).

advisors also may need to gain a deeper knowledge of retirement and estate planning considerations. Practitioners may want to consider augmenting firm training with earning a professional credential such as the Certified Financial Planning (CFP®) designation or the Certified Trust and Financial Advisor (CTFA) designation. Additionally, technology enhancements will probably need to be made. Goals-based planning and reporting technology as well as tax-optimization software may need to be sourced and implemented within firms that formerly focused only on investment management.

The transition to a goals-based investing framework may also be challenging for clients who are accustomed to the traditional advisory approach. This is because clients of traditional practices normally view their investment advisory engagement as an outsource decision – meaning the client is hiring the advisor to manage her assets versus a do-it-yourself approach to investing. Accordingly, the investor views her role as minimal in this type of advisory relationship. Since goals-based investing demands a high level of client engagement and transparency, certain clients may be uncomfortable with this significant change. Others may simply be disinterested in a collaborative approach or too time constrained to be actively involved in the process on a consistent basis.

Another reason that moving to a goals-based framework is difficult for some clients is because the measurement of success is redefined from relative performance to personal goal achievement. Performance-focused clients may view this new metric for success as an unwanted change. They may feel as if the advisor has moved the goalposts or changed the rules of the game, and consequently may struggle to see the value and benefits of this new approach.

Although migrating to a highly collaborative experience can be hard for advisors and clients used to traditional practices, this change offers many rewards for practitioners and investors willing to adapt to a different way of viewing wealth management. Goals-based investing, when effectively executed, generally leads to increased client retention, more referrals, and higher wallet share – the percentage of client assets managed by the advisor.

From a client's perspective, an advisory experience centered on personal goal achievement provides a pathway for improved decision making amid turbulent market environments. Also, this collaborative approach – wherein clients are more vested in the advisory process – frequently translates to higher client engagement and overall satisfaction with the relationship. Moreover, since goals-based investing often creates more value for clients in the form of tax savings and increased probability of goal attainment, advisors are typically able to maintain existing fee levels amid an environment where fees are increasingly coming under pressure.

The challenges of change for advisors and clients are typically more than offset by the benefits of moving to a collaborative, goals-based experience. For advisors willing to embark on this journey, five recommendations for making this transition easier and more effective are listed below.

1. Communicate purpose

Setting a clear vision with a well-articulated purpose enables people to understand the rationale behind change. Understanding does not necessarily diminish the pain of change. But it can help those impacted be less inclined to fight against the new direction.

Six years ago, my wife and I decided to move back to the Midwest after having spent five years in Arizona. When we shared this decision with our three teenagers, the news was not well received. Many tears were shed for what felt like an overwhelming loss to them. To help our kids accept this change, my wife and I spent time with each of them explaining why this move was necessary.

A leadership opportunity had opened up for me at a bank that culturally was aligned with my beliefs, and my current job prospects were not ideal amid the severe economic downturn in Phoenix at the time. In many ways, this decision was about helping our children – we wanted to give them the best shot of success as they transitioned to adulthood. My wife and I were committed to helping our kids get through college debt free, and this change would give us the opportunity to do just that.

At the time, when we communicated this purpose, our teenagers still struggled with making the move. However, with the benefit of hindsight, they now can see the change was worth the hardship. Our oldest daughter just graduated from college with no debt. Our other two kids are on the same course. As I look back on this experience, because we were honest with our children amid change and held true to our purpose, my wife and I have been able to maintain great relationships with all three of our kids.

I believe practitioners, when making a move toward goals-based investing, should take a similar approach with staff and clients. Smart financial advisors recognize the less-than-ideal environment of remaining anchored in the past, and can see the future benefits for clients and themselves by transitioning to a more holistic approach to wealth management.

Invest the time to clearly communicate the purpose of transitioning from an investment-centric focus to a goals-based approach. It is crucial that associates and investors alike understand the *why* behind this change. Without such knowledge, people will be inclined to passively or outwardly resist the new direction. Some may even leave the practice when purpose is not adequately explained. Although communicating rationale will not eliminate the difficulties associated with transition, this recommendation should make it easier for team members and clients to be willing to move forward with you on this path.

2. Involve the advisory team and clients in the process

A second key to effectively making change is to involve those impacted, and to do so early and often. When people are able to be active participants in a transition, higher engagement and buy-in to the change tend to emerge. Moreover, when individuals feel like they have a voice in the process, in effect they become co-owners of the change. In fact, involving others can even turn the worst naysayers into the most compelling advocates.

A measure of true leadership is found in those who proactively involve others to assume leadership and responsibility for improving processes and a company as a whole. *Turn the Ship Around!*, by US Navy submarine commander David Marquet, is a real-life story of creating leaders at every level of an organization. In this book, the commander shares how the crew completely turned the nuclear submarine around, going from the worst in the navy to the top performing vessel by moving from command-and-control authority to give-control empowerment.

Likewise, financial advisors should involve their team and clients in the process of transitioning to a goals-based approach. Once purpose is clearly conveyed, proactively engage associates and clients to help drive this change forward. Solicit their feedback and decisions around processes, supporting technology, and reporting.

Doing this may be easier internally than externally with clients. One way some advisors include clients in the decision-making process is to create a client advisory board. This group of hand-picked clients typically meet a couple of times per year with the advisory practice. Listening to the voice of the client and soliciting their input are important components in effectively implementing change.

3. Make changes incrementally

A third recommendation of transition management is to move forward incrementally versus making wholesale changes all at once. Not only is a sink-or-swim mentality unnecessary when moving to a goals-based approach, it can also jeopardize the long-term success of adoption.

For example, clients may appreciate continued access to performance reports, especially those who engaged their advisors under the premise that investment results were the key metric for success. If this type of reporting was entirely removed without sufficient time for clients to accept the goals-based approach, advisors run the risk of alienating or losing clients.

Making changes incrementally also creates an environment where input from others can be tested and absorbed rapidly into the transition process. Having spent part of my career inside fintech companies, I have seen firsthand the benefit of this approach in software development versus traditional approaches involving long development cycles and regimented processes. This newer approach, also known as agile software development, leverages collaboration and cross-functional teams, promoting rapid and flexible responses to change and continuous improvement. The benefit of this dynamic, iterative approach is that testing and client feedback occur real time alongside ongoing development efforts. Improvements occur faster, ultimately making the solution more useable for end clients.

In a similar manner, advisors can introduce new goals-based initiatives incrementally to clients through a pilot launch or small focus group. This method allows advisors to quickly know which tools and processes connect well with clients and which ones do not. With this knowledge, advisory practices can fine-tune their approach and make any necessary improvements before doing a firm-wide introduction of goals-based investing.

4. Measure and track progress

Another best practice for transitioning to a new client experience is to measure and track progress of these efforts. This can take many different forms. One example is to track how many clients have been introduced to the goals-based process. Introductions may be as simple as discussing a wealth roadmap or as complex as undertaking a comprehensive goals-based plan. Measuring the extent to which an advisor has had these initial conversations across his book of business is a useful tool for assessing transition progress.

Another example may be to quantify the impact that goals-based investing has had on deepening the level of client engagement. For instance, tracking changes to referral rates and the percentage of overall client assets being managed by the advisor can highlight whether or not the goals-based experience is enhancing client engagement and improving business results of the practice.

5. Celebrate successes

Changing a traditional investment-centric practice to a goals-focused approach requires a significant amount of hard work. And progress may feel very slow along the way. For these reasons, it is important that financial advisors remember to celebrate successes as they make this journey. Acknowledging progress reminds individuals affected by the change that their sacrifices are worth the efforts.

Cause for celebration – especially early on in this transition – does not need to be a result of a newsworthy outcome. An experience as simple as a previously unengaged client becoming an active participant in the goal planning process should be showcased amongst the advisory team. Likewise, if a client buys-in to this transition and begins to improve her probability of goal attainment, the advisor should intentionally recognize this progress with the client. Practitioners have found that regular encouragement of clients helps them remain committed to this new approach to managing wealth.

Evidence suggests an increasing number of clients desire a collaborative experience with their financial advisors. Goals-based investing fits well with these changing client expectations. Moreover, the traditional advisory model centered on investment management capabilities continues to experience fee pressures and diminishing value from clients. Accordingly, smart financial advisors are making the transition to goals-based investing and creating a more collaborative and interactive experience for their clients in this process. Practitioners willing to undertake such efforts are positioning their practices to thrive in the future.

16

Fintech Solutions to Enhance Practice Growth and the Investor Experience

Harnessing technology to increase advisory value

Do a Google search on the word 'fintech' and more than 21 million results are found. Yet, the term – a portmanteau of financial technology – did not even exist in the English language until the early 21st century. Now, fintech is all the rage. For proof, just look to venture capitalists and where they are investing funds. Financial technology companies across the globe raised $36 billion in 2016, nearly a 90% increase on the $19 billion recorded in 2015, according to data compiled by Financial Technology Partners and KPMG.[109]

Technology initially was used by financial institutions to support operational processes. Increasingly, though, fintech represents applications that are disrupting the financial services sector, including mobile payments, money transfers, lending, fundraising, and investment management. Agile fintech start-ups are able to quickly innovate and upend slow-moving, brick-and-mortar financial institution behemoths. According to a study published by Citigroup in 2016, new technologies could eliminate up to 30% of banking industry jobs over the next decade.[110]

---

[109]　Elena Mesropyan, 'Global FinTech Funding Reached $36 Bn in 2016 With Payments Companies Securing 40% of Total Funds', www.letstalkpayments.com (January 2, 2017); and 'Fintech funding hits all-time high in 2015, despite pullback in Q4: KPMG and CB Insights', www.kpmg.com (March 9, 2016).

[110]　Citi GPS, 'Digital Disruption: How FinTech is Forcing Banking to a Tipping Point', www.ir.citi.com (March 2016).

Banking is not the only financial services industry in the crosshairs of fintech entrepreneurs. So is wealth management. For example, consider the rise of robo advisors. This new breed of online wealth management service providers automates portfolio management using algorithm-based decision logic with minimal to no human intervention. In less than a decade, robo-advisor startups such as Betterment and Wealthfront have amassed billions of dollars in assets under management. And the likes of Vanguard, Schwab, and BlackRock have launched their versions of digital advice, garnering billions of dollars in assets to these technology-driven solutions in just a few years.

Given the rapid rise of robo advisors, some wealth managers perceive that technology diminishes the role of human advisors. This myth, however, is far from true. If anything, technology can greatly enhance personal interactions with investors. When used effectively, it enables advisors to spend more time with clients and less time on manual tasks. And in turn, these tech-savvy practitioners are able to know their clients better, understand investor goals and total wealth with more clarity, and provide highly tailored advice to clients.

Moreover, the 2016 Planning and Progress Study conducted by Northwestern Mutual revealed that human advice paired with technology is the advisory format preferred by the majority of investors. The study found that 54% of people view a human relationship coupled with technology as ideal, whereas only 33% desired solely a human relationship and just 11% preferred an exclusively digital advisory engagement.[III]

Financial advisors cannot ignore these trends. Practices that adapt by intelligently embracing fintech solutions will be better positioned for survival in the digital era, whereas advisory firms that ignore emerging technologies will likely encounter a grimmer fate.

This chapter shows how advisors can avoid irrelevancy and thrive by becoming tech-savvy. Fintech strategies to help advisors prosper amid industry disruption are unpacked. Also, strategies to augment the client experience with collaborative-enabling technology are highlighted. Fintech applications that complement the six components of the goals-based investing process are then recapped.

Next, emerging fintech trends, including digital advice, gamification, and machine learning are reviewed from an advisor's perspective. The chapter concludes by showcasing ways advisors can enhance their advisory value and client relationships through technology adoption.

[III] 'Planning and Progress Study 2016', www.northwesternmutual.com (2016).

Realizing better practice results with fintech

Fidelity Institutional conducted a study that evaluated how advisors use technology to support their practices, focusing on a subset of professionals that were particularly tech savvy. This group of practitioners, representing approximately 30% of the overall advisory population, demonstrated key technology usage patterns within their businesses, including:

- Using tablets, laptops, or videoconferencing in client meetings.

- Offering a collaborative client experience via co-planning and an interactive client portal.

- Automating workflows to increase in-house efficiencies.

- Using data aggregation to provide clients with a complete picture of their net worth.

- Providing clients with automated email alerts.

- Communicating with clients and promoting their practices via social media.

- Leveraging interactive, goals-based reporting.

- Tracking client and prospect interactions via customer relationship management (CRM) systems.

- Using online risk and compliance tools.

The primary purpose of Fidelity's study was to determine how the business results differed between the tech-savvy advisors and the group of advisors who did not deploy technology well. The findings clearly point to the thriving and prosperous nature of practitioners who fully embrace digital innovation within their businesses. For example, Fidelity found that tech-savvy advisors managed 40% more assets and served 55% more clients than other advisors. Moreover, the tech-enabled practitioners had more millionaire clients as a percentage of their client base (35% versus 28%) and served more Gen X/Y clients as a percentage of their books (37% versus 31%).[112]

Figure 16.1 shows more results from Fidelity's study on the positive business impact of smart technology utilization within advisory practices. As shown, tech-savvy advisors tend to attract and retain more clients, grow their businesses better, and have a wider geographic footprint than non-tech advisors. These positive outcomes are likely the result of technology freeing advisors from labor-

---

112   Fidelity Investments, 'eAdvisors Take the Lead: How some advisors leverage technology to help spur outsized productivity and growth' (2015).

intensive, low-value activities, enabling advisors to focus on high-value added services such as goals-based investing and planning.

Figure 16.1. Technology helps tech-savvy advisors enhance their businesses

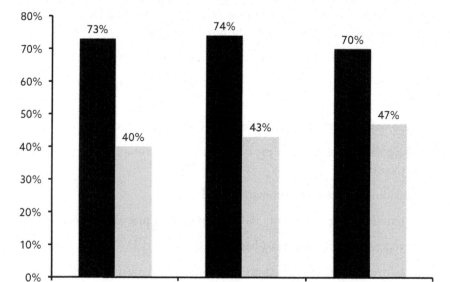

Source: Fidelity Investments, 'eAdvisors Take the Lead: How some advisors leverage technology to help spur outsized productivity and growth' (2015).

The Aite Group, an independent research and consulting firm, conducted research similar to Fidelity's study to identify digitally-savvy advisors and compare their practices to the total advisor population. They found a smaller percentage of advisors – a mere 10% – were fully leveraging technology within their practices. By reviewing performance metrics of advisory firms and changes in client assets over a 12-month period as of October 2015, the Aite Group discovered that advisors providing digital services outperformed traditional practices.

For instance, 92% of tech-savvy advisors increased their assets under management during the one-year period, as compared to only 78% of traditional advisors reporting asset growth. Tech-enabled practices also saw higher revenue growth during this time. Over 70% of these practices increased revenue by 5% or more.

In comparison, just over half of the other group of advisors experienced growth of 5% or more.[113]

Enhancing advisor-client collaboration with technology

Not only do tech-savvy advisors generate better business results than their peers, but they also tend to excel at delivering an exceptional client experience. Investing in digital solutions that enhance the advisor-client relationship is rapidly becoming a top priority for financial advisors.

For example, an advisor technology study by *Investment News* found that an increasing number of advisors rank client experience as a top consideration when investing in technology. In a span of two years, this ranking increased more than 50%, as 22% ranked client experience technology a top consideration in 2013 and 33% did in 2015. According to the study:

> "Clearly advisors recognize the increasing expectations from clients who are digital natives and who have 'appified' their personal lives. The new focus on client experience is an essential response, as well, to the competitive threat of robo advisors, whose 24/7, self-service access is seen as an amenity by many younger investors – and some older ones as well. In this sense, harnessing technology correctly is a tool for client retention as well as productivity and growth."[114]

One type of advisory application that focuses on the client experience is the client portal – a customer website or mobile app that serves as an electronic gateway to client-specific information and facilitates a sharing mechanism between advisors and investors. Portals allow clients to view basic information about their accounts without calling or having to meet with their advisor. And when portals include account aggregation capabilities with real-time data feeds from multiple custodians, clients are able to view a complete picture of their wealth from a single access point.

This holistic view of client wealth enables goal progress to be tracked. It also serves as a foundation for deeper engagement between financial advisors and their clients. Additionally, some client websites allow investors to digitally share their portal data with accountants and attorneys to aid in tax preparation, estate planning, and other professional services.[115]

---

[113] 'The Emerging Digital Advisor', www.pershing.com.
[114] Investment News, '2015 Advisor Technology Study: Driving Efficiency, Profitability & Growth'.
[115] Stuart DePina, 'Five Ways a Client Portal Can Transform Your Practice', www.

Another technology solution that facilitates advisor-client collaboration and enhances client engagement is goals-based financial planning software. Over the past decade, significant advancements have been made in planning technology and such tools are enabling advisors to demonstrate more value to their clients through collaborative, goals-based planning. These applications, consequently, are supplanting investment and portfolio management solutions as the value hub and core offering of advisory practices.

Moreover, financial planning software typically has an extremely loyal advisor following. As evidence of this loyalty, an SEI survey of financial advisors found that 87% of respondents indicated that they are satisfied with their current financial planning tool, and only 11% indicate they are planning to change. A surprising 29% of respondents, however, still rely on spreadsheets or do not use financial planning software, indicating the market is far from saturated.[116]

As noted in the last chapter, goals-based planning software helps support client engagement through an interactive and dynamic process. For example, using planning technology, advisors are able to walk clients through *what if* scenarios to evaluate the impact of different retirement ages, saving targets, spending levels, goal requirements, risk preferences, and portfolio strategies. The advisors and clients are able to review the impact of these changes in real time. With this information, they collectively decide the best path forward by establishing new goals-based plans or making adjustments to existing plans if necessary. As a result, clients are highly engaged in this co-planning process, with technology serving as the central driver of this experience.

Fintech applications for goals-based investing

Throughout Part 2, fintech solutions were referenced that support one or more of the six components of the goals-based investing process. The following section encapsulates these prior references (as well as additional providers) in one place, groups them according to the goals-based components, and provides brief descriptions of the solutions.

This list is not meant to be comprehensive, as the line-up of existing applications is expansive and new fintech entrants are continually emerging. Nor is the list an endorsement for any of the technologies. Rather, the purpose of this section is to highlight representative examples of fintech solutions available to enhance goals-based advisory practices and the overall client experience.

wealthmanagement.com (February 9, 2017).
[116]   Raef Lee, John D. Anderson and Michael Kitces, 'The Next Wave of Financial Planning', www.onefpa.org (2015).

Solutions for defining goals

- **Advicent Figlo** – a goals-based financial planning application with the flexibility of cash-flow planning, empowering advisors to engage clients at each stage of the relationship with client-centric financial planning technology. (www.advicentsolutions.com/Products/Figlo)

- **Advisor Software goalgamiPro** – a financial planning solution, enabling advisors to quickly assemble household balance sheets for clients, create goals-based plans, and generate client reports in ten minutes or less. (advisorsoftware.com/solutions/goalgami-pro)

- **eMoney emX Pro** – an integrated platform with cash-flow planning, estate planning, goals-based planning, digital vault, aggregation, practice management, investment planning, and retirement income. (www.emoneyadvisor.com/Products)

- **Envestnet Finance Logix** – a comprehensive goals-based and cash-flow planning solution with advisor efficiency tools, client-advisor communication suite, document management, reporting suite, client portal, and data aggregation. (www.financelogix.com)

- **FIS WealthStation** – a modular front office platform, providing advisors with tools for client management, financial planning, investment management, asset allocation, data aggregation, trading and rebalancing, reporting, client access, and compliance. (www.sungard.com/solutions/wealth/advisor-services/wealthstation)

- **inStream** – a goals-based planning application, featuring an advisor dashboard, automated alerting, safe saving rate analysis, wealth management calculators, and a business intelligence virtual forum for peer networking and staying abreast of industry trends. (instreamwealth.com)

- **MoneyGuidePro** – a leading goals-based planning platform that enables advisors to streamline data gathering, evaluate health care costs, maximize Social Security benefits, demonstrate the impact of risk and loss tolerance to client plans, interactively recommend scenarios to increase probability of success, and provide access to a client planning portal. (www.moneyguidepro.com)

- **Wealthcare Financeware** – a goals-based investing application, aligning advisor and investor interests through an interactive life-goals selector, the "What If" Command Center, and the Comfort Zone® indicator powered by a Monte Carlo simulation engine. (www.wealthcarecapital.com/index.php/what-we-do/financeware)

Solutions for identifying assets

- **eMoney emX Pro** – an aggregation tool integrated with eMoney's other products that consolidates a client's financial accounts for a complete financial picture, updated in real time. (www.emoneyadvisor.com/Products)

- **Envestnet Yodlee** – a data aggregation and data analytics platform powering personalized financial applications and services for advisors, investors, and consumers. (www.yodlee.com)

- **Morningstar ByAllAccounts** – a software application that aggregates transactions, positions, and balances from thousands of custodians and integrates data with the Morningstar Advisor Workstation. (byallaccounts.morningstar.com)

- **Pershing Albridge** – a technology solution that aggregates financial data to provide a consolidated view of assets and supports dynamic data analysis and consolidated wealth management reporting. (www.albridge.com)

- **Quovo** – a comprehensive financial account aggregation application, covering personal financial accounts, held-away client accounts, and custodial feed consolidation. (www.quovo.com)

- **Wealth Access** – a mobile personal financial management application that aggregates account data from thousands of institutions, integrates with portfolio accounting and financial planning systems, and includes data mining features for advisors. (www.wealthaccess.com)

Solutions for assessing risk

- **Finametrica** – a risk profiling application that helps financial advisors find the optimal level of investment risk for clients, considering their risk required, risk capacity, and risk tolerance, and expressing risk tolerance scores in terms of an advisor's asset allocation strategies. (www.riskprofiling.com/US)

- **Riskalyze** – a risk alignment platform, enabling practitioners to capture a quantitative measurement of client risk tolerance and use that data to win new clients, capture and meet expectations, and quantify suitability. (www.riskalyze.com)

- **Tolerisk** – a risk tolerance assessment tool that allows advisors to measure a client's actual ability to take risk separately from their willingness to assume risk, combining them scientifically to create an actionable investment risk directive recommendation. (www.tolerisk.com)

Solutions for determining the optimal mix of assets

- **eVestment** – a flexible suite of cloud-based solutions that help investment professionals capitalize on global investment trends, select and monitor investment managers, and intelligently construct portfolios using optimization technology. (www.evestment.com)

- **FIS WealthStation Allocation Master** – a module within the WealthStation platform, enabling investment advisors to develop financial profiles, generate simulations, optimize portfolios, and create specific implementation proposals. (allocationmaster.wealthstation.sungard.com)

- **Morningstar Direct** – a web-based investment analysis platform built specifically around the workflows of asset managers and financial advisors to help position and market products, construct portfolios, analyze investments, and connect with investors. (www.morningstar.com/company/direct)

- **Zephyr AllocationADVISOR** – comprehensive asset allocation, optimization, and portfolio simulation software, equipping advisors with tools to determine the optimal investment allocations for client portfolios and to produce reports and presentations that contain efficient frontiers, projections, and Monte Carlo analyses. (www.informais.com/solutions/investment-analytics-and-reporting/zephyr-allocationadvisor)

Solutions for implementing a goals-based plan intelligently and tax-efficiently

- **Envestnet Tamarac** – a web-based platform that integrates portfolio management, performance reporting, billing, tax-efficient rebalancing, and trading software with an online client portal and an enterprise-level CRM. (www.tamaracinc.com)

- **FolioDynamix** – a turnkey platform solution that helps advisors generate investment proposals, automate account opening, manage investment models, trade accounts, tax-efficiently rebalance portfolios, and report performance. (www.foliodynamix.com)

- **InvestEdge-Northfield** – portfolio management technology that leverages an alliance with Northfield Information Systems, automating tax-aware rebalancing with tools for monitoring portfolio risk and optimizing portfolios to models with minimal turnover and capital gains. (www.investedge.com/what-we-do/simple-rebalancing)

- **LifeYield** – a software solution that optimizes the implementation of a client's financial plan by suggesting tax-smart management across the household's taxable and tax advantaged accounts when money is invested or withdrawn, or when a portfolio needs to be rebalanced; includes a module that shows investors how to file and maximize Social Security benefits. (www.lifeyield.com)

- **Retiree Inc. Income Solver** – a software application that focuses exclusively on creating tax-efficient retirement income for clients, enabling advisors to extend portfolio longevity, reduce tax liability for clients, maximize Social Security benefits, minimize Medicare surcharges, compare withdrawal strategies side-by-side, and demonstrate these benefits through client reporting. (www.incomesolver.com)

- **Smartleaf Investment Engine** – an automated tax optimization and portfolio rebalancing platform that enables financial advisors to efficiently implement investment decisions across client accounts while simultaneously supporting customization and tax management. (www.smartleaf.com/smartleaf-solutions#investment-engine)

Solutions for reviewing goal progress

- **FirstRate** – a performance measurement and client reporting solution, providing financial advisors with customizable investment analytics, portfolio oversight, GIPS compliance, and client reporting capabilities – including goal progress reporting. (firstrate.com)

- **InvestEdge** – a suite of tools that automates key front-office functions that include advisor dashboard, alerts, portfolio management, performance measurement, goals-based reporting, compliance monitoring, trade/rebalancing, and data aggregation, and offers a client portal and a digital marketplace of third-party model portfolios. (www.investedge.com)

- **SEI** – an integrated wealth management platform that enables advisors to manage client assets in a goals-based framework and allows investors to gain a picture of their total wealth and to track their progress towards achieving specific goals via an online portal. (www.seic.com/enUS/private-banks.htm)

- **Smartleaf Client Experience Engine** – an interactive client portal that allows advisors to show each client a personalized record that includes portfolio health checks, explained trading and rebalancing activity, taxes saved reports, and goal progress. (www.smartleaf.com/smartleaf-solutions#experience-engine)

- See the listing of fintech applications noted in the 'Solutions for defining goals' subsection above. Each of these providers also offer some form of goal progress reporting.

Benefits and drawbacks of point solutions versus integrated platforms

Within the preceding list, certain technology providers are listed in multiple categories. These broader-scope solutions are sometimes referred to as integrated platforms – technology that combines different functional applications into a single operational platform that may sit on top of a common database. Modules may include client relationship management, account aggregation, goals-based planning, risk tolerance scoring, asset allocation optimization, portfolio management, goal progress reporting, and client portal options. In contrast, point solutions are applications with a singular focus such as risk assessment, tax-smart rebalancing, or performance measurement.

The advantage of integrated platforms is the efficiency that results from information stored on a common database. The advisory team ideally enters information only once, and this data is then accessible across the entire platform modules. Other benefits include easier archiving and retrieval of client data, and potential reduction in a firm's efforts around compliance oversight.

A disadvantage of integrated platforms is the limited options that may be available to support various advisory functions. For example, the tax-management capabilities of an integrated platform solution may not provide the full-array of tax-efficient functionality desired by the advisor. Alternatively, this advanced functionality may be available in a point solution that focuses solely on tax-aware portfolio management. However, best-of-breed applications that specialize in one area of practice management typically do not afford the same efficiencies provided by integrated platforms. Given these trade-offs, advisory practices must evaluate whether utilizing the specialization of point solutions or leveraging the scalability of platform technology best fits with the mission and value proposition of the firm.[117]

Emerging fintech trends: digital advice, gamification, and machine learning

Innovation within the wealth management industry continues to accelerate at a rapid pace. In this dynamic environment, practitioners can no longer afford to remain anchored to legacy technology. Smart, tech-savvy advisors are continually surveying the digital landscape for ways to grow their practices and engage more effectively with clients. Below are brief reviews of three emerging technologies within the wealth management industry: digital advice, gamification, and machine learning.

[117]   David L. Lawrence, 'Integrated Advisor Platforms', www.fa-mag.com (May 1, 2006).

Digital advice

Automated investment services, also known as robo advisors or digital-advice solutions, are online wealth managers that use complex algorithms to trade, rebalance, and tax-manage investor portfolios. Normally, investors complete an online questionnaire about their investment amount, risk preferences, and financial goals. Once assets are transferred to the digital advisor, the money is invested into a mix of assets based on the investor's questionnaire responses, often using low-cost ETFs. The cost for this automated investment service is a fee based on assets managed – typically ranging from 0.25%–0.75% – plus the expenses of the underlying investment vehicles. Periodically, the service rebalances investor assets back to their target mixes and may include additional capabilities such as automatic tax-loss harvesting. These online services can deliver investment advice and manage portfolios with no human intervention, or can be augmented with advisor support.[118]

According to a 2016 research report by KPMG, projected robo-advisor assets under management in the US may grow to $2.2 trillion by 2020. This represents a 68% annual growth rate over five years. In another digital-advice report from Business Insider Intelligence, robo advisors are forecasted to manage around 10% of total global assets under management by 2020. This equates to about $8 trillion in worldwide assets being managed by automated investment services.[119]

Given such high forecasted growth rates, are robo advisors friends or foes of human advisors? Although this question continues to be debated, I believe that digital advice is more complementary to existing advisory services than a replacement of face-to-face advice. For instance, a number of large asset management and wealth management firms are starting to launch their versions of robo advisors, facilitating the segmentation of their offerings between mass affluent, high net worth, and ultra-affluent clients. These digital-advice solutions typically coexist with the firms' existing professional advisory services.

It is likely that a majority of investors above the mass affluent segment will continue to value in-person advice. As a matter of course, evaluating the trade-offs associated with client goals, risk preferences, tax strategies, and other factors often involve choices where no clear answers exist. Client preferences and understanding of the underlying assumptions are as important to the decision-making process as investment algorithms in such circumstance. Accordingly,

[118] Citi GPS, 'Digital Disruption: How FinTech is Forcing Banking to a Tipping Point', (March 2016).
[119] Daniel O'Keefe, Jonathan Warmund and Ben Lewis, 'Robo advising: Catching up and getting ahead', www.kpmg.com (2016); and Sarah Kocianski, 'The Robo Advising Report: Market forecasts, key growth drivers, and how automated asset management will change the advisory industry', www.businessinsider.com (June 9, 2016).

competent professionals are better able than computers to help clients navigate this ambiguity.

However, wealth management services offered by advisors to the mass affluent market may be more suited to digital-advice platforms. For this market segment, automated investment services enable advisors to service more clients and increase productivity. Some advisors are augmenting their existing service model with a robo-advice offering to acquire and manage assets of younger and less affluent investors. Absent the efficiencies and scalability of digital advice, these advisors would not be able to practically service this client segment – even though many of these investors will need full personalized advice as their wealth increases over time.

Other companies with large, non-advisory consumer bases, such as banks, insurance companies, and brokerage firms, see robo-advice solutions as a way to cross-sell investment management services to their existing customers, creating a new source of revenue for these firms. As evidence of this trend, nearly every major US bank – including Bank of America, Wells Fargo, and Citigroup – have announced or launched digital advice offerings through their consumer channels.

Gamification

Another emerging fintech category is gamification – the use of game techniques and experience design to digitally interact, engage, and motivate investors to achieve their financial goals. Apis Partners, a private equity fund manager focused on investing financial services and fintech companies, conducted a study on gamification within the financial services industry. The firm identified three primary developments that have led to the rise of gamification: an increasingly interconnected world of smart devices, rise of tech-savvy consumers, and the mass popularity of gaming. These three trends show no signs of abating, likely resulting in the continual rise of fintech gamification in the future.[120]

The focus of gamification is about engaging clients. People are more inclined to adapt their behaviors when they are engaged in entertaining, goal-oriented tasks that reinforce positive action rewards. Gamification solutions capitalize on these patterns of human behavior and incorporate fun, digital interactions to encourage consumers to take certain actions. Gaming techniques have been successfully used in a variety of industries. For example, airline and lodging industries offer customer programs, whereby consumers earn points for their loyalty. Other examples can be found in fitness and weight loss companies such

---

[120] Matteo Stefanel and Udayan Goyal, 'Gamification of Financial Services: Current Trends and Future Possibilities', www.apis.pe.

as Weight Watchers and Fitocracy, and on travel sites like TripAdvisor, where review badges can be received.[121]

Within the wealth management industry, gamification is being used by advisors to create engaging experiences with clients to help determine and prioritize financial goals. Also, interactive, goal-progress reporting and alerting are being used to reward and motivate investors to take action through the use of game-like scenarios. As financial planning software increasingly moves from being an advisor-centric tool to a real-time collaborative solution, gamification techniques within these applications will likely become more commonplace.

Michael Kitces, director of planning research at the Pinnacle Advisory Group, believes the next phase of fintech gamification will be the utilization of up-to-date client data to provide instantaneous feedback normally found in well-designed digital games. Kitces believes that delaying feedback about goal progress by a few weeks or longer – such as waiting until the next advisor-client meeting to review results – will have far less effect than providing real-time information to clients. As fintech solutions begin to enable investors to immediately know their goal status and the impact their spending and saving has on the probability of their success, investor behavior will likely begin to change more rapidly, too.[122]

Machine learning

Besides robo advisors and gamification, machine learning is another emerging fintech concept that advisors should be watching. Machine learning is a type of artificial intelligence, whereby computers learn to make predictions and solve problems without being explicitly programmed to do so. It also entails the development of computer-generated programs that adapt when exposed to new information.

A well-known example of this type of cognitive technology is IBM Watson – a question-answering computer system able to process natural language. In 2011, IBM Watson went head to head in *Jeopardy!* against two of the game's top champions and won. Since then, IBM has continued to significantly invest in its machine learning initiatives and now has an entire team dedicated to developing Watson for the wealth management industry. IBM has engineered an advisory offering using Watson that is capable of analyzing personal behaviors and preferences to identify investment opportunities of likely interest to specific

---

[121]   Carolyn Nees, 'How gamification can help get clients to plan for retirement', www.investmentnews.com (May 15, 2015).

[122]   Michael Kitces, 'Making A Game Out Of Financial Planning', www.kitces.com (September 10, 2012).

investors. Also, the system can predict which clients are most apt to leave a practice, enabling the advisor to proactively reach out to these individuals before it is too late.[123]

Will Trout, senior analyst with Celent's wealth management practice, believes artificial intelligence will continue to expand its reach within the financial services industry. "Wall Street firms are already using machine learning to automate report writing and replace their analysts," Trout says. He went on to predict, "Soon they will replace their qualitative research people who do the fund selection. This will be completely automated."

However, machine learning likely will not displace financial advisors – at least not any time soon. Instead, this emerging technology is expected to free practitioners from repetitive tasks, helping to create efficiencies in compliance, risk oversight, and investment management. Hence, artificial intelligence should help advisory practices get more done with fewer resources while serving more clients. It also should enable advisors to make better decisions about client and prospect behavior by leveraging the predictive analytics associated with cognitive technologies.[124]

Actions advisors can take to enhance their value through technology

Fintech undoubtedly is transforming wealth management. Smart financial advisors recognize this reality and are harnessing technology to grow their practices and enhance the client experience. But the majority of wealth management professionals continue to underutilize technology to their detriment.

If you are among this latter group, stop viewing technology as merely a necessity for doing business and start embracing it as a crucial component to your long-term success as an advisor. More than likely, your clients are increasingly using technology in their daily lives. And if you do not keep up, you will probably get left behind. Moreover, technology – when utilized effectively – liberates you from routine tasks, enabling you to commit more time to helping clients achieve their financial goals.

Do not let the rapid pace of digital change overwhelm you and keep you on the sidelines. Instead, consider the following ideas and actions to enhance your

---

123   Ryan W. Neal, 'Beyond Robos', www.wealthmanagement.com (December 26, 2016).
124   Suleman Din, 'AI-powered robo adviser takes aim at the richest clients', www.financial-planning.com (October 19, 2016).

advisory value and client relationships by using technology intelligently within your practice.[125]

Ways to enhance operational efficiencies with technology

- Make workflows consistent and automate them to efficiently manage administrative tasks and client onboarding.

- Use automated rebalancing software to tax-efficiently manage portfolios, allocations, and withdrawals.

- Plan platform integration carefully. Too many disparate point solutions make scalability challenging. Consolidation to a single platform may not be practical or feasible, but reducing the number of standalone applications can increase practice management efficiencies.

- Leverage a CRM solution to track client and prospect interactions and help prioritize daily work activities.

Ways to enhance the client experience with fintech

- Leverage interactive, goals-based investing and planning tools to promote a co-planning environment and increase client engagement.

- Give your clients access to a portal that supports secure communication with you, includes account aggregation functionality, and is integrated with your goals-based planning technology.

- Evaluate your conference meeting space, including flat screen technology. Make connecting digitally easy and use the screen to develop client plans and review goal progress. Secure access to a collaborative conferencing solution to conduct client meetings remotely when necessary.

- Let your clients choose how they interact with you – via video conferencing, in person, or over the phone.

Fortunately, you do not need to be a digital savant to implement these fintech recommendations within your firm. However, you must make these actions a priority, or they will easily get crowded out amid the other tasks involved in managing your practice. Becoming a tech-savvy advisor definitely takes commitment and hard work, but the efforts are worthwhile when your practice grows and your client relationships flourish.

---

[125] 'eAdvisors Take the Lead: How some advisors leverage technology to help spur outsized productivity and growth' (2015).

17

Two Stories of Transformation

Advisor and client journeys to goals-based success

> "Change is the end result of all true learning."
>
> – Leo Buscaglia

HOPEFULLY, BY READING this book, you have gained new insights about goals-based investing and improving investor outcomes. You now should be able to quickly spot common hazards of traditional investment approaches and understand how goals-based investing overcomes these dangers. Also, you should be able to recognize the necessity for advisor-investor collaboration within a goals-based framework and how technology can facilitate a highly engaging client experience.

But this newly acquired knowledge is of little value if not acted upon. Over the course of my career, I have seen multiple groups of advisors exposed to these concepts and best practices. Some learn, adapt, and reap the benefits of transitioning their practices. Many, however, choose to ignore the ideas and resist making the necessary changes for future success.

You may find yourself somewhere between these two extremes – intrigued by goals-based investing, but not entirely convinced that you should adopt this framework. As you contemplate what actions to take, if any, please consider the two closing examples of transformation in this chapter. To preserve confidentiality of the individuals referenced, their names have been changed, and case circumstances have been slightly modified. Still, the stories reliably represent real-life, transformative change that I have seen take place with advisors and investors.

The first story is about a financial advisor who courageously reversed course, risking his livelihood in the process of this transition. Resulting financial metrics are summarized. However, the qualitative benefits experienced by this advisor and the clients he served are the most inspiring parts of this narrative.

The second illustration examines an investor contemplating a life-altering decision. To determine her path forward, she consults a trusted partner – her financial advisor. The story highlights how a goals-based approach brings clarity to ambiguity and confidence where doubt previously prevailed.

Perhaps these final two stories will serve as an allegorical tipping point, persuading you to fully embrace goals-based investing and related fintech solutions within your practice.

A courageous advisor

Joe, a 45-year-old financial advisor, spent the first decade of his 15-year advisory career building his book into a profitable business. From the start, Joe positioned his value as a financial professional who enriched investors by skillfully navigating volatile markets, taking advantage of trends and theses he identified before others did. As a result, his clients came to expect him to recommend compelling investment ideas – ones that sidestepped bear markets and led the pack during bull markets. In this traditional, brokerage-focused model, Joe found himself continually spinning investment stories backed by past performance to generate client transactions. Sometimes his ideas worked out, but frequently they did not. Joe became adept at convincingly rationalizing his picks, enabling his practice to sustain momentum and modest growth.

Despite making a good living, Joe became increasingly dissatisfied with his career. His discontent developed into a professional midlife crisis about five years ago. He questioned what authentic value his practice brought to clients and began viewing his job as that of a glorified salesman. Making matters worse, Joe felt stuck – he and his family had become accustomed to a nice lifestyle. They lived in a prestigious neighborhood, belonged to the city's premier country club, and drove luxury vehicles. Additionally, his three kids attended a private school and were doing well academically and socially. When considering the financial impact of starting over in a new career, Joe did not feel right about making such a choice.

Although he kept his professional struggles private, Joe's wife could tell something was wrong. She suggested he take some time off work and go on a golf trip with a few of his guy friends. Two weeks later Joe was headed to Arizona for three days of winter golf in sunny, 70-degree weather. During the first round, Joe and his two golfing companions got paired with a local single who happened to be a financial planner. Joe and the local quickly connected. They exchanged stories about their professional experiences as they played the course.

The local expressed a much different view about being an advisor. He spoke about helping clients attain their financial aspirations and the personal satisfaction he felt from serving as a trusted advisor to his clients and their families. The golfer clearly explained the concept of goals-based investing and shared how he transitioned his practice to this approach a few years earlier. By the 18th hole, Joe felt a renewed optimism about his profession. At the close of the round, the two golfers had drinks in the clubhouse, exchanged business cards, and went their separate ways.

Joe will never know for sure whether that day's encounter was fate or merely circumstantial. However, he does know with certainty that the chance meeting was a pivotal moment in his career. Upon returning home, Joe started researching goals-based investing methodologies and best practices. He also enrolled in the CFP® program to expand his professional knowledge. Shortly thereafter, Joe purchased goals-based planning software, obtained the required fee-based licensure, and began mapping out a plan for introducing this approach to his clients.

What happened next took Joe by complete surprise. To his dismay, many of his existing clients were disinterested in a fee-based, planning engagement and did not share in his newfound enthusiasm about goals-based investing. They had become mesmerized by his promising stories of investment gains and were unwilling to pay for holistic advice. In essence, Joe's former success as a commission-based broker ironically became his biggest obstacle to overcome in this transition to a goals-based approach.

Joe soon realized he faced a very difficult choice. He could revert back to a transaction-focused practice and remain stuck with a dissatisfying career, but avoid disrupting his book of business and lifestyle. Or he could continue focusing on his new path forward, risk losing a number of clients, and potentially experience a sharp drop in income. Rather than internalize his dilemma this time, Joe sought his wife's input, especially since the decision could dramatically impact her and the kids. After considering the options, his wife encouraged him to not compromise on his convictions. She had seen the positive changes in Joe at home – he was much more engaged with the family and a lot more fun to be around recently. She understood the financial risks, but knew even greater consequences to their family could emerge over time if Joe felt trapped in an unrewarding job.

Courageously, with the support of his wife, Joe chose to continue transitioning his practice to a goals-based approach. He did lose some clients – about a quarter of his book – but not as many as he had feared. Certainly, the first few years of the transition were challenging. Joe had to learn new systems and quickly broaden his professional knowledge. His income also took a hit from loss of clients and the lower initial payout associated with fee-based advice. Nonetheless, Joe felt a sense of purpose about his work for the first time in his advisory career. He found enabling clients to confidently retire, to adequately fund their children's and grandchildren's college education, and to leave a financial legacy to family and charitable causes, to be exceptionally rewarding.

Five years after boldly making this transition to goals-based investing, Joe's practice is now thriving. He has nearly 15% more clients than prior to the switch – mostly originating from referrals of clients who stuck with him through the change. Furthermore, the majority of Joe's clients use his aggregation tool, providing him with a complete picture of their wealth. Not only does this information allow him to give better advice, but it also provides Joe with clarity on the percentage of his clients' wallet share that he is managing. Although Joe did not previously have this data, he knows confidently that he now oversees a much higher percentage of his clients' assets based on the amount of new additions he has received in the past few years.

Looking back, Joe is glad that he listened to his wife's counsel and proceeded to change his practice. Regaining and subsequently surpassing his prior income level was a nice milestone. But by far the most satisfying part of this journey has been moving from a peddler of investment ideas to a trusted advisor for the families he serves. And similar to the financial planner he met on an Arizona golf course five years earlier, Joe now passionately advocates for goals-based investing among his advisory peers.

When promoting this approach with other practitioners, Joe willingly shares how to make such a transition successful and which obstacles to watch out for. Below are a few of the lessons he learned along the way:

Clearly communicate your transition story

An essential first step Joe discovered when moving to a goals-based approach is to adequately prepare clients for this change. He believes it is important for advisors to identify a clear message that articulates the client benefits of this new model. They should emphasize how the change represents expanded, more comprehensive services for them. If transitioning from a commission-based practice, advisors must explain to investors the benefits of a fee-based model and how this compensation structure aligns with their best interests.

Joe admits that fewer clients likely would have left his practice if he had communicated the purpose of the transition more effectively. He wrongly believed that simply having discussions about expanded services would be enough to convince his clients to make this change with him. Existing clients may need time to process this transition. Advisors should be prepared to have multiple conversations with investors on the topic, taking time to answer their questions and engaging them in the dialogue. Openly explain why the shift is being made now. For instance, demonstrate how recent advancements in technology enable you to better deliver goals-based investing than previously possible.

Understand goals-based investing is a time-intensive model

When considering switching to a goals-based approach, Joe encourages advisors to consider the amount of increased client servicing that is necessary with this model. Initially, he underestimated how much time it would take to collaboratively work with clients to develop and monitor their financial plans. The combination of more effort and potentially lower pay during the transition can be discouraging to many advisors, especially those who are not fully committed to this change.

Furthermore, staff changes may be required to effectively support a service-based model. Skilled, professional talent is needed to manage increased client expectations and to hold investors accountable to saving and spending targets associated with their goals-based plans. For some advisors this may require additional staff training, possibly letting certain individuals go if unwilling or unable to make the necessary changes, and potentially hiring new team members. Additionally, like Joe, advisors may find pursuing advanced education – such as earning the CFP®, CTFA, or CFA designations – to be a worthwhile investment. However, each of these considerations necessitates that advisors take time away from meeting with clients and prospects to adequately develop themselves and their teams.

Recognize that a goals-based approach works better for some clients than others

Another lesson Joe learned was that goals-based investing was not feasible for all clients. Given the time commitment of this model, he quickly discovered that he could not afford to deliver a high service level to clients with lower wealth totals and little promise of additional assets. This reality forced Joe to segment his clients and determine a reasonable level of service for each group. Last year, Joe was able to partner with a digital advice provider to efficiently deliver a fee-based model to the lower end of his book, enabling him to concentrate his efforts with high net worth clients with complex planning needs.

Reflecting back on his transition, Joe now recognizes the importance of educating clients about the differences between traditional, investment-centric models and goals-based investing approaches. He recommends informing clients and prospects about the distinctions between a planning-focused advisor and an investment manager and explaining how these separate roles entail different levels of advisor-client engagement. Some clients may decide that a holistic, highly interactive advisory approach is not for them. Discovering this early on in the transition is better for both parties than creating misunderstanding and frustration later in the process.

Moreover, similar to Joe, consider segmenting your book, recognizing what level of service will be required by different groups of clients. Create service models for each segment that you and your team can realistically support. This may require you to offload some clients to junior advisors, or to launch a digital advice solution within your practice.

Increase advisory value through goals-based investing

A gratifying outcome Joe realized from changing his practice's focus was the increased value he now is able to offer his advisory clients. While making this transition, Joe ran across several studies that quantified the value of a goals-based advisor. One such study was Vanguard's 'Advisor Alpha' research. The results of this study show the value added by competent advisors is about 3% per year – generated from behavioral coaching, tax-efficient asset location, and smart withdrawal strategies. However, Vanguard suggests that the 3% added value is not normally achieved in a consistent manner, but instead is lumpy and most concentrated when fear and greed abound. Joe's professional experiences validate that he tends to earn his keep the most during times when investor emotions are highly elevated.[126]

Another similar study Joe ran across was Morningstar's 'Alpha, Beta, and Now… Gamma'. The term *gamma* refers to the extra return investors can earn by making smarter financial decisions with the help of their advisors. Morningstar estimated this added value to be around 1.8% per year in outperformance, resulting from goals-based advice and tax-smart strategies.[127]

Based on these studies, as well as other research and professional practice, Joe is proud of his work as an advisor and the additional value he is able to create

---

[126] Francis M. Kinniry Jr., Colleen M. Jaconetti, Michael A. DiJoseph, Yan Zilbering and Donald G. Bennyhoff, 'Putting a value on your value: Quantifying Vanguard Advisor's Alpha®', www.advisors.vanguard.com (September 2016).

[127] David Blanchett and Paul Kaplan, 'Alpha, Beta, and Now… Gamma' www.corporate.morningstar.com (August 28, 2013).

for his clients. He now views his career as a noble profession – efforts that truly enrich the lives of the families he works for. Previously, Joe's clients came to him for ideas, but not advice. But that has changed. Today, his clients seek him out for his counsel. They see him as a steward of their resources – someone who will help guide them in pursuit of their financial and life goals.

One of Joe's most rewarding experiences that highlights this increased trust and confidence in him is the story of a client facing a life-altering decision. In fact, Joe was among the first professionals this client and her family sought advice from after discovering their distressing news. Below is the story of Rebecca, one of Joe's clients, who experienced firsthand the benefits of goals-based advice during a critical stage in her life.

An uncertain investor

Rebecca, an OB/GYN doctor in her mid-fifties, met Joe three years ago after being referred to him by another physician. Following a second meeting with Joe, she engaged him to manage $1.5 million of her wealth. Rebecca appreciated his collaborative process and how his investment recommendations were specifically tailored to meet her retirement goals. This advisory relationship was much different than her past experience with other financial advisors. She was accustomed to being sold investment ideas that appeared attractive at the time, but often did not pan out as expected. In contrast, her conversations with Joe started and ended with her financial needs, desires, and aspirations – not investment products. Rebecca found this interactive, consultative approach to be highly engaging. She trusted Joe and his professional expertise.

About a year after meeting Joe, Rebecca was diagnosed with breast cancer. Fortunately, she caught it early enough that her chance of survival was relatively high. Nonetheless, this news was very disturbing to her and her family. Surgery and radiation were the prescribed treatments. And, at least for a while, Rebecca needed to focus on overcoming this disease instead of her medical practice.

This illness-induced time off created space for Rebecca to reevaluate her life's priorities. Her 70-hour work week left little time for anything else. Her husband had recently retired from a civil service career, and her children were now grown and beginning to start their families. Although Rebecca enjoyed practicing medicine, her cancer diagnosis made her realize there were many more things she would like to do – travel with her husband, spend more time with her children and new grandchild, and volunteer at the local pregnancy crisis center. However, she was not sure if it was financially prudent for her to retire. Rebecca and her husband had saved reasonably well, but for the past 25 years her physician's income provided nice cash flow to comfortably support their lifestyle.

Rebecca did not want to make an uninformed, emotion-driven decision regarding her future. So she called Joe, shared with him the news of her diagnosis, and set a time for her and her husband to meet with him. She knew Joe would be able to preload her family's net worth into his planning technology, since it was linked to the client portal where Rebecca aggregated her held-away accounts. A few days later, the three met at Joe's office. Before launching the technology, Rebecca and her husband expressed to Joe their concerns and uncertainty about their future. Through the course of this conversation, Rebecca questioned the feasibility of retiring early from her practice.

After Joe updated her husband's new pension income in the planning software, Rebecca was handed the keyboard and mouse to navigate several *what if* scenarios viewable on the conference room's large flat screen. She chose to first change her retirement age from 65 to her current age using an interactive slider on the goals-based tool. Their probability of success to fund all goals fell from 99% to under 70% – a number that was outside their comfort zone. With Joe's instruction, Rebecca considered several other options and evaluated results in real time. They looked at the impact of reducing several goals, including their desired retirement income and legacy gifts to family and charity. They also considered how changing their portfolio mix affected success rates and risk. By the end of this process, Rebecca confidently knew what to do next.

Today, Rebecca is cancer free. She also is no longer working 70 hours per week. Following the pivotal planning meeting with Joe a few years earlier, Rebecca had the confidence to approach the other physicians in her practice about job sharing. Concurrently, the practice was in the process of recruiting two new physicians who also had expressed interest in working fewer hours than normal to give them more time with their young families. Rebecca knew if reducing her patient load and cutting back her hours was not agreed upon, she could afford to retire early by modifying a few of her longer-term goals. Fortunately, the practice agreed to a job-sharing arrangement with her and the new recruits, and Rebecca now has the flexibility to travel with her husband, spend time with friends and family, and volunteer on a biweekly basis.

If cancer had not found her, Rebecca likely would still be working as hard as ever. The crisis prompted her to reevaluate her priorities. And Joe, her trusted advisor, gave her the much-needed clarity and confidence to make life changes amid a period of significant ambiguity.

Closing thoughts

As the stories of Joe and Rebecca illustrate, goals-based investing is much more than a new approach to navigating the markets and selecting investments. It is truly about changing lives. Goals-based investing connects wealth to investor hopes, dreams, and aspirations. It provides purpose to investing, and mutually engages advisors and clients throughout the process. Additionally, this approach enables advisors and investors to avoid many of the hazards that erode wealth and negatively affect desired outcomes.

However, goals-based investing would not be nearly as impactful without the recent advancements in fintech. With emerging technology, advisors and investors are now able to solve problems collaboratively and evaluate multiple scenarios in real time. Technology used in this manner gives investors confidence in the advisory process. It also makes clients feel like co-owners rather than inactive participants. As a result, clients are more engaged and satisfied with the advisory experience, and practice growth for advisors is a natural by-product of these stronger relationships.

In closing, consider the following questions as you reflect on your future:

- How will your professional story end?

- Will you be upended by disruptive technology, clinging tightly to the traditional investment-centric model?

- Or will your narrative be filled with future success, enabling clients to reach their desired outcomes through goals-based investing and fintech solutions?

I sincerely thank you for taking time to read this book. Hopefully, the concepts and ideas have given you the courage to join me in this journey – moving away from a traditional, investment-centric approach towards a fintech-inspired, goals-based framework. Although changing course is not easy, I have witnessed firsthand countless advisors and investors experience the transformational benefits of embracing goals-based investing.

My desire is that your path forward will be equally as rewarding. Cheers!

Index

THANKS
FOR READING!

Our readers mean everything to us at Harriman House.
As a special thank-you for buying this book let us help
you save as much as possible on your next read:

If you've never ordered from us before, get £5 off your
first order at **harriman-house.com** with this
code: `sf5a1`

Already a customer? Get £5 off an order of £25 or
more with this code: `2sf5a`

Get 7 days' FREE access to hundreds of our books at
volow.co – simply head over and sign up.

Thanks again!
from the team at

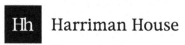

Lightning Source UK Ltd.
Milton Keynes UK
UKOW01n0809201017
311330UK00003B/148/P